FOURTH EDITION

# Soccer

## *STEPS TO SUCCESS*

Joseph A. Luxbacher, PhD

**HUMAN KINETICS**

**Library of Congress Cataloging-in-Publication Data**

Luxbacher, Joe.
  Soccer : steps to success / Joseph A. Luxbacher, PhD. -- Fourth edition.
    pages cm
  1.  Soccer.  I. Title.
  GV943.L87 2013
  796.334--dc23

                              2013015442

ISBN-10: 1-4504-3542-4 (print)
ISBN-13: 978-1-4504-3542-0 (print)

The web addresses cited in this text were current as of April 2013, unless otherwise noted.

**Acquisitions Editor:** Tom Heine; **Managing Editor:** Amy Stahl; **Assistant Editors:** Tyler Wolpert, Elizabeth Evans; **Copyeditor:** Patsy Fortney; **Graphic Designer:** Keri Evans; **Cover Designer:** Keith Blomberg; **Photographers (cover and interior):** © Human Kinetics; **Visual Production Assistant:** Joyce Brumfield; **Photo Production Manager:** Jason Allen; **Art Manager:** Kelly Hendren; **Associate Art Manager:** Alan L. Wilborn; **Illustrations:** © Human Kinetics; **Printer:** Versa Press

We thank Unity High School in Tolono, Illinois, for assistance in providing the location for the photo and video shoot for this book.

Human Kinetics books are available at special discounts for bulk purchase.  Special editions or book excerpts can also be created to specification.  For details, contact the Special Sales Manager at Human Kinetics.

Printed in the United States of America    10 9 8 7 6 5 4 3 2 1

The paper in this book is certified under a sustainable forestry program.

**Human Kinetics**
Website: www.HumanKinetics.com

*United States:* Human Kinetics
P.O. Box 5076
Champaign, IL 61825-5076
800-747-4457
e-mail: humank@hkusa.com

*Canada:* Human Kinetics
475 Devonshire Road Unit 100
Windsor, ON N8Y 2L5
800-465-7301 (in Canada only)
e-mail: info@hkcanada.com

*Europe:* Human Kinetics
107 Bradford Road
Stanningley
Leeds LS28 6AT, United Kingdom
+44 (0) 113 255 5665
e-mail: hk@hkeurope.com

*Australia:* Human Kinetics
57A Price Avenue
Lower Mitcham, South Australia 5062
08 8372 0999
e-mail: info@hkaustralia.com

*New Zealand:* Human Kinetics
P.O. Box 80
Torrens Park, South Australia 5062
0800 222 062
e-mail: info@hknewzealand.com

E5788

This book is dedicated to two very special people in my life—my late father, Francis Luxbacher, my first and finest coach, and my late mother, Mary Ann Luxbacher. My dad introduced me to the game, taught me its subtleties, and instilled in me a lifelong respect and passion for the sport. My mom was my strongest supporter in everything that I attempted, from playing sports to writing books, and gave me the confidence to follow my passions. Their presence will forever be with me.

# Contents

# Climbing the Steps to Soccer Success

The fact that you are reading this book suggests that you have a passion for the game of soccer—and you are definitely not alone. Soccer is far and away the most popular pastime on the planet. It is a game that evokes excitement and emotion unparalleled within the realm of competitive sport. More than 150 million registered athletes, including more than 10 million women, play the sport on an official basis. Millions more kick the ball around on an unofficial basis, on sandlots, in playgrounds, and on the back streets of small towns and large cities. Legions of rabid fans follow their favorite teams and players by attending games or viewing the action on television and through other media. For example, the 2010 FIFA World Cup, played in South Africa, was televised in every single country and territory on Earth, including Antarctica and the Arctic Circle, generating record-breaking viewing figures around the world. The in-home television coverage of the competition reached more than 3.2 billion people around the world, or nearly half of the households on Earth. These numbers reinforce the fact that soccer is deserving of its unofficial title of "The World Game."

The immense popularity of soccer does not mean that it is an easy game to play successfully. In reality, soccer poses several physical and mental challenges for participants. With the exception of the goalkeeper, there are no specialists on the soccer field—and even the keeper must be adept in foot as well as hand skills. As in the sport of hockey, all soccer players must be able to defend as well as attack. They must control the ball using a variety of foot skills, and they do so under the pressures of restricted space, limited time, physical fatigue, and the determined challenge of opponents. Decision-making abilities are constantly tested as players respond to rapidly changing situations during play. Players face many challenges. Individual performance and ultimately team success depend on each player's ability to meet these challenges. Such ability does not occur by chance—it must be developed. *Soccer: Steps to Success* is written with that goal in mind.

Whether you're at the purely recreational or highly competitive level, you will improve your performance and enjoy the game more as you develop greater competency in the skills and strategies required for successful play. The fourth edition of *Soccer: Steps to Success* provides a progressive plan for developing soccer skills and gaining a more thorough understanding of the individual and group strategies underlying team play. Here is a sequence you should follow at each step in this book:

1. Read the explanation of the skill covered in the step, why the step is important, and how to execute the step.

2. Study the full-color photos, which show exactly how to position your body to execute the skill successfully.

3. Read the instructions for each drill. Practice the drill and record your score.

4. Have a qualified observer—a teacher, coach, teammate, or trained partner—evaluate your basic skill technique once you've completed each set of drills. The observer can use the success checks with each drill to evaluate your execution of the skill.

5. At the end of the step, review your performance and total your scores from the drills. Once you've achieved the indicated level of success with the step, move on to the next step.

This updated and expanded version is organized into 12 clearly defined steps that enable you to advance at your own pace. Each step provides an easy and logical transition to the next step. You cannot leap to the top of the staircase! You get to the top by climbing one step at a time. The first few steps provide a foundation of basic skills and concepts. As you progress through the book, you will learn how to use those skills to execute tactics and work with teammates. Numerous photos and illustrations further clarify the proper execution of soccer skills and tactics, including those used by the goalkeeper. Drills are sprinkled throughout each step so that you can practice and master fundamental skills and tactical concepts before engaging in more pressure-packed simulated game situations. At the completion of all 12 steps, you will be a more experienced and accomplished soccer player.

*Please note:* 1 yard equals 0.9144 meter. In this book most measurements are approximate. If I write to place a player 10 yards from the goal, then 10 meters will also be about right.

# Acknowledgments

The writing and publishing of a book truly require a team effort. In that regard, I am deeply indebted to a number of people for their help and support with the latest edition of *Soccer: Steps to Success*. Although it is not possible to mention everyone by name, I would like to express my sincere appreciation to the staff at Human Kinetics, particularly Tom Heine and Amy Stahl, for their assistance in the development and completion of the book; to my coaching colleagues at the University of Pittsburgh and Shoot to Score Soccer Academy for their willingness to share thoughts and ideas; and last, but certainly not least, to my lovely wife, Gail, and children, Eliza and Travis, for their constant love and support.

# The Sport of Soccer

Without question, soccer is the most popular team game in the world, played and watched by millions of people each year. In a global society divided by physical and ideological barriers, soccer's popularity is not limited by age or sex or by political, religious, cultural, or ethnic boundaries. Known internationally as football, soccer is the major sport of nearly every country in Asia, Africa, Europe, and South America. The game provides a common language among people of diverse backgrounds and heritages.

Soccer is popular for many reasons. First and foremost is the fact that soccer players come in all shapes and sizes, so virtually everyone is a potential player. Pelé, considered by most to be the greatest soccer player ever, is only average in height and weight. A more recent example is Lionel Messi, star forward for Barcelona and Argentina, who stands at 5 feet 7 inches (170 cm) tall and weighs approximately 70 kilograms (155 lb). Although physical attributes such as speed, strength, and stamina are essential for high-level performance, so too are a player's technical ability, tactical knowledge, ability to anticipate, savvy, and overall game sense. And although team success ultimately depends on the coordinated efforts of teammates, each player is afforded the opportunity to express his individuality within the team structure. Soccer offers something for everyone. The fact that it is considered a player's game as opposed to a game dominated by coaches is probably the overriding reason for its universal appeal.

The Fédération Internationale de Football Association (FIFA) is the governing body of world soccer. Founded in 1904, FIFA is arguably the most prestigious sport organization in the world with more than 200 member nations. In 1913 the United States Soccer Football Association (USSFA) was founded and approved as a member of FIFA. The name was later changed to the United States Soccer Federation (USSF). The various professional and amateur associations in the United States are organized under the auspices of the USSF. In 1974 the United States Youth Soccer Association (USYSA) was established as an affiliate of the USSF to administer and promote the sport for players under 19 years of age.

A soccer game, generally referred to as a match, is played between two teams of 11 players each; one of the players on each team is designated as the goalkeeper. Each team defends a goal and can score by kicking or heading the ball through the opponent's goal. The goalkeeper's primary job is to protect the team's goal, although she also plays an important role in initiating team attack. The goalkeeper is the only player allowed to control the ball with the hands and can do so only within the penalty area, which is 44 yards wide and 18 yards out from the end line of the field. Field ("out") players may not use their hands or arms to control the ball. Instead, they must use their feet, legs, bodies, or heads. Each goal counts as 1 point, and the team that scores more goals wins the match.

Soccer is played on a field area, commonly called a pitch, that is both longer and wider than an American football field. A regulation game consists of two 45-minute periods with a 15-minute halftime intermission. A coin toss generally determines which team kicks off to start the game. Once play begins, the action is virtually continuous. The clock stops only after a goal is scored, on a penalty kick, or at the discretion of the referee. There are no official time-outs, and substitutions are limited. Field players often cover more than 6 miles (9.7 km) during a regulation match, much of that distance at sprinting pace. It is not surprising that soccer players are among the most highly conditioned of all athletes.

The organization of the 10 field players is generally referred to as a system of play, or formation. Formations can vary from one team to another and even from one game to the next, depending on the strengths and weaknesses of the individual players, the roles and responsibilities assigned to each player, and the personal philosophy of the coach. Most modern systems deploy three or four defenders; three, four, or five midfielders; and one, two, or three forwards. Field players are not restricted in their movement, although each has specific responsibilities within the system of play employed by the team. (See step 12, Understanding Player Formations, Roles, and Responsibilities, for more information on team organization.)

The strategies of team play have undergone modifications during the evolution of the sport. The goalkeeper is generally considered the one true specialist on the soccer team, the final barrier between the team's goal and an opponent's score. The keeper is the only player allowed to use the hands to control the ball. In the not-so-distant past, the field players fulfilled more specialized roles than they do today. Forwards were expected to stay up front and score goals. Defenders were expected to "stay home" and do whatever was necessary to keep the ball out of their goal. They rarely ventured forward into the attack. But over the past couple of decades, all that has changed, for the better, I might add. The modern game places greater emphasis on the complete soccer player, the individual who can defend as well as attack. With the exception of the goalkeeper, the days of the soccer specialist are history.

# THE SOCCER FIELD

The official field of play must be 100 to 130 yards long and 50 to 100 yards wide. The length must always exceed the width. For international matches, the length must be 110 to 120 yards and the width 70 to 80 yards. Distinctive lines no more than 5 inches (12.7 cm) wide mark the *field area*. As shown in figure 1, the end boundaries of the field are called the *goal lines* and the side boundaries are called the *touchlines*. The *halfway line* divides the playing area into two equal halves, and the *center spot* marks the center of the field. A *center circle* with a radius of 10 yards surrounds the center spot.

A *goal* is positioned at each end of the field on the center of the goal line. The dimensions of each goal are 8 feet (2.4 m) high and 24 feet (7.3 m) wide. The *goal area* is a rectangular box drawn along each goal line. The goal area is formed by two lines drawn at right angles to the goal line, 6 yards from each goalpost. These lines extend 6 yards onto the field of play and are joined by a line drawn parallel to the goal line.

The *penalty area* is a rectangular box drawn along each goal line formed by two lines drawn at right angles to the goal line 18 yards from each goalpost. The lines extend 18 yards onto the field of play and are joined by a line drawn parallel with the goal line. The goal area is enclosed within the penalty area. Located within the penalty area is the *penalty spot*. The penalty spot is marked 12 yards front and center of the midpoint of the goal line. Penalty kicks are taken from the penalty spot. The penalty arc, with a radius of 10 yards from the penalty spot, is drawn outside the penalty area. A corner area, with a radius of 1 yard, is marked at each corner of the field. Corner kicks are taken from within the corner area.

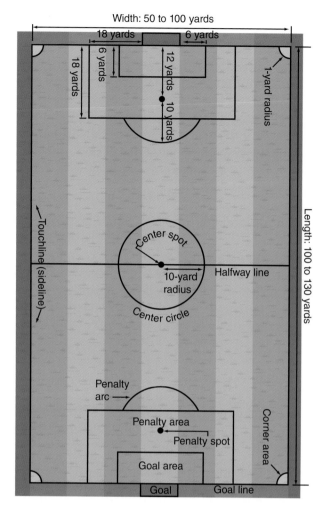

**Figure 1** The soccer field.

# EQUIPMENT

The soccer ball is spherical and made of leather or other approved materials. The regulation-size adult soccer ball is designated internationally as the size #5 ball. The official FIFA #5 ball is 27 to 28 inches (69 to 71 cm) in circumference and weighs between 14 and 16 ounces (397 to 454 g). Smaller balls (size #4 and size #3) are sometimes used for youth games. The required uniform for field players consists of a jersey or shirt, shorts, and socks that match those of their teammates and contrast with those of their opponents. Shin guards are worn underneath the socks. The goalkeeper often wears a long-sleeve jersey and shorts with padding at the elbows and hips. The colors should distinguish the goalkeeper from the field players and the referee. All players must wear some type of soccer shoes during play. Players are not permitted to wear any article of clothing that the referee determines to be a potential danger to another player (e.g., watches, chains, or other forms of jewelry).

# RULES OF THE GAME

Soccer is a simple game with only 17 fundamental rules. The official FIFA *Laws of the Game* are standard throughout the world and pertain to all international competition. Minor modifications of the FIFA laws are permissible for youth and school-sponsored programs in the United States. These modifications may involve the field size, size and weight of the ball, size of the goals, number of substitutes allowed, and duration of the game. The following is an abbreviated discussion of the rules governing play.

## Start of Play

The match begins with a placekick from the center spot of the field. Every player on the kicking team must be in her own half of the field. Opponents must position themselves outside the center circle and within their own half of the field. The ball is considered in play when it travels into the opponent's half of the field the distance of its own circumference. The initial kicker is not permitted to play the ball a second time until another player touches it. A similar placekick restarts the game after a goal has been scored and also begins the second half of play. A goal may be scored directly from the kickoff.

## Ball In and Out of Play

The ball is considered out of play when it completely crosses a touchline or goal line (whether on the ground or in the air) or when the referee stops the game. The ball is in play at all other times, including during

- rebounds from a goalpost, crossbar, or corner flag onto the field of play;
- rebounds off the referee or linesmen when they are in the field of play; and
- intervals while a decision is pending on a supposed infringement of the laws (e.g., the "play-on" situation).

When the referee is unsure of who last touched a ball that traveled out of the field area, or when a temporary stoppage occurs during the run of play (because of a severe injury to a player, for example), play is restarted with a *drop ball* at the spot where the ball was last in play. The referee drops the ball between two opposing players, who cannot kick the ball until it contacts the ground.

When the ball travels out of play over a sideline, either on the ground or in the air, it is returned into play by a *throw-in* from the spot where it left the playing field. A player from the team opposite that of the player who last touched the ball takes the throw-in. The thrower must hold the ball with both hands and deliver it from behind and over the head. The player must face the field of play with each foot touching the sideline or the ground outside the sideline at the moment the ball is released. The ball is considered in play immediately after it crosses the touchline onto the field of play. The thrower may not touch the ball a second time until it has been touched by another player. A throw-in is awarded to the opposing team if the ball is improperly released onto the field of play. A goal cannot be scored directly from a throw-in.

A ball last touched by a member of the attacking team that passes over the goal line, excluding the portion of the line between the goalposts and under the crossbar, is returned to play by a *goal kick* awarded to the defending team. The goal kick is spotted within the half of the goal area nearer to where the ball crossed the goal line.

The ball is considered in play once it has traveled outside the penalty area. The kicker cannot play the ball a second time until a teammate or an opponent touches it. A goal kick cannot be played directly to the goalkeeper within the penalty area. All opposing players must position themselves outside the penalty area when a goal kick is taken. A goal cannot be scored directly off a goal kick.

A ball last touched by a member of the defending team that passes over the goal line, excluding the portion of the line between the goalposts and under the crossbar, is returned to play by a *corner kick* awarded to the attacking team. The corner kick is taken from within the quarter circle of the corner nearer the spot where the ball left the playing area. Defending players must position themselves at least 10 yards from the ball until it is played. The kicker is not permitted to play the ball a second time until another player touches it. A goal may be scored directly from a corner kick.

## Scoring

A goal is scored when the whole ball passes completely over the goal line, between the goalposts, and under the crossbar, provided it has not been intentionally thrown, carried, or propelled by the arm or hand of a player of the attacking team. Each goal counts as 1 point. The team scoring more goals wins the game. The game is termed a *draw* if both teams score an equal number of goals during regulation time.

# RULE VIOLATIONS AND SANCTIONS

An appointed *referee* officiates at each game and has ultimate authority on the field. The referee enforces the rules and decides on any disputed point. The referee is assisted by two *assistant referees,* who take positions along opposite touchlines. Assistant referees indicate when the ball is out of play (subject to the decision of the referee) and determine which team is entitled to the throw-in, goal kick, or corner kick. Assistant referees also assist the referee in determining when offside violations have occurred, and they alert the referee when a substitute wishes to enter the game.

Players need to be aware of the rule violations and penalties that may be called. A penalty at the wrong time can be devastating for a team, resulting in loss of momentum, a turnover, or even a goal for the other team. Learn the following rule violations and penalties, and work to avoid them during play.

## Offside

All players should be familiar with the offside law. A player is in an *offside position* if she is nearer the opponent's goal line than the ball is at the *moment the ball is played* unless

- the player is in her own half of the field, or
- the player is not nearer to the opponent's goal line than at least two opponents.

Just because a player is in an offside position does not mean that he must be whistled offside by the referee. A player is declared offside and penalized for being in an offside position only if, at the moment the ball touches or is played by a teammate, the referee judges the player to be interfering with play or with an opponent or gaining an advantage by being in an offside position. A player is not offside merely because he is in an offside position or receives the ball directly from a goal kick, corner kick, or throw-in.

The punishment for infringement of the offside law is an indirect free kick awarded to the opposing team at the spot where the offside occurred. The referee shall judge offside at the instant the ball is played and not at the moment the player receives the ball (see figure 2). For example, a player who is in an onside position at the moment the ball is played does not become offside if she moves forward into an offside position to receive the pass while the ball is in flight.

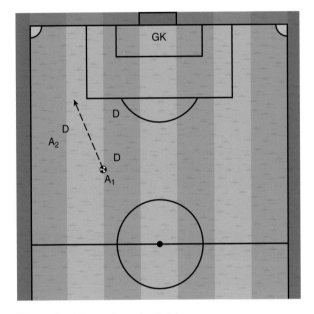

**Figure 2**   Player is not offside.

# Free Kicks

The two classifications of free kicks are direct and indirect. A goal can be scored directly by the kicker from a *direct free kick*. To score from an *indirect free kick*, a player other than the kicker (who can be a member of either team) must play or touch the ball before it passes over the goal line. Defending players must position themselves at least 10 yards from the ball for both direct and indirect free kicks. The only instance in which defending players can get in position closer than 10 yards to the ball is when the attacking team has been awarded an indirect free kick spotted within 10 yards of the defending team's goal. In that situation defending players can stand on their goal line between the goalposts to attempt to prevent the ball from entering the goal.

When a player takes a free kick from within his penalty area, all opposing players must remain outside the area and be at least 10 yards from the ball. The ball must be stationary when the kick is taken and is considered in play once it has traveled the distance of its circumference and beyond the penalty area. The goalkeeper may not receive the ball into his hands and then kick it into play. If the ball is not kicked directly into play beyond the penalty area, the kick must be retaken. If the kicker touches the ball a second time before another player touches it, then the opposing team is awarded an indirect free kick.

# Fouls and Misconduct

Fouls are either *direct* or *indirect*. A player who intentionally commits any of the following offenses will be penalized by the award of a direct free kick to the opposing team at the spot where the foul occurred:

- Spitting at an opponent
- Kicking or attempting to kick an opponent
- Tripping an opponent
- Jumping at an opponent
- Charging an opponent in a violent or dangerous manner
- Charging an opponent from behind unless the opponent is obstructing the player from the ball
- Striking or attempting to strike an opponent
- Holding an opponent
- Pushing an opponent
- Carrying, striking, or propelling the ball with a hand or arm (this violation does not apply to the goalkeeper within her penalty area)

When a player on the defending team intentionally commits an offense of a direct free kick within his own penalty area, he is penalized by the award of a *penalty kick* to the opposing team. Indirect free kicks result from the following rule infractions:

- Playing in a manner the referee considers dangerous to the offending player or another player, referred to as "dangerous play"
- Charging an opponent with the shoulder when the ball is not within playing distance of the players involved (charging with the shoulder is legal when attempting to play the ball)
- Intentionally impeding the progress of an opponent when not attempting to play the ball, commonly referred to as "obstruction"
- Intentionally preventing the goalkeeper from releasing the ball
- Violating the offside rule
- Charging the goalkeeper except when she has possession of the ball or has moved outside of the goal area

An indirect free kick is awarded to the attacking team if the goalkeeper engages in any of the following:

- Violating the six-second rule, in which the goalkeeper, while in possession of the ball, fails to release it into play within six seconds
- Indulging in tactics that the referee rules are designed to waste time, delay the game, and give an unfair advantage to the goalkeeper's own team
- Violating the goalkeeper back-pass rule (see the next section)

## Goalkeeper Back-Pass Rule

The *Laws of the Game* state that the goalkeeper is not permitted to receive the ball in her hands after it has been deliberately kicked to her by a teammate. The kick must be a deliberate pass for this rule to take effect; a deflection, for example, is not penalized. Violation of the back-pass rule results in the award of an indirect free kick to the opposing team at the spot of the infraction.

Players may use the head, chest, or knees to intentionally pass the ball to their goalkeeper. However, if a player deliberately attempts to circumvent the rule (such as by using the feet to flip the ball in the air to head it to the goalkeeper), then the player will be guilty of unsporting conduct and will be officially cautioned. In that situation the opposing team is awarded an indirect free kick from the place where the foul was committed.

## Cautions and Ejections

It is at the referee's discretion to reprimand a player who continually commits flagrant violations of the laws. The referee issues a *yellow card* to officially caution a player. A yellow card violation conveys a warning to the player that he will be ejected from the game if similar violations continue. The referee issues a *red card* to signal that a player has been ejected from the game. A player can be shown the red card and sent off the field if, in the opinion of the referee, the player

- is guilty of violent conduct,
- is guilty of serious foul play,
- spits at an opponent or any other person,
- uses foul or abusive language,
- receives a second caution in the same match,
- denies the opposing team a goal or an obvious goal-scoring opportunity by deliberately handling the ball (this does not apply to the goalkeeper within her own penalty area), or
- denies an obvious goal-scoring opportunity to an opponent moving toward the player's goal by an offense punishable by a free kick or penalty kick.

The player who receives a red card cannot return to the game and may not be replaced by a substitute.

## Penalty Kick

The most severe sanction for a direct foul, other than ejection from the game, is the penalty kick. A penalty kick results when a player commits a direct foul offense within his team's penalty area. (*Note:* A penalty kick can be awarded irrespective of the position of the ball.) The kick is taken from the penalty spot 12 yards front and center of the goal. All players except the kicker and the goalkeeper must position themselves outside the penalty area at least 10 yards from the penalty spot. The goalkeeper must stand between the goalposts with feet touching the goal line. The keeper is permitted to move sideways along the line before the kick but may not move forward off the line until the ball has been played. The player taking a penalty kick must kick the ball forward and cannot touch it a second time until it has been played by another player (the second player can be the goalkeeper). The ball is in play once it has traveled the distance of its circumference. A goal can be scored directly from a penalty kick. Time should be extended at halftime or the end of regulation time to allow a penalty kick to be taken.

# WARM-UP AND COOL-DOWN

Before every practice session or game, you should perform a warm-up to prepare yourself both physically and mentally for the more strenuous training to follow. *Warm-up* activities elevate muscle temperature, stimulate increased blood flow to the muscles, and stretch the major muscle groups. A thorough warm-up improves muscular contraction and reflex time, increases muscle suppleness, prevents next-day soreness, and reduces the likelihood of muscle and joint injuries.

The intensity and duration of the warm-up can vary from one situation to another and from one person to the next. Environmental conditions, such as ambient temperature and humidity, should be taken into account. For example, you probably will not have to warm up as long or as hard on a hot, humid afternoon in June as you would on a cold, blustery day in November. As a general rule, you should warm up for 15 to 20 minutes at sufficient intensity to break a sweat. Sweating indicates an elevation in muscle temperature.

Before stretching, begin your warm-up by increasing the blood flow to the muscles. Any form of aerobic activity that involves the large muscle groups will suffice, although from a practical standpoint it is to your advantage to use soccer-specific movements and activities whenever possible. Skill-related drills that involve dribbling maneuvers combined with sudden changes of speed and direction, or passing the ball among teammates who are moving throughout the field area, are a great means of getting the blood moving. For example, many of the dribbling drills described in step 1 are appropriate as soccer-specific warm-up activities.

Once your muscles are sufficiently warmed, perform a series of stretching exercises that target all the major muscle groups used in soccer. Don't bounce or jerk! Slowly extend the muscle or group of muscles to its greatest possible length without discomfort. A slow, steady extension of the muscle inhibits the firing of the stretch reflex, the body's built-in safeguard against overstretching. Hold the stretch for 30 seconds, relax, and then move gently into a deeper stretch for another 30 seconds. Stretch each muscle group twice, focusing on the hamstrings, quadriceps, back, groin, calves and Achilles tendons, and neck.

At the end of every practice and game, take a few minutes to allow your heart rate and body functions to gradually return to their normal resting state. The *cool-down* can include light aerobic exercise, such as a slow jog with or without the ball, combined with stretching exercises that target the most-used muscle groups. Stretching after a hard training session may actually be more beneficial than prepractice stretching in preventing next-day soreness.

# Key to Diagrams

| | |
|---|---|
| GK | Goalkeeper |
| D | Defender |
| A | Attacker |
| X | Player |
| 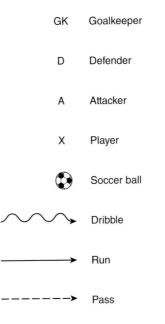 | Soccer ball |
| ∿∿∿→ | Dribble |
| ⟶ | Run |
| – – – → | Pass |

# Dribbling, Shielding, and Tackling

**D**ribbling in soccer serves the same basic function as dribbling in basketball—it enables the player to maintain control of the ball while running past opponents or accelerating into open space. Depending on the situation, you will use different surfaces of the foot (inside, outside, instep, and sole) to control the ball. It is also essential that, when in possession of the ball, you are able to evade, or ward off, the challenge of opponents attempting to steal it. *Shielding skills* are used to accomplish that objective.

Three dribbling styles are commonly observed in game situations: dribbling to penetrate past—or bypass—opponents; dribbling for close control, or possession, when in tight spaces; and dribbling for speed when advancing with the ball in open space. Shielding skills are often used in conjunction with dribbling skills to protect, or hide, the ball from opponents challenging for possession. Shield the ball by positioning your body between the ball and the opponent and controlling the ball with the foot farther from the challenging player. This technique may also be referred to as screening the ball.

Although the ability to dribble and take on opponents is an essential part of every player's attacking skill set, you must never lose sight of the fact that excessive dribbling in inappropriate situations serves no useful purpose and can actually undermine your team's efforts. Refrain from taking on opponents (i.e., attempting to dribble past them) in the defending third of the field nearest your own goal; in this area the reward for beating an opponent on the dribble is not worth the potential consequences associated with the loss of possession. Dribbling skills are used to best advantage in the attacking third of the field near the opponent's goal; in this area the potential reward for beating an opponent outweighs the risk of getting stripped of the ball. If you can dribble past an opponent in the attacking third, there is a good chance that you've created a scoring opportunity for yourself or your team.

Soccer players, much like hockey and basketball players, must be able to defend as well as attack. You cannot be a "one way" player and expect to succeed at the higher levels of competition. When your team does not have the ball, you must do your part to win it back. You can do this in two ways: by intercepting an opponent's pass or by tackling the ball away from the player in possession. Tackling is the defensive technique used to strip, or steal, the ball from an opponent with possession. The term tackle has a different meaning in soccer than it has in American football. Soccer players tackle the ball, not the opposing player.

Three different techniques—block tackle, poke tackle, and slide tackle—are used to dispossess an opponent depending on the game situation and the defender's angle of approach. The block tackle is generally preferred because it allows for greater body control and puts the defender in a position to counterattack quickly once she gains possession of the ball. This technique is typically used when closing down the dribbler from the front. When chasing an opponent from behind or approaching from the side, the poke and slide tackle techniques are generally used in an attempt to dispossess the dribbler.

# DRIBBLING SKILLS

There is not one single method or style of dribbling. For that reason dribbling in soccer is sometimes referred to as an art rather than a skill because players can express themselves in many ways. Players are free to develop their own styles, or dribbling personalities, so to speak, so long as they achieve the desired objectives. Some players dribble using long, fluid strides, whereas others, such as three-time World Player of the Year Lionel Messi, prefer short, choppy steps coupled with explosive changes of speed and deceptive foot movements. Whatever works for you is right for you.

Dribbling to beat an opponent (figure 1.1) is the first fundamental dribbling situation we cover. In modern soccer, dribbling has assumed an even more important role in team attack as defenses have become more organized and difficult to break down. For that reason exceptional dribblers such as Cristiano Ronaldo (Portugal), Kaká (Brazil), and Arjen Robben (Netherlands), players who have the ability to weave through opposing defenses with the ball seemingly glued to their feet, are extremely valuable to their respective teams. Single-handedly, they can break down even the most compact defenses with bursts of dribbling brilliance to create scoring opportunities where none existed. Although you may never achieve the same level as a Ronaldo or Robben, you most certainly can improve your dribbling ability and in doing so become an important asset to your team. Most great dribblers have perfected a handful of moves that freeze defenders and are virtually impossible to stop, and you can do the same. It simply takes practice—and lots of it.

## Figure 1.1 DRIBBLING TO BEAT AN OPPONENT

*Approach*

1. Dribble directly at defender.
2. Maintain balance and body control.
3. Keep ball within range of control.
4. Keep head up with vision on opponent.

*Execution*

1. Attack (dribble at) defender at speed.
2. Use deceptive body and foot movements.
3. Use sudden change (burst) of speed to unbalance defender.
4. Push ball past defender.

*Follow-Through*

1. Accelerate past defender.
2. Take most direct route to goal.

### MISSTEP

You slow down when dribbling at the defender.

### CORRECTION

Take on the defender at top speed to commit him to you; then push the ball past him and accelerate.

### MISSTEP

The ball gets tangled between your feet as you approach the defender.

### CORRECTION

Don't be too fancy or attempt too many deceptive movements. Become proficient at a few dribbling maneuvers; then couple those moves with sudden changes of speed and direction.

# Beat an Opponent Dribbling Drill 1
## Dribble the Slalom

Partner with a teammate. Set up a line of six to eight markers spaced 2 yards apart. One player works while the other rests. Begin at the first marker and dribble in and out of the markers until you get to the last one; then turn and dribble in and out of the markers back to the starting line. Keep the ball within a tight range of control at all times, and complete the slalom as quickly as possible. Exchange the ball with your partner and rest while he dribbles the circuit. Repeat the slalom dribble course 20 times each. The ball contacting a marker is considered a dribbling error. Award yourself 1 point for each complete circuit without error.

### To Increase Difficulty

- Position markers 1 yard apart.
- Place markers in random (zigzag) pattern.

### To Decrease Difficulty

- Increase distance between markers.
- Reduce number of markers.
- Slow dribbling pace.

### Success Check

- Maintain balance and body control.

- Keep ball tight to feet while cutting around markers.
- Use inside and outside surfaces of foot to cut ball sharply while weaving through slalom.
- Keep head up with vision on field as much as possible.

### Score Your Success

0 to 12 points = 0 points

13 or 14 points = 1 point

15 to 17 points = 3 points

18 to 20 points = 5 points

Your score ___

# Beat an Opponent Dribbling Drill 2
## Unbalance the Defender

Place two markers 10 yards apart on the sideline or end line of the field. Partners face one another on opposite sides of the line, midway between the markers. One player (attacker) has the ball while the other plays as the defender. The attacker attempts to dribble the ball laterally to either marker before the defender can position there. Neither player may cross the line that separates them. Play continuously for 30 seconds. After a short rest, players exchange possession of the ball and repeat. The attacker scores 1 point each time she beats the defender to a marker with the ball under control. Each partner plays 10 times as the attacker. The player who scores more points wins the game.

### To Increase Difficulty

- Position markers 15 yards apart.
- Increase each round to 60 seconds.

### To Decrease Difficulty

- Decrease distance between markers.
- Reduce number of repetitions.
- Slow pace.

### *Success Check*

- Maintain balance and body control.
- Keep ball tight to feet.

- Incorporate sudden changes of speed and direction to unbalance defender.
- Use inside and outside surfaces of foot to control ball.
- Keep head up with vision on defender as much as possible.

### *Score Your Success*

0 to 3 points = 0 points

4 to 6 points = 3 point

7 to 10 points = 5 points

Your score ___

# Beat an Opponent Dribbling Drill 3
## Take On a Passive Defender

Twelve to 20 players station within the penalty area of the field; each pair has one ball. On the coach's command, all players begin jogging within the area. Those with a ball dribble, and those without a ball act as passive (half-speed) defenders. As dribblers move throughout the area, they dribble at and take on defenders at every opportunity, rehearsing the deceptive foot and body movements used to beat an opponent on the dribble. Dribblers perform at near-game (full) speed. Passive defenders are just that—jogging at 50 percent speed—and do not attempt to win the ball from the dribblers. Play for five minutes, after which dribblers exchange possession of the ball with defenders and repeat.

*(continued)*

Beat an Opponent Dribbling Drill 3 *(continued)*

### To Increase Difficulty

- Reduce size of area to restrict open space in which to dribble.
- Allow defenders to tackle ball.

### To Decrease Difficulty

- Increase size of area to create more open space.
- Require that defenders be completely stationary.

## Success Check

- Keep close control of ball.
- Keep head up, aware of surroundings.

- Attack defender at game speed.
- Use deceptive movements coupled with change of direction to unbalance opponent.
- Accelerate past defender.

## Score Your Success

Lose control of the ball 6 or more times = 1 point

Lose control of the ball 3 to 5 times = 3 points

Lose control of the ball 0 to 2 times = 5 points

Your score ___

# Beat an Opponent Dribbling Drill 4
# End-to-End Game

Compete against a partner within a 10- by 20-yard grid. Position on opposite end lines of the grid; your partner has the ball. To begin, she serves (kicks) the ball to you and immediately moves forward as the defender. You receive and control the ball; then attempt to dribble past your opponent (defender) and beyond her end line. You must stay within the 10-yard-wide lane when attempting to beat the defender on the dribble. Award yourself 1 point for successfully dribbling past the defender and over the end line with possession of the ball. After each attempt, return to your respective end lines and repeat. Partners alternate playing as dribbler and defender. Continue the exercise until each player has attempted to take on her opponent 20 times. The player scoring more points wins.

### To Increase Difficulty for Attacker

- Decrease width of field so dribbler has less space in which to maneuver.
- Add second defender, creating a 1v2 situation in which dribbler must beat two opponents on the dribble.

### To Decrease Difficulty for Attacker

- Require defender to assume a "crab" position (sitting position with weight supported by hands and feet) to limit mobility.
- Increase width of field to increase available space for dribbler.

### Success Check

- Attack defender at game speed.
- Use deceptive body feints to unbalance opponent and dribbling movements such as step-overs and scissors moves.
- Employ sudden changes of speed and direction.
- Accelerate past defender.

### Score Your Success

0 to 7 points = 0 points

8 to 11 points = 1 point

12 to 14 points = 3 points

15 or more points = 5 points

Your score ___

---

# Beat an Opponent Dribbling Drill 5
## Score by Dribbling Only

Form two equal teams of five to seven players each. Play on a field area approximately 50 by 35 yards. Regular soccer rules apply except for the method of scoring. Goals are scored by dribbling the ball over the opponent's end line rather than by shooting. There are no goalkeepers. The entire length of the end line is considered the goal line. Award 1 team point each time a player dribbles the ball over the opponent's end line. Play for 20 minutes and keep track of points. The team scoring more points wins.

### To Increase Difficulty for Attacking Team

- Decrease width of field to reduce available space.
- Add two neutral players who always play with defending team to provide two-player numerical advantage.

### To Decrease Difficulty for Attacking Team

- Increase width of field to provide more space in which to maneuver.
- Add two neutral players who always play with attacking team to provide two-player advantage.

### Success Check

- Use dribbling skills in appropriate situations and areas of field.
- Maintain close control of ball.
- Attack defender at speed.
- Employ sudden changes of speed and direction to unbalance defender.
- Push ball past defender and accelerate into open space.

### Score Your Success

Each player on the winning team is awarded 1 point for each goal scored, up to a maximum of 6.

Each player on the losing team is awarded 1 point for each goal scored, up to a maximum of 3.

Your score ___

# Beat an Opponent Dribbling Drill 6
## Tactical Dribbling

Divide into two equal teams of five to eight players. Use markers to outline a 60- by 40-yard field with a regulation goal on each end line. Divide the field lengthwise into three 20- by 40-yard zones. Designate one player from each team as a goalkeeper who positions in the goal. Begin with a kickoff from the center of the field. Teams score 1 point for kicking the ball through the opponent's goal and 1 point each time an attacker dribbles past a defender in their attacking third of the field. Regular soccer rules apply except for the following zone restrictions:

- Players may use only one- and two-touch passes in the zone nearest their goal.
- In the middle zone, players may dribble to advance the ball into open space but may not take on and beat opponents.
- Dribbling to take on an opponent is mandatory in the attacking third of the field, an area in which players must beat an opponent on the dribble before passing to a teammate or shooting on goal.

Violation of a zone restriction is penalized by loss of possession to the opponents. Play for 20 minutes. The team scoring more points wins the game.

### To Increase Difficulty for Attacking Team

- Reduce field size to restrict space and time available.
- Add one neutral player who plays with defending team to provide one-player numerical advantage.

### To Decrease Difficulty for Attacking Team

- Increase field size to provide dribblers more space in which to maneuver.
- Allow three or fewer touches of ball before passing in defending third of field.
- Add two neutral players who play with attacking team to provide two-player numerical advantage.

### Success Check

- Maintain close control of ball at all times.
- Keep head up to recognize available options.
- Employ sudden changes of speed and direction to unbalance opponent.
- Dribble in appropriate situations and in appropriate areas of field.

### Score Your Success

Each player on the winning team gets 2 points for the win and 1 additional point for each time he successfully dribbles past an opponent in the attacking third of the field. Each player on the losing team gets 0 team points but is awarded 1 point each time he successfully dribbles past an opponent in the attacking third of the field.

0 to 5 points = 1 point

6 to 10 points = 3 points

11 or more points = 5 points

Your score ___

# DRIBBLING TO MAINTAIN POSSESSION

At times you will find yourself with very little room to maneuver, as when being pressured by two or even three opposing players. In this situation your immediate concern becomes possession rather than penetration. You can retain control of the ball by dribbling out of trouble so that you can pass the ball to an available teammate. By combining sudden changes of speed and direction with deceptive foot and body movements, you can unbalance opponents and create space in which to dribble and maneuver with the ball. It is imperative that you keep the ball under very close control at all times (see figure 1.2).

## Figure 1.2    DRIBBLING TO MAINTAIN POSSESSION

### Preparation

1. Assume crouched position with knees bent and ball within close control.
2. Maintain low center of gravity and wide base.
3. Display balance and body control.
4. Keep head up and be aware of immediate surroundings.

### Execution

1. Respond to pressure of opponents.
2. Use body feints and deceptive foot movements to unbalance opponent.
3. Control ball with appropriate surface of foot.
4. Position body to create distance between opponent and ball.
5. Change speed, direction, or both.

### Follow-Through

1. Maintain close control of ball at all times.
2. Move away from pressure.
3. Release ball to teammate.

### MISSTEP

The ball rolls away from your control and into the path of a defending opponent.

### CORRECTION

Keep the ball beneath your body as you dribble, as close to your feet as possible. From that position you can change direction quickly, and the ball is always within your immediate control.

### MISSTEP

You fail to recognize pressure and expose the ball to an opponent.

### CORRECTION

This error can occur when your vision is focused entirely on the ball and you are not aware of your immediate surroundings. Keep your head up as much as possible when dribbling, and try to maintain a wide base of support to keep distance between the ball and the opponent. Maintaining good field vision is just as important as maintaining close control of the ball.

## Possession Dribbling Drill 1   Small Circles

Each player has a ball. Everyone finds an open area approximately 4 feet (1.2 m) in diameter to work in. Perform a continuous series of sole-of-the-foot rollbacks, quarter turns, V-outs, and similar movements with the ball. Practice pushing and pulling the ball, and tight turning with the ball. The objective is to have the ball "on a string" (i.e., always within close control) while quickly changing positions. Complete five 90-second training bouts with a 30-second rest between bouts. Score 1 point for each 90-second bout without loss of control of the ball.

### To Increase Difficulty

- Change both speed and direction with each touch of ball.
- Reduce size of playing area.

### To Decrease Difficulty

- Increase size of playing area.
- Reduce speed of movement.
- Reduce bouts to 60 seconds.

### *Success Check*

- Maintain close control of ball.
- Use various surfaces of foot to control ball.

- Keep knees bent and center of gravity low.
- Combine sudden changes of speed with change of direction.
- Practice deceptive foot and body movements.

### *Score Your Success*

4 or 5 losses of possession = 1 point

2 or 3 losses of possession = 3 points

0 or 1 loss of possession = 5 points

Your score ___

# Possession Dribbling Drill 2    Unopposed Dribble

Randomly position 15 to 20 markers to represent stationary defenders within a 20-by 20-yard area. Dribble unopposed within the area, using various surfaces of your foot to control the ball as you quickly move between and around the imaginary defenders. Incorporate sudden changes of direction into your dribbling pattern. For example, quickly change direction by cutting the ball around a marker with the instep of your right foot; then accelerate into open space by pushing the ball with the outside of your left foot. Begin slowly and gradually increase the pace to game speed. Dribble for five minutes continuously, rest for 60 seconds, and repeat. Keep track of the number of markers you contact while dribbling.

## To Increase Difficulty

- Place markers closer together to reduce available space.
- Change both speed and direction with each touch of ball.
- Increase dribbling speed.

## To Decrease Difficulty

- Position markers farther apart.
- Reduce dribbling speed.

## Success Check

- Maintain close control of ball.
- Keep knees bent and a center of gravity low.

- Combine sudden changes of speed and direction.
- Incorporate deceptive foot movements.

## Score Your Success

Contact 11 or more markers in five minutes = 1 point

Contact 6 to 10 markers in five minutes = 3 points

Contact 0 to 5 markers in five minutes = 5 points

Your score ___

# Possession Dribbling Drill 3    Magnets

Use markers to outline a 25- by 25-yard area. All players station within the area, each with a ball. On the coach's command, begin dribbling randomly within the area, maintaining close control of the ball at all times. Consider yourselves magnets with similar charges; that is, you repel each other. When you come near another dribbler, immediately change course as you are "repelled" off in a different direction. Play for three minutes. Earn 1 point each time you repel off another player (i.e., change direction).

## To Increase Difficulty

- Reduce playing area and available space.
- Perform at game speed.

## To Decrease Difficulty

- Increase size of area.
- Dribble at half speed.

*(continued)*

Possession Dribbling Drill 3 *(continued)*

## Success Check

- Use various surfaces of foot to control ball.
- Use explosive changes of speed and direction to repel away from other players.
- Always maintain distance between ball and nearby players.

## Score Your Success

20 to 25 points in a three-minute game = 1 point

26 to 39 points in a three-minute game = 3 points

40 or more points in a three-minute game = 5 points

Your score ___

# Possession Dribbling Drill 4   Takeovers

Use markers to outline a rectangular area 25 by 30 yards. All players position within the area, with one ball for every two players. On command, all players begin to move randomly throughout the playing area. Those with a ball dribble; those without a ball jog at three-quarter speed. Dribblers look to exchange possession of the ball with one of the free players by dribbling directly at that player and using the "takeover" maneuver. As two players exchange a ball, they should execute the "same foot" takeover—that is, if a player has the ball on her right foot, the teammate taking the ball does so with her right foot. The same procedure applies when the ball is on the left foot. Players are awarded 1 point for each successful takeover with a teammate. Perform as many takeovers as possible in the time allotted.

## To Increase Difficulty

- Reduce available space.
- Dribble and perform takeovers at game pace.
- Add defender who attempts to prevent takeovers.

## To Decrease Difficulty

- Increase size of area.
- Dribble at half speed.

## Success Check

- Dribble directly at a teammate who does not have a ball.
- Use same-foot takeover maneuver.
- Avoid colliding with teammates.

## Score Your Success

20 to 25 points in a five-minute game = 1 point

26 to 39 points in a five-minute game = 3 points

40 or more points in a five-minute game = 5 points

Your score ___

# Possession Dribbling Drill 5
## Avoid the Challenge

Use markers to outline a 30- by 30-yard area. Designate two players as chasers who station outside of the area, without soccer balls. All other players, each with a ball, position within the area. Each player within the area tucks a colored scrimmage vest into the back of his shorts so that it hangs out. All players within the square begin dribbling randomly. On the coach's command, the chasers sprint into the area to chase the dribblers and pull the scrimmage vests from their shorts. Dribblers use sudden changes of speed, direction, or both, to evade the chasers. If a dribbler's vest is pulled out, he immediately becomes a chaser and attempts to steal another dribbler's vest. The original chaser tucks the vest in his shorts and becomes a dribbler. Dribblers must maintain close possession of the ball at all times; they are not permitted to leave the ball to evade the chasers. A dribbler is penalized 1 point each time his vest is stolen by a chaser. Play for five minutes continuously.

### To Increase Difficulty for Dribblers

- Reduce size of area.
- Add additional chasers.

### To Decrease Difficulty for Dribblers

- Increase size of field area so dribblers have more space in which to maneuver.

### Success Check

- Keep ball under close control at all times.

- Employ sudden changes of speed and direction.
- Keep head up with vision on field and chasers.
- Recognize defensive pressure and respond accordingly.

### Score Your Success

Vest stolen 6 or more times = 1 point

Vest stolen 3 to 5 times = 3 points

Vest stolen 2 or fewer times = 5 points

Your score ___

# Possession Dribbling Drill 6   Knockout

Play this game with 8 to 10 teammates. All players but three station within the center circle of the soccer field, each with a ball. The three players without balls (defenders) station outside the circle. On the coach's command, the defenders enter the area and attempt to kick the dribblers' balls out of the circle. Dribblers use sudden changes of speed and direction coupled with close control of the ball to keep possession and ride off the challenge. A dribbler whose ball is kicked out of the circle should quickly retrieve it and return to play. Play for three minutes continuously; then rotate three new players as defenders, and repeat. Continue three-minute games until all players have served one game as a defender. Keep track of how many times your ball is kicked out of the circle.

*(continued)*

Possession Dribbling Drill 6 *(continued)*

### To Increase Difficulty for Dribblers

- Reduce size of area.
- Add additional chasers to reduce available space.

### To Decrease Difficulty for Dribblers

- Increase size of area so dribblers have more space in which to maneuver.

## *Success Check*

- Keep ball under close control.
- Shield ball from challenging defender.

- Employ sudden changes of speed and direction.
- Keep head up with vision on field.
- Maintain balance and body control.

## *Score Your Success*

Ball kicked out of circle 6 or more times = 1 point

Ball kicked out of circle 3 to 5 times = 3 points

Ball kicked out of circle 0 to 2 times = 5 points

Your score ___

# DRIBBLING FOR SPEED

In some situations dribbling speed takes priority over close control of the ball, as when you find yourself behind the opponent's defense in a breakaway situation. In this case your primary aim is to get to the goal as fast as possible. Use either the outside surface of your instep or your full instep to push the ball ahead into the open space, sprint to it, and then push it again (see figure 1.3).

### MISSTEP

You use short, choppy steps to advance with the ball.

### CORRECTION

Push the ball out ahead and away from your feet. Stride to the ball and push it again. Do not touch the ball every step or two as you would when dribbling for close control.

## Figure 1.3 DRIBBLING FOR SPEED

### Preparation

1. Keep head up with vision on field.
2. Maintain upright running posture.
3. Push ball ahead but within range of control.

### Execution

1. Use outside surface of instep to contact ball.
2. Push ball several strides forward and sprint to it.
3. Take most direct route toward goal.

### Follow-Through

1. Use long, smooth running strides.
2. Accelerate to ball and push again.

# Speed Dribbling Drill 1    Speed Dribble Relay

Partner with two teammates. You and one teammate station on the goal line, while the third player positions on the edge of the penalty area (18-yard line) facing you. You have the ball. Begin the relay by dribbling as quickly as possible to the top edge of the penalty area. Exchange possession of the ball with the player positioned there. Remain at that spot while the other player dribbles to the goal line and exchanges possession with the player there. That player completes the cycle by dribbling the ball back to you. Continue the relay until each player has dribbled 20 lengths. Award yourself 1 point each time you dribble the 18-yard distance at top speed and exchange possession of the ball without error. An error occurs if the ball bounces out of your range of control as you dribble or as you exchange possession with a teammate.

### To Increase Difficulty

- Increase dribbling distance to 30 yards.
- Increase number of repetitions performed.
- Add extra player who chases dribbler from behind.

### To Decrease Difficulty

- Reduce dribbling distance.
- Dribble at half speed.

## Success Check

- Maintain upright running posture.
- Push ball several steps ahead with each touch using outside surface of instep.
- Accelerate to ball at top speed.
- Slow pace when exchanging ball with teammate.

## Score Your Success

Fewer than 10 lengths without error = 0 points

10 to 14 lengths without error = 1 point

15 to 17 lengths without error = 3 points

18 to 20 lengths without error = 5 points

Your score ___

# Speed Dribbling Drill 2
# First to the Penalty Area

Players are in pairs within the center circle of the soccer field, one with a ball and one without. The player with possession pushes the ball toward one of the goals and attempts to dribble at top speed into that penalty area. The other player, the chaser, pauses for a count of 1 and then tries to catch the dribbler and kick the ball away before the dribbler can reach the penalty area. The chaser must stay on his feet at all times; sliding from behind to dislodge the ball is prohibited. The dribbler is awarded 1 point for entering the penalty area with possession of the ball. Players return to the halfway line, switch roles, and repeat the drill. Continue the drill until each partner has taken 10 turns as the dribbler.

### To Increase Difficulty

- Do not require chaser to pause for a count of 1 before leaving center circle.
- Require dribbler to reach goal line to score.

### To Decrease Difficulty

- Shorten distance to be dribbled.
- Reduce number of repetitions.
- Require chaser to pause for a count of 2 before leaving center circle.

## Success Check

- Maintain upright dribbling posture.

- Push ball several feet ahead and accelerate to it.
- Push ball forward with outside surface of instep.
- Take most direct route to the goal.
- While dribbling, position your body to cut off defender's path to ball.

## Score Your Success

0 to 4 points = 1 point

5 to 7 points = 3 points

8 to 10 points = 5 points

Your score ___

# Speed Dribbling Drill 3    Attack or Defend

Form two equal teams of four to six players each. Use markers to outline a 30- by 40-yard playing area bisected by a midline. Position a supply of soccer balls, one ball for every two players, evenly spaced along the midline. Teams station on opposite end lines with players spread an equal distance apart. On the coach's command, players from both teams sprint to the midline and compete for possession of a ball. Players who win a ball then attempt to return it over their own end starting line by dribbling. Players who fail to gain possession of a ball can prevent scores by chasing the dribblers and kicking their balls away before they can dribble them over the end line. Players score 1 point for dribbling a ball over their end line. The round ends when all balls have been dribbled over an end line or have been kicked out of the area. Play 10 rounds with a short rest between them. Players keep track of their own points.

### To Increase Difficulty

- Increase length of field.
- Add two extra defenders to chase dribblers.

### To Decrease Difficulty

- Place two balls for every three players on midline to decrease number of chasing defenders.

## Success Check

- Be first to a ball.
- Quickly turn and begin dribbling back to starting end line.

- Push ball out from feet and accelerate forward.
- Position your body between ball and defender attempting to win it.
- Follow most direct route to end line.

## Score Your Success

Return 0 to 2 balls over end line = 1 point

Return 3 to 5 balls over end line = 2 points

Return 6 or more balls over end line = 3 points

Your score ___

## Speed Dribbling Drill 4
## Dribble Through the Open Goal

Use markers to outline a 30- by 30-yard area. Station 8 to 10 players, each with a ball, along one sideline, with 2 to 3 yards between players. Use cones or discs to make a series of mini-goals, 2 yards wide, on the opposite sideline. There should be *three fewer mini-goals* than there are players with a ball. On command, the players dribble as fast as they can across the square and through an open goal. Once a dribbler goes through an open goal, that goal is closed to any other dribbler. Dribblers earn 1 point each time they dribble through an open goal. Repeat 20 times. Players keep track of their own points.

### To Increase Difficulty

- Increase distance to goals.
- Add defenders to chase dribblers.

### To Decrease Difficulty

- Shorten distance to goals.
- Use two fewer goals than players.

### Success Check

- Be first through a goal.
- Push ball out from your feet and accelerate forward.
- Follow most direct route to goal.

### Score Your Success

4 to 8 points = 1 point

9 to 12 points = 2 points

13 or more points = 3 points

Your score ___

# SHIELDING SKILLS

There will be times when you simply can't dribble fast enough to lose an opponent who is chasing you down. Or possibly an opponent is challenging for possession in an area where there is no available space in which to dribble away from pressure. In these situations you must be able to fend off the challenge until an available passing option presents itself. Doing so requires strength, balance, and proper positioning of your body between the ball and the opponent, a technique commonly referred to as shielding the ball (figure 1.4).

Position sideways to the opponent and assume a slightly crouched posture with knees bent and a low center of gravity. In this position you can establish a wide base of support and create greater distance between the opponent and the ball. Control the ball with the foot farther from the opponent, and use body feints, deceptive foot movements, and sudden changes of direction to unbalance the defender, as explained earlier in this chapter. Keep the ball under close control at all times.

Figure 1.4   **SHIELDING THE BALL**

*Preparation*

1. Position sideways to defender.
2. Assume crouched posture with knees bent.
3. Place feet to create a wide base of support.
4. Extend arm nearer to defender to make yourself wider.
5. Keep head up for maximum field vision.

*Execution*

1. Control ball with foot farther from opponent.
2. Manipulate ball with outside, inside, or sole of foot.
3. Maintain wide base of support.
4. Respond to opponent's pressure.
5. Use body feints to unbalance opponent.

*Follow-Through*

1. Readjust body position in response to pressure from opponent.
2. Use sudden changes of direction to maintain distance between ball and defender.
3. Release ball to nearby teammate to alleviate pressure.

**MISSTEP**

You expose (show) the ball, and the defender pokes it away.

**CORRECTION**

Keep the ball as far from the defender as possible but within your range of control. Constantly reposition your body between the ball and the defender to hide the ball.

### MISSTEP
You are knocked off balance by an opponent's legal shoulder charge and lose possession of the ball.

### CORRECTION
Poor balance can result from standing too upright with feet too close together. Maintain a crouched posture with feet approximately shoulder-width apart (i.e., a wide base of support) and weight evenly distributed. Proper balance leads to increased strength on the ball.

## Shielding Drill 1   1v1 Possession

Partner with a teammate and play within a 12- by 12-yard area. You are the attacker; your partner plays the defender. Attempt to shield the ball from the defender while moving within the field area. The defender marks (covers) tightly but applies only passive (50 percent) pressure and does not actually try to win the ball, instead forcing you to quickly reposition in response to the pressure. Play for 60 seconds. Penalize yourself 1 point each time the ball leaves the field area or each time it rolls outside of your range of control where the defender could poke it away. Play five 90-second rounds with a short rest between them; then switch roles and play five more rounds. Keep a tally of your penalty points.

### To Increase Difficulty
- Decrease size of playing area.
- Increase duration of round to 90 seconds.
- Permit defender to apply maximum pressure to win ball.

### To Decrease Difficulty
- Increase size of playing area.
- Shorten rounds to 30 seconds.

### Success Check
- Position yourself sideways to opponent with your body between ball and opponent.

- Control ball with foot farther from opponent.
- Use sudden changes of speed and direction coupled with deceptive body feints.
- Move away from defensive pressure.

### Score Your Success

15 or more penalty points in five rounds = 1 point

11 to 14 penalty points in five rounds = 3 points

0 to 10 penalty points in five rounds = 5 points

Your score ___

# Shielding Drill 2   Evade the Double Team

Form groups of three. Each player has a ball. Use markers to outline a 25- by 25-yard playing area. Designate one player as "it"; the others are chasers. The player who is "it" dribbles into the field area. The chasers closely follow, dribbling their balls, and attempt to pass and contact the "it" player's ball with their own. The "it" player uses sudden changes of speed and direction and positions his body to shield the ball from the chasers. Play for 90 seconds. The "it" player is assessed 1 penalty point each time his ball is contacted by one of the chaser's balls. Play three 90-second rounds, with a different player designated as "it" for each round.

## To Increase Difficulty

- Decrease size of playing area to restrict available space.
- Add third chaser.

## To Decrease Difficulty

- Shorten duration of rounds to 60 seconds.
- Use only one chaser with ball.

## Success Check

- Maintain close control of ball at all times.

- Use sudden changes of speed and direction to lose chasers.
- Shield ball with body.
- Feel pressure and move away from it.

## Score Your Success

6 or more penalty points per round = 1 point

3 to 5 penalty points per round = 3 points

0 to 2 penalty points per round = 5 points

Your score ___

# Shielding Drill 3   All Versus All

Use markers to outline a 30- by 30-yard playing area. Sixteen to 20 players, each with a ball, dribble within the playing area. On a signal from the coach, the game becomes "all versus all." Each player must protect her ball while attempting to kick the other players' balls out of the field area. A player whose ball leaves the area is eliminated from the game. This exercise emphasizes proper execution of shielding and dribbling skills. The game continues until only one player remains in possession of a ball. Eliminated players should immediately retrieve their balls and practice ball juggling or dribbling maneuvers outside of the field area until the game ends. Repeat for several rounds.

## To Increase Difficulty

- Adjust size of playing area to reduce available space.
- Add additional chasers who are not dribbling.

## To Decrease Difficulty

- Increase size of playing area.

*(continued)*

Shielding Drill 3 *(continued)*

## *Success Check*

- Keep head up with vision on opponents.
- Feel pressure and react accordingly.
- Control ball with foot farther from challenging opponent.
- Position body between challenging defender and ball.
- Use dribbling skills to create additional space and time in which to maneuver.

## *Score Your Success*

One of final eight players eliminated = 1 point

One of final six players eliminated = 2 points

One of final four players eliminated = 3 points

Last player standing = 5 points

Your score ___

# TACKLING SKILLS

It is quite obvious that your team can't score goals if the other team has possession of the ball. You can regain possession for the team by intercepting passes or by tackling the ball from an opponent. Three basic skills are used for tackling the ball: the block, the poke, and the slide tackle. Successful execution of each technique requires balance and body control, proper timing of the challenge, sound judgment, and confidence.

In my 30-plus years as a player, coach, and camp director, I have witnessed few players demonstrate adequate tackling skills. This is because these important defensive skills are somewhat difficult to execute, and also because players simply do not practice them as often as they should. Granted, it is probably more fun to practice shooting and dribbling skills, but you won't get a chance to use either of those skills in actual match situations unless you first gain possession of the ball.

## Block Tackle

Use the block tackle (figure 1.5) to win the ball from an opponent who is dribbling directly at you. Quickly close the distance to the ball and position your feet in a staggered stance with one foot slightly ahead of the other. Assume a slightly crouched posture with a low center of gravity and your arms out to the sides. In this position you will have good balance and be able to react quickly to the dribbler's sudden movements or changes of direction. Tackle the ball by contacting it with the inside surface of your blocking foot. Position the blocking foot sideways with your toes pointed slightly upward. Keep the foot and ankle firmly positioned as you generate momentum forward and drive the inside surface of your foot powerfully through the center of the ball.

## Figure 1.5 **BLOCK TACKLE**

### Approach

1. Quickly close distance to dribbler.
2. Assume staggered stance with weight balanced over balls of feet.
3. Maintain crouched posture with low center of gravity.
4. Keep shoulders slightly angled to dribbler.

### Execution

1. Position blocking foot sideways with toes pointed slightly upward.
2. Keep blocking foot and ankle firm.
3. Drive inside surface of foot through center of ball.
4. Shift weight forward.

### Follow-Through

1. Generate momentum through point of contact.
2. Win ball.
3. Initiate counterattack.

Once you've made the decision to challenge for possession, you must commit yourself to the tackle with power and determination. When doing so, you must play the ball, not the opponent. If the referee judges that you are intentionally contacting the opponent before contacting the ball, you will be signaled for a rule violation.

### MISSTEP

The opponent pushes the ball through your block and races past you.

### CORRECTION

Keep your body compact with your knees flexed and a low center of gravity. Block the ball with a short, powerful snap of your leg. Transfer your full body weight forward through the point of contact.

## Poke Tackle

Use the poke tackle technique (figure 1.6) to dispossess an opponent when approaching from the side or slightly behind the dribbler. Quickly close the distance to the dribbler, extend the leg and foot nearer to the ball, and poke the ball away with your toes. Be sure to play the ball, not the opponent. Kicking the opponent when trying to set the ball free is a foul.

### MISSTEP

You make a reckless challenge and physically contact the dribbler before tackling the ball.

### CORRECTION

Maintain body control at all times. As you close the distance to the dribbler, keep a clear view of the ball. At the appropriate moment, extend your leg and foot to poke the ball away. Focus on the ball.

## Figure 1.6  **POKE TACKLE**

*Approach*

1. Close distance to dribbler.
2. Maintain balance and body control.
3. Focus on ball.

*Execution*

1. Extend nearer leg and foot toward ball.
2. Bend balance leg.
3. Poke ball away with toes.
4. Avoid physical contact with dribbler prior to contacting ball.

*Follow-Through*

1. Maintain balance and body control.
2. Chase after and collect ball.

## Slide Tackle

The slide tackle technique (figure 1.7) is generally used to dispossess an opponent when you are approaching from the side, or in some cases from behind, the dribbler. The body action looks similar to that of a baseball player sliding into a base. As you near the dribbler, leave your feet and slide on your side to a position slightly ahead of the ball. At the same time, snap your leg straight and kick the ball away using the instep of your foot. It is important that you contact the ball first, before making any contact with the dribbler; if not, the referee will probably whistle a foul and award a free kick to the opposing team.

### MISSTEP
You take down the opponent when attempting to win the ball.

### CORRECTION
Do not attempt to execute the slide tackle from directly behind the dribbler. Angle your approach from one side or the other before leaving your feet to slide ahead of the ball. Hook your leg around from the side to kick the ball away.

### Figure 1.7  SLIDE TACKLE

*Approach*

1. Approach dribbler from side or from behind.
2. Maintain balance and body control.
3. Slow approach slightly as you near ball.

*Execution*

1. Leave feet and slide on your side.
2. Place arms to sides for balance.
3. Extend sliding (lower) leg ahead of ball with foot extended.
4. Bend opposite leg at knee.
5. Snap sliding leg and foot into ball.
6. Contact ball on instep.

*Follow-Through*

1. Jump up immediately after dislodging ball.
2. Chase and collect ball.

## Hook Slide Tackle

The hook slide tackle (see figure 1.8) is a slight variation of the standard slide tackle. This technique is typically used to dispossess an opponent when approaching from behind. As you get near the dribbler, slide on your side past him. Snap your blocking (upper) foot on a slightly downward plane with the ankle locked. Contact the ball with the instep of the upper foot. Time your challenge to tackle the ball when it separates from the dribbler's feet so you avoid contact with the dribbler before contacting the ball. After executing the tackle, jump quickly to your feet and initiate a counterattack.

In most instances the standard slide tackle and the hook tackle variation are not the preferred options. These techniques are appropriate in situations in which the block tackle is not possible, such as when an opponent has beaten you on the dribble and there is little hope of catching him or when an opponent is dribbling past you along a touchline and you leave your feet to kick the ball out of bounds. Because you must go to the ground to challenge for the ball, you are in a poor position to recover should you fail to execute the tackle successfully.

**Figure 1.8** Hook slide tackle.

# Tackling Drill 1    Block Tackle

Face a teammate who stands 3 yards away with a ball at her feet. Practice the block tackle technique as your partner walks the ball toward you. Close the distance to the ball, position the blocking foot sideways, and tackle the ball with the inside surface of your foot. Maintain a low center of gravity, and keep your foot firm as it contacts the ball. Execute 25 block tackles with your favorite foot. Award yourself 1 point for each correct execution of the technique.

## To Increase Difficulty

- Increase number of repetitions.
- Attempt to tackle ball from player dribbling at you at speed.

## To Decrease Difficulty

- Practice block tackle on stationary target.

## Success Check

- Assume crouched posture with knees bent.
- Maintain balance and body control.
- Position blocking foot firmly sideways.
- Tackle with power and commitment.
- Generate momentum forward through point of contact with ball.

## Score Your Success

Fewer than 20 correct executions = 0 points

21 to 24 correct executions = 1 point

25 correct executions = 3 points

Your score ___

# Tackling Drill 2    Deny Penetration

Use markers to outline a 5- by 10-yard playing area. You and a partner get in position at opposite ends of the area; your partner has the ball. On command, your partner dribbles at you from a distance of 10 yards. Move forward to close the distance to the dribbler and attempt to block tackle or poke tackle the ball. You may tackle with either foot, depending on the dribbler's angle of approach. Repeat 20 times, after which you switch roles with the dribbler and repeat. Award yourself 1 point for each successful tackle that prevents the opponent from dribbling the ball over your end line.

## To Increase Difficulty for Defender

- Increase width of area.

## To Decrease Difficulty for Defender

- Decrease width of area.
- Require dribbler to advance at half speed.

## Success Check

- Assume crouched posture with low center of gravity.
- Maintain balance and body control.
- Keep blocking foot firm.
- Contact center of ball.
- Avoid contact with opponent before contacting ball.

### Score Your Success

0 to 8 points = 0 points

9 to 11 points = 1 point

12 to 15 points = 3 points

16 to 20 points = 5 points

Your score ___

---

# Tackling Drill 3    Hot Box

Use discs or cones to mark the corners of a 10- by 10-yard square. Divide players into two teams (A and B) of three players each. Teams face each other in single-file lines, on opposite sides of the square. Each player has a ball to use when in an attacking role. Team A stations one player inside the square as the first defender (without a ball), facing team B. On command, the first player from team B attempts to dribble through the square to the opposite sideline. The defender must prevent the attacker from dribbling past him by tackling the ball. If the attacker succeeds in dribbling through the square to the opposite sideline, the defending team is penalized 1 team point. Once beaten, the defender immediately turns to face the second player from the team B line who tries to dribble through the square. If the defender successfully tackles the ball, he is awarded 1 point, and immediately goes to his team's line of dribblers and becomes an attacker. The team B player immediately positions within the square as a defender to face a dribbler from team A. Play for 10 minutes and keep track of points scored.

### To Increase Difficulty for Defender

- Increase width of area.

### To Decrease Difficulty for Defender

- Decrease width of area.

### Success Check

- Assume crouched posture with low center of gravity.
- Channel dribbler to one side (toward sideline) of square.
- Maintain balance and body control.

- Keep blocking foot firm.
- Contact center of ball with momentum forward.
- Avoid contact with opponent before contacting ball.

### Score Your Success (team score)

0 to 6 points = 0 points

7 to 10 points = 1 point

11 to 14 points = 3 points

15 or more points = 5 points

Your score ___

---

# Tackling Drill 4  Slide Tackle

Partner with a teammate, and play on one end of a regulation field. You position at the top edge of the penalty area, 18 yards from goal, facing the end line. Your partner (server) positions directly behind you, about 20 yards from goal, with a supply of balls. The server kicks a rolling ball toward the end line. You immediately sprint after the ball and execute a slide tackle to prevent the ball from rolling over the end line; then return and repeat. Perform 10 repetitions. Award yourself 1 point for each successful execution of the slide tackle technique.

## To Increase Difficulty

- Server dribbles ball toward end line and you attempt to slide tackle ball.

## To Decrease Difficulty

- Reduce distance of recovery run.

## Success Check

- Slide ahead of ball.

- Place arms at sides for balance and body control.
- Snap lower leg and contact ball on instep.

## Score Your Success

0 to 3 points = 1 point

4 to 6 points = 2 points

7 to 10 points = 3 points

Your score ___

# Tackling Drill 5  Tackle All

Position markers to designate a field area of approximately 30 by 30 yards. Divide the group into two teams of equal numbers (at least six players per team). Members of one team play as defenders and initially station outside of the area; members of the other team are attackers. Each attacker has possession of a ball within the area. To begin, the attackers dribble in random fashion within the field area. On the coach's command, the defenders sprint into the area and attempt to tackle dribblers' balls. Defenders may use either the block or the poke tackle technique. Slide tackles are prohibited in this drill because of the restricted space. If a defender successfully tackles a ball, she kicks it out of the area and immediately tries to dispossess another dribbler. Defenders are awarded 1 point for each ball they kick out of the area. A dribbler who loses her ball should retrieve it immediately and reenter the game. Play for three minutes; then teams switch roles and repeat. Defenders keep track of their own points.

## To Increase Difficulty for Defenders

- Increase size of playing area.
- Use fewer defenders than dribblers.

## To Decrease Difficulty for Defenders

- Reduce size of playing area.
- Use fewer dribblers than defenders.

## Success Check

- Quickly close distance to ball.
- Ensure balance and body control.
- Maintain low center of gravity.
- Commit to tackle with power and determination.
- Avoid contact with dribbler before tackling ball.

## Score Your Success

0 to 4 points scored as defender = 1 point

5 or more points scored as defender = 3 points

Your score ___

# SUCCESS SUMMARY

Players who can consistently take on and beat opponents on the dribble play a vital role in team attack. Although some players are by nature better dribblers than others, everyone can develop effective dribbling skills. It simply takes practice. All you need is a ball and a patch of open ground. Keep in mind that dribbling is an individual art that can be expressed in a variety of ways. Rehearse your moves against stationary cones, imaginary defenders, or live defenders when training with teammates. Pay particular attention to how quickly you can change speed and direction, how effective your body feints and foot movements are, and how you position your body to protect the ball from an opponent challenging for possession. Review the photos and the success checks in the drills to evaluate your overall performance and get helpful hints for improvement.

It's also important to develop individual defensive skills. Practice the block, poke, and slide tackle techniques in both practice and actual game situations. If possible, watch a video of yourself in training or an actual game competition to evaluate your ability to execute the various tackling techniques.

Each of the drills in this step has been assigned a point value so you can evaluate your performance and chart your progress. Enter your score in the following table and total your points.

### Beat an Opponent Dribbling Drills

| | |
|---|---|
| 1. Dribble the Slalom | _____ out of 5 |
| 2. Unbalance the Defender | _____ out of 5 |
| 3. Take On a Passive Defender | _____ out of 5 |
| 4. End-to-End Game | _____ out of 5 |
| 5. Score by Dribbling Only | _____ out of 6 |
| 6. Tactical Dribbling | _____ out of 5 |

## Possession Dribbling Drills

1. Small Circles ___ out of 5
2. Unopposed Dribble ___ out of 5
3. Magnets ___ out of 5
4. Takeovers ___ out of 5
5. Avoid the Challenge ___ out of 5
6. Knockout ___ out of 5

## Speed Dribbling Drills

1. Speed Dribble Relay ___ out of 5
2. First to the Penalty Area ___ out of 5
3. Attack or Defend ___ out of 3
4. Dribble Through the Open Goal ___ out of 3

## Shielding Drills

1. 1v1 Possession ___ out of 5
2. Evade the Double Team ___ out of 5
3. All Versus All ___ out of 5

## Tackling Drills

1. Block Tackle ___ out of 3
2. Deny Penetration ___ out of 5
3. Hot Box ___ out of 5
4. Slide Tackle ___ out of 3
5. Tackle All ___ out of 3

**Total** ___ **out of 111**

A combined score of 90 or greater indicates that you are prepared to move on to meet the challenges presented in step 2. A score in the range of 65 to 89 is considered adequate. You can move on to step 2 after additional practice of the dribbling, shielding, and tackling skills in step 1. If you scored 64 or fewer points, you have not sufficiently mastered the skills covered in step 1. Review, practice, and improve your performance of all of these skills before moving on to step 2.

# Passing and Receiving Rolling Balls

The soccer ball is a precious commodity. Every player on the pitch wants a piece of it, and without it your team cannot score goals. The fact remains, however, that there is only one ball to be shared among 22 players, and that sharing is accomplished through a variety of passing skills.

It is important to realize that the soccer team is much more than a group of talented individuals each doing their own thing. Although flashes of individual brilliance can and sometimes do decide the outcome of a game, at the end of the day team success ultimately depends on players' working in combination. Even the most talented players can't do it alone! To maximize team performance, players must mesh their individual talents to create a smooth, functioning whole. Passing and receiving skills form the vital thread that allows 11 individuals to play as one—that is, the whole to perform greater than the sum of its parts.

To perform successfully at higher levels of competition, players must be able to pass and receive the ball accurately under the game pressures of limited time and space, physical fatigue, and challenging opponents. Passing and receiving skills are generally grouped together for the simple reason that they complement one another. Each passed ball should, in theory, be received and controlled by a teammate. The mastery of passing and receiving skills enables teammates to maintain possession of the ball, dictate the tempo of the game, and ultimately create scoring opportunities. Top-flight professional teams such as Barcelona and Manchester United clearly demonstrate how this can be done—watch them!

Successful passing combinations are characterized by passes that are accurate, correctly paced, and properly timed. The team cannot generate the combination play required to score goals if its players cannot pass the ball accurately among themselves. Correct pace has to do with the speed, or weight, of the pass. The pass should be at a speed that allows the receiving player to easily control and prepare the ball for the next action. Timing has to do with the moment of release. The pass should arrive at a teammate's feet so that he does not have to break stride. Passes that arrive too early or too late often result in loss of possession.

Once the passer has done her job, it is up to the receiving player to follow suit. Players must become adept at controlling balls arriving on the ground and through the air. Ground balls are most often controlled with the inside or outside surface of the foot. In rare instances the sole of the foot can also be used to receive a rolling ball. In all cases the receiving player must present a "soft target." By withdrawing the receiving surface as the ball arrives, you can cushion the impact and control the ball close to your feet. When receiving the ball, do not stop it completely. Soccer is a fluid game; as such, the ball should rarely be stopped dead during a match. In most instances you should receive and control the ball in the direction of your next movement or into the space away from a challenging opponent.

# PASSING GROUND BALLS

A variety of passing techniques can be observed during a soccer game. Some passes travel along the ground; others are driven through the air. In most situations, ground passes are preferred because they are easier to control and usually can be played with greater accuracy. Three fundamental techniques—the push pass, the outside-of-the-foot pass, and the instep pass—are used to pass the ball along the ground. While more flashy passing skills such as the deceptive heel pass—where a player steps over the ball and heels it backward to a teammate—may also be utilized in certain situations, the three fundamental techniques listed above are used more frequently and are of greater importance. Your choice of technique will depend on the situation and the distance over which the ball must be played.

The most basic type of pass, and the first that you should become comfortable with, is the push pass (figure 2.1). The push pass is used for playing the ball over distances of 5 to 10 yards and can also be used for slipping the ball past an opposing goalkeeper when a close-in shot requires accuracy rather than power.

### MISSTEP
The ball pops upward and leaves the ground.

### CORRECTION
You have leaned back and contacted the ball too far forward on your foot, near the toes. Wedging your toes beneath the ball will cause it to pop up into the air. Strike the horizontal midline of the ball with the large inside surface of your kicking foot between the ankle and toes.

### MISSTEP
Accuracy is poor.

### CORRECTION
Plant your balance foot beside the ball and pointed toward the target. Square your hips and shoulders. Keep your head steady as you contact the ball. Follow through directly toward the target.

## Figure 2.1  **PUSH PASS**

### Approach

1. Square up with target.
2. Plant balance foot beside ball and pointed toward target.
3. Keep shoulders and hips square.
4. Position kicking foot sideways.
5. Keep arms out to sides for balance.
6. Keep head steady with vision on ball.

### Execution

1. Position body square to target.
2. Swing kicking leg forward.
3. Keep ankle locked and kicking foot firm.
4. Contact center of ball with inside surface of foot.

### Follow-Through

1. Transfer weight forward.
2. Generate momentum through ball.
3. Perform short and smooth follow-through.

As you approach the ball, face the target with your shoulders square. Plant your balance (nonkicking) foot beside the ball with your knee bent and toes pointed toward the target. Position your passing foot square to the target with your toes pointed slightly up and away from the midline of your body. Contact the center of the ball with the inside surface of your foot. Keep your ankle locked and foot firmly positioned. Follow through with a short, powerful kicking motion.

Soccer players are rarely stationary for any length of time during a match. For this reason they must be able to release accurate passes while running with the ball. In these situations the outside-of-the-foot pass (figure 2.2) is usually the best choice; it can be used for both short- and medium-distance passes.

To perform the outside-of-the-foot pass, plant your balance foot slightly behind and to the side of the ball. Draw back the kicking leg with the foot extended and rotated slightly inward. Use an inside-out kicking motion to contact the inside half of the ball with the outside surface of your instep. Keep your kicking foot firmly positioned and your arms out to your sides for balance. Use a snaplike kicking motion of the lower leg (from the knee) for short-range passes. Use a more complete follow-through to generate greater distance on the pass.

### Figure 2.2 OUTSIDE-OF-THE-FOOT PASS

*Approach*

1. Plant supporting foot slightly behind and to side of ball.
2. Flex balance leg at knee.
3. Draw kicking leg back behind balance leg.
4. Position kicking foot down and rotated inward.
5. Keep head steady with vision on ball.

*Execution*

1. Keep knee of kicking leg over ball.
2. Snap kicking leg forward at knee.
3. Keep foot extended and firm.
4. Contact inside half of ball on outside surface of instep.

*Follow-Through*

1. Transfer weight forward.
2. Use inside-out kicking motion.
3. Use snaplike follow-through of kicking leg.

### MISSTEP

The ball leaves the ground.

### CORRECTION

Position the knee of your kicking leg over the ball at the moment of contact. Position your kicking foot down and keep it rotated inward. Lean forward as you kick the ball.

### MISSTEP

The pass lacks pace.

### CORRECTION

Contact the ball with as much foot surface as possible just left or right of the ball's vertical midline. Keep your kicking foot firm and use a short, powerful kicking motion.

The instep of the foot (*i.e., the area directly underneath the shoelaces*) provides a hard, flat surface that you can use to pass the ball over longer distances, both on the ground and through the air. The technique used to pass the ball along the ground (figure 2.3) is as follows: Approach the ball from behind at a slight angle. Plant your balance (nonkicking) foot beside the ball with your leg slightly bent at the knee and toes pointed toward the target. Draw back the kicking leg with the foot extended and firmly positioned. Keep your head steady with your vision on the ball. Square your hips and shoulders to the target as you drive the instep through the ball. The kicking foot is pointed down at the moment of contact. The kicking mechanics are very similar to those used when shooting the ball at goal.

### MISSTEP

The ball travels upward into the air.

### CORRECTION

This misstep occurs when you plant your nonkicking foot behind the ball. To pass the ball along the ground, you must place your balance foot beside the ball as you kick it. This will enable you to position the knee of your kicking leg over the ball with the foot fully extended and toes pointed down as the foot contacts the ball.

### MISSTEP

Accuracy is poor.

### CORRECTION

Square your shoulders and hips with the target as you kick the ball. Keep the kicking foot firm. Strike the ball directly through its center with the large, flat surface of the instep. Use a complete follow-through motion toward the target to generate distance on the pass.

Figure 2.3 **INSTEP PASS**

*Approach*

1. Approach ball from behind at a slight angle.
2. Plant balance foot beside ball with knee bent.
3. Square shoulders and hips to target.
4. Draw back kicking leg with foot extended and firm.
5. Keep knee of kicking leg over ball.
6. Keep arms out to sides for balance.

*Execution*

1. Keep head steady with vision on ball.
2. Transfer weight forward.
3. Initiate kicking motion.
4. Keep foot extended and firm.
5. Contact center of ball with instep.

*Follow-Through*

1. Generate momentum forward through ball.
2. Keep body weight centered over ball of balance foot.
3. Follow-through motion of kicking goes to waist level or higher.

# Passing on the Ground Drill 1
## Push Pass Off the Rebound Wall

Get in position with a ball 5 yards from a wall or kickboard. Use the inside-of-the-foot (push pass) technique to pass the ball off the wall so that it rebounds back to you. As the ball rolls toward you, pass it off the wall again. This is commonly referred to as one-touch passing. Repeat for 50 consecutive passes. When possible, alternate using your right and left feet.

### To Increase Difficulty

- Move 10 yards from wall.
- Increase speed or number of repetitions, or both.
- Perform all passes with weaker (nondominant) foot.

### To Decrease Difficulty

- Move closer to wall.
- Stop ball before passing it (two-touch passing).
- Make all passes with stronger (dominant) foot.

## Success Check

- Plant nonkicking foot beside ball and point it toward target.

- Keep passing foot firmly positioned.
- Square shoulders and hips to target.
- Contact horizontal midline of ball with inside surface of foot.
- Follow through toward target.

## Score Your Success

Fewer than 25 one-touch passes off the wall without error = 0 points

25 to 34 one-touch passes off the wall without error = 1 point

35 to 44 one-touch passes off the wall without error = 3 points

45 or more one-touch passes off the wall without error = 5 points

Your score ___

# Passing on the Ground Drill 2   Rapid Fire

Play with two teammates. Two servers (A and B), each with a ball, face one another at a distance of 16 yards. Markers are set up to represent a 2-yard-wide goal directly in front of each server. You position midway between the servers. Server A begins the drill by passing the ball to you (the middle player); use the inside-of-the-foot passing technique to return the ball through the goal to server A. After passing the ball, immediately turn to play a ball arriving from server B that you return in the same manner. Execute 40 one-touch push passes before switching positions with one of the servers. Continue the drill until each player has taken a turn in the middle.

### To Increase Difficulty

- Increase distance between servers to 20 yards.
- Increase number of repetitions.
- Reduce width of goal to 1 yard.

### To Decrease Difficulty

- Decrease distance between servers to 12 yards.
- Allow middle player two touches to receive and pass ball.
- Increase width of goal to 3 yards.

*(continued)*

Passing on the Ground Drill 2 *(continued)*

### *Success Check*

- Square shoulders and hips to target.
- Step toward ball as it arrives.
- Firmly position the passing foot sideways.
- Contact horizontal midline of ball.
- Follow through toward the target.

### *Score Your Success*

Fewer than 25 one-touch passes through goals = 0 points

25 to 29 one-touch push passes through goals = 1 point

30 to 34 one-touch push passes through goals = 3 points

35 or more one-touch push passes through goals = 5 points

Your score ___

# Passing on the Ground Drill 3
## Two-Touch Pass and Support Run

Form two groups of four to six players each. Groups line up in single file facing each other at a distance of 15 yards. The first player in line 1 passes the ball to the first player in line 2 and immediately sprints forward to the end of line 2 in support of (to follow) the pass. The first player in line 2 moves forward a step or two to meet the ball, prepares it with a first touch, passes it to the next player in line 1 with a second touch, and immediately sprints to the end of line 1 in support of the pass. Continue the drill until each player has passed 30 balls. Players use two-touch passes only.

### To Increase Difficulty

- Increase passing distance to 20 yards.
- Pass with weaker foot only.
- Increase speed or number of repetitions, or both.
- Require one-touch passes only.

### To Decrease Difficulty

- Reduce passing distance.
- Allow three touches to control and pass ball.

### *Success Check*

- Move forward to meet ball.
- Square shoulders and hips to target.
- Contact horizontal midline of ball.
- Follow through toward target.
- Sprint forward to support pass.

### *Score Your Success*

Fewer than 15 passes accurately played to the opposite line = 0 points

15 to 19 passes accurately played to the opposite line = 1 point

20 to 24 passes accurately played to the opposite line = 3 points

25 or more passes accurately played to the opposite line = 5 points

Your score ___

# Passing on the Ground Drill 4  **6v2 Keep-Away**

Use markers to outline a 12- by 15-yard playing area. Designate six players as attackers and two as defenders. The defenders position within the area. Attackers spread out along the inside perimeter of the square; one has possession of the ball. The six attackers attempt to keep the ball away from the two defenders within the playing area. Attackers may use inside-of-the-foot or outside-of-the-foot techniques to pass the ball. Attackers are restricted to two- or one-touch passes only. If a defender steals the ball or the ball is played out of the field area, the attacker who committed the error becomes a defender, and the defender becomes an attacker. Play for 15 minutes continuously. Keep a tally of the number of individual errors (loss of possession).

## To Increase Difficulty for Attackers

- Require one-touch passes only.
- Decrease size of playing area.
- Add third defender.

## To Decrease Difficulty for Attackers

- Increase size of playing area.
- Use only one defender.

## Success Check

- Keep head up with vision on field.

- Square shoulders and hips to target.
- Keep passing foot firm and in correct position.
- Play ball firmly to target.
- Constantly reposition to make yourself available to receive passes.

## Score Your Success

9 or more errors in 15 minutes = 1 point

6 to 8 errors in 15 minutes = 3 points

0 to 5 errors in 15 minutes = 5 points

Your score ___

# Passing on the Ground Drill 5
## One–Two Combination in the Box

The entire team can participate in this drill. Players pair up, and each pair takes position within a penalty area of the field. Each pair has a ball. All players jog randomly within the penalty area; those with balls dribble. Dribblers look to execute give-and-go (wall) passes with any players who do not have balls. Dribblers make eye contact with their intended targets, who check toward the dribblers to receive short, crisp passes. Dribblers then immediately sprint forward to collect one-touch passes from the receivers, control the ball, and then continue to dribble while looking for other free players with whom to execute one–two (wall) passes. Dribblers' initial passes must be made with the outside of the foot, the most appropriate passing surface for executing a wall pass. Continue for five minutes, after which players switch roles and play for another five minutes. Keep a tally of inaccurate passes, such as passes that disrupt the one–two combination.

*(continued)*

Passing on the Ground Drill 5 *(continued)*

### To Increase Difficulty

- Reduce size of area.
- Add defender to pressure dribblers.

### To Decrease Difficulty

- Increase size of area.
- Perform drill at half speed.

## Success Check

- Dribble toward target.

- Pass ball with outside surface of foot.
- Sprint forward to collect return pass.

## Score Your Success

7 or more inaccurate passes = 1 point

4 to 6 inaccurate passes = 3 points

0 to 3 inaccurate passes = 5 points

Your score ___

# Passing on the Ground Drill 6
## Score Through Multiple Gates

Form two teams of four to six players each. Use markers to outline a playing area 40 by 40 yards. Position cones or flags to represent six small goals randomly spaced throughout the area. Each goal is 2 yards wide. Teams can score in all six goals and must defend all six goals. To score, a player must complete a pass through a goal to a teammate positioned on the opposite side. Each goal scored earns the passer 1 point. Players may pass the ball through either side of a goal, but not twice consecutively through the same goal. Regular soccer rules apply except that teams do not change possession of the ball after a goal, and the offside law is waived. All scores must be made with the outside- or inside-of-the-foot technique. Play for 15 minutes. Keep track of your points.

### To Increase Difficulty

- Decrease size of playing area.
- Reduce width of goal to 1 yard.
- Add one neutral player who always joins defending team, providing defenders an advantage over the attackers.

### To Decrease Difficulty

- Make goals larger.
- Increase number of goals.
- Add one neutral player who always plays with team in possession, giving attackers a one-player advantage over defenders.

## Success Check

- Combine with teammates to maintain possession.
- Strive for accuracy and correct pace of passes.
- Attack goal least defended.

## Score Your Success

0 or 1 point = 0 points

2 to 5 points = 2 points

6 or more points = 4 points

Your score ___

# Passing on the Ground Drill 7
## One-Touch Pass to Open Teammate

Three players (servers) position side by side 2 yards apart. The fourth player (target player) faces the servers at a distance of 7 yards. Servers 1 and 2 each have a ball at their feet; server 3 does not have a ball to begin. Server 1 begins by passing the ball to the target player, who returns it using a first-time (one-touch) inside-of-the-foot or outside-of-the-foot pass to the server without a ball (server 3). Server 2 immediately plays a ball to the target player, who returns it to server 1, who is without a ball. Continue the exercise at maximum speed for 40 passes, after which one of the servers switches position with the target player. Repeat until each player has taken a turn as the target player. Earn 1 point for each one-touch pass traveling directly to an open server. Keep track of points scored.

**To Increase Difficulty**

- Use four servers and three balls.
- Increase passing distance.

**To Decrease Difficulty**

- Use only two serves and one ball.
- Decrease passing distance.
- Permit two touches to return ball.

**Success Check**

- Keep feet moving (jogging motion).
- Square shoulders and hips to target.

- Firmly position kicking foot.
- Step forward to meet ball.
- Follow through toward target.

### Score Your Success

24 or fewer points = 1 point

25 to 29 points = 3 points

30 to 34 points = 5 points

35 to 40 points = 7 points

Your score ___

---

# Passing on the Ground Drill 8   Moving Targets

Play this game with the entire team. Use markers to outline a playing area of approximately 30 by 30 yards. Designate five players as chasers who get in position outside the area, each with a ball. The remaining players (moving targets), without balls, get in position within the area. On command, the chasers dribble into the area to pass off moving targets. The objective is to contact a moving target below the knees with a passed ball. The targets use sudden changes of speed and direction to avoid being "caught" by chasers. Any target contacted with a passed ball immediately locates a loose ball and becomes a chaser; the original chaser becomes a target. A chaser is awarded 1 point for each opponent contacted below the knees with a passed ball. Play for 10 minutes continuously. Use any of the passing techniques discussed thus far. Keep a tally of points scored as a chaser.

*(continued)*

Passing on the Ground Drill 8 *(continued)*

### To Increase Difficulty for Chasers

- Enlarge playing area.
- Pass only with nondominant foot.

### To Decrease Difficulty for Chasers

- Reduce size of playing area.

## Success Check

- Choose appropriate passing technique.

- Keep passing foot properly positioned.
- Follow through toward target.

## Score Your Success

0 to 2 points = 1 point

3 or 4 points = 3 points

5 or more points = 5 points

Your score ___

# Passing on the Ground Drill 9
# Pass and Move to Open Space

Position four markers to represent the corners of an area 30 by 30 yards. Place an additional marker near the center of the square. Four players participate: one player stations at each corner marker; the central marker is open. One player has a ball. To begin, the player with the ball passes to any of the other players and then sprints to the open (unoccupied) marker. The player receiving the ball immediately passes to another player and then sprints to the unoccupied marker. The drill continues with players passing to a teammate and then sprinting to the unoccupied marker, which is constantly changing. Earn 1 point for each accurate pass to a teammate (i.e., a pass that does not require the teammate to move more than 1 yard from the marker to receive the ball). Perform the drill at near-game speed. Continue until each player has made 30 or more passes.

### To Increase Difficulty

- Increase passing distance.
- Require all passes to be with nondominant foot.
- Require all one-touch passes.

### To Decrease Difficulty

- Reduce passing distance to 15 yards.
- Perform drill at half speed.
- Permit unlimited touches to receive and pass.

## Success Check

- Keep passing foot firm and properly positioned.
- Square shoulders and hips to target.
- Follow through with the kicking motion toward target.
- Sprint to unoccupied marker after passing ball.

0 to 14 points = 1 point

15 to 19 points = 3 points

20 to 25 points = 5 points

Your score ___

# Passing on the Ground Drill 10
## Third Player Passing

Position four markers to create a field in the shape of a diamond, with 15 yards between markers. Five players participate: two players position at the first marker (one has the ball), and one player positions at each additional marker (these players do not have balls). To begin, the player with the ball passes to the player at the next (second) marker; then sprints to support (follow) the pass. The player receiving the ball makes a short one-touch pass back to the original passer, who then passes to the player at the next (third) marker and then runs and positions at the second marker. The player who originally was at the second marker runs toward the receiving player (at the third marker), receives a short pass from that player, and then passes to the player stationed at the fourth marker. This passing sequence continues as each player passes to the player at the next marker, receives a short return pass, and then passes to the next (third) player in the sequence. Continue until each player has made 40 passes. Earn 1 point for each accurate pass to the third player in the sequence.

### To Increase Difficulty

- Increase passing distance.
- Require all one-touch passes.

### To Decrease Difficulty

- Reduce passing distance to 10 yards.
- Perform drill at half speed.
- Permit unlimited touches to receive and pass.

### Success Check

- Keep passing foot firm and properly positioned.
- Square shoulders and hips to target.
- Follow through with the kicking motion toward target.
- Sprint forward to receive return pass after passing ball.

### Score Your Success

20 to 25 accurate passes = 1 point

26 to 30 accurate passes = 3 points

31 or more accurate passes = 5 points

Your score ___

# RECEIVING GROUND BALLS

As discussed earlier, passing and receiving skills are like opposite sides of the same coin; they are linked in the sense that one relies on the other to create value. If players lack proper receiving skills, the team will not be able to string together the passing combinations required to create scoring opportunities. Likewise, if passing skills are deficient, then receiving skills are of little use. The two are inexorably linked.

Rolling (ground) balls are usually received and controlled with the inside or outside surfaces of the foot, and on occasion with the sole of the foot. I have observed the sole-of-the-foot technique used more often in indoor soccer, where the space is restricted and players are almost always under challenge of an opponent as they receive the ball. However, this technique can also be used outdoors on the larger field to roll the ball away from a challenging opponent and to quickly change the direction of play.

## Receiving With the Inside Surface of the Foot

For the inside-of-the-foot reception (figure 2.4), as the name implies, use the inside surface of the foot to receive and control the ball. This technique is typically used when you are not under immediate pressure from an opponent. Move forward to meet the ball as it arrives. Extend your receiving leg and position your receiving foot sideways with toes pointed up and away from the midline of your body. To cushion the impact of the ball (i.e., to create a "soft target"), withdraw your foot as the ball arrives. Rarely should you stop (trap) the ball completely. In most situations it is to your advantage to receive and control the ball in the direction of your next movement, or into the space away from a nearby opponent.

### MISSTEP
The ball bounces off your foot and out of your range of control.

### CORRECTION
You must provide a "soft target" when receiving the ball. To cushion the impact, withdraw your foot as the ball arrives and control the ball in the direction of your next movement.

### MISSTEP
The ball rolls under your foot.

### CORRECTION
This can occur because you improperly positioned your receiving foot or took your eyes off the ball. As the ball arrives, keep your head steady and focus on the point of contact. Raise your receiving foot only about an inch (2.5 cm) or so off the ground, and contact the horizontal midline (center) of the ball with the inside surface of your foot.

## Figure 2.4   INSIDE-OF-THE-FOOT RECEPTION

*Preparation*

1. Move (check) toward ball.
2. Extend receiving leg to meet ball.
3. Position receiving foot sideways.
4. Keep ankle locked and receiving foot firm.
5. Keep head steady with vision on ball.

*Reception*

1. Receive ball on inside surface of foot.
2. Withdraw foot to cushion impact as ball arrives.
3. Turn with ball into space away from nearby opponent.

*Follow-Through*

1. Push ball in direction of next movement.
2. Keep head up with vision on field.

# Receiving With the Outside Surface of the Foot

At times during a match you will receive the ball while tightly marked by an opponent challenging for possession. In this situation the inside-of-the-foot technique may not be the most appropriate choice because the defending player may be able to reach in with a foot to kick the ball free. You can position your body to create space between the ball and a challenging opponent by receiving it with the outside surface of your foot (figure 2.5). Position yourself sideways and receive the ball with the foot farther from the opponent. Rotate your receiving foot inward and downward and receive the ball on the outside surface of your instep. Turn the ball into the space away from the opponent, which will give you additional time to pass the ball or dribble away to alleviate pressure.

## Figure 2.5 OUTSIDE-OF-THE-FOOT RECEPTION

*Preparation*

1. Move (check) toward ball.
2. Position sideways between ball and opponent.
3. Maintain semi-crouched posture with low center of gravity.
4. Receive ball with foot farther from opponent.
5. Keep head steady with vision on ball.
6. React to pressure from opponent.

*Reception*

1. Extend receiving foot down and rotate inward.
2. Receive ball on outside surface of instep.
3. Withdraw receiving leg slightly to cushion impact.
4. Turn ball into space away from challenging opponent.

*Follow-Through*

1. Readjust body position as needed to shield ball from opponent.
2. Keep head up to view field and opponent.
3. Push ball in direction of next movement.

**MISSTEP**

You fail to protect the ball as you receive it, and an opponent reaches in with her foot and kicks the ball away from you.

**CORRECTION**

Position sideways to create space between the ball and the opponent. Control the ball with the foot farther from the opponent. Readjust your position in response to the opponent's movement.

**MISSTEP**

The defender steps in front of you to intercept the pass.

**CORRECTION**

Always move toward (check to) the ball as you prepare to receive it. The first player to the ball always wins the prize.

## Receiving With the Sole of the Foot

You can also use the sole-of-the-foot reception (figure 2.6) effectively to control the ball when an opponent is challenging for the ball from behind. You can maintain maximum distance between the ball and the opponent by leaning back into him, extending your receiving leg to meet the ball, and controlling the ball with the sole of your foot. Square your hips and shoulders to the ball, angle your receiving foot upward, and pin the ball to the ground with the sole of your foot. In that position you can manipulate the ball by rolling it forward or sideways with the sole of your foot to evade the opponent's challenge.

**MISSTEP**

You feel awkward and immobile when receiving the ball with the sole of your foot.

**CORRECTION**

Keep your supporting leg bent at the knee with arms out to the sides for balance. This will ensure a low center of gravity and enhance your mobility. From this posture you will be able to react more quickly to the movements of the opponent.

**MISSTEP**

The defender kicks the ball away.

**CORRECTION**

Lean into the challenging opponent to create distance between her and the ball. Move the ball in response to defensive pressure.

## Figure 2.6   SOLE-OF-THE-FOOT RECEPTION

### Preparation

1. Move (check) toward ball.
2. Keep hands out to sides for balance.
3. Flex knees with and keep low center of gravity.
4. Extend receiving leg toward ball.
5. Angle receiving foot upward.

### Reception

1. Lean back into defender as ball arrives.
2. Control ball with sole of foot.
3. Maintain distance between ball and defender.

### Follow-Through

1. React to pressure of opponent.
2. Manipulate ball by rolling with foot.
3. Relieve pressure by moving away from opponent.

# Receiving Ground Balls Drill 1    Dancing Feet

Partners face one another at a distance of 5 yards. One player has the ball to begin. On command, partners pass the ball back and forth along the ground as many times as possible in 60 seconds. Players must use two touches to control and return the ball. Use the inside- or outside-of-the-foot technique to receive, prepare, and return the ball. You are assessed 1 penalty point each time you use more than two touches. Keep track of your penalty points. Perform five 60-second rounds with short breaks between them.

### To Increase Difficulty

- Increase duration to 90 seconds.
- Increase passing distance to 10 yards.

### To Decrease Difficulty

- Allow three touches to receive, control, and return ball.

## Success Check

- Select proper receiving technique early.
- Provide a "soft target" (withdraw receiving surface).

- Receive ball in one fluid movement.
- Use first touch to prepare ball; second touch to pass.

## Score Your Success

7 or more penalty points in five rounds = 2 points

3 to 6 penalty points in five rounds = 3 points

0 to 2 penalty points in five rounds = 4 points

Your score ___

# Receiving Ground Balls Drill 2
# Turn, Dribble, and Pass On

Play with the entire team. Players station on half of a regulation field, with one ball for every two players. On command, all players begin moving throughout the area. Those with balls dribble at pace for a few yards before passing to players who are moving without balls. Players receiving balls must turn them left or right with their first touch; then dribble for a few yards in that direction before passing to players without balls. Passes can be received and controlled with either the inside or outside surface of the foot. Players are required to turn the ball right or left with their first touch; they should not stop the ball dead. A player who uses more than one touch to turn with the ball in a different direction is penalized 1 point. Play for 10 minutes continuously, keeping a tally of your penalty points.

### To Increase Difficulty

- Add several defenders who challenge receiving players for ball.

### To Decrease Difficulty

- Allow two or three touches to receive, control, and turn ball.
- Perform drill at half speed.

*(continued)*

Receiving Ground Balls Drill 2 *(continued)*

## Success Check

- Move toward ball to receive it.
- Change direction with ball in one fluid movement.
- Withdraw receiving surface as ball arrives.
- Keep ball in close control as you turn.

## Score Your Success

10 or more penalty points = 1 point

6 to 9 penalty points = 3 points

0 to 5 penalty points = 5 points

Your score ___

# Receiving Ground Balls Drill 3
# Two-Touch Keep-Away

Use markers to outline a 12- by 12-yard playing area. Four players form an attacking team and try to keep the ball away from a fifth player (defender) within the square. Attacking players are allowed only two touches to receive and pass the ball. Players use the receiving technique most appropriate for the situation. Attacking players are penalized 1 point each time they make errors that result in loss of possession to defenders. An error occurs if the defender steals the ball, the ball is played outside of the square, or an attacker uses more than two touches to receive and pass the ball. The attacker who commits the error becomes a defender, and the defender becomes an attacker. Play for five minutes.

## To Increase Difficulty for Attackers

- Reduce playing area to 8 by 8 yards.
- Add second defender.

## To Decrease Difficulty for Attackers

- Enlarge playing area to 15 by 15 yards to give attackers more space and time.
- Allow attackers three touches to pass and receive ball.
- Add fifth attacker.

## Success Check

- Choose appropriate receiving technique.
- Provide soft receiving surface.
- Control ball into space away from defender.
- Keep play fluid—do not stop ball.

## Score Your Success

10 or more errors committed in a five-minute game = 1 point

6 to 9 errors committed in a five-minute game = 3 points

0 to 5 errors committed in a five-minute game = 5 points

Your score ___

# Receiving Ground Balls Drill 4
## Bump, Spin, Do It Again

Players 1 and 2 (receivers) position back to back midway between players 3 and 4 (servers), who are 15 yards apart, each with a ball. The drill begins with the receiving players checking (moving) toward the servers they are facing. Servers play a firm ground pass to the checking players, who receive and control the ball with their first touch, return (pass) the ball to the servers with their second touch, and then spin away and check toward the opposite server to repeat the drill. Continue at maximum speed for 90 seconds, after which the receivers and servers switch roles and repeat the drill. Checking players must use two-touch receiving and passing. Each player takes four turns as a receiving player. Players are penalized 1 point each time they use more than two touches to receive and return a ball to a server. Keep track of your penalty points.

### To Increase Difficulty for Receiving Player

- Add third server, to increase number of passes.
- Increase duration to 120 seconds per round.

### To Decrease Difficulty for Receiving Player

- Permit three touches to receive and return ball.
- Perform drill at half speed.

### Success Check

- Check hard toward server.
- Maintain balance and body control at all times.
- Prepare ball with first touch.
- Keep ball within range of control at all times.

### Score Your Success

8 or more total penalty points in the four 90-second rounds = 1 point

4 to 7 penalty points = 3 points

0 to 3 penalty points = 5 points

Your score ___

# Receiving Ground Balls Drill 5
## Receive Through Channels

Play on a field area of 50 by 50 yards. Use markers to designate six to eight small goals (3 yards wide) positioned randomly throughout the field. Players are in pairs, with one ball per pair. Partners move throughout the field area playing combinations and passing through the goals to one another as often as possible. Partners are not permitted to pass through the same goal twice in succession. After completing a pass through a goal, the receiving player dribbles off toward a different goal and the partner sprints forward to receive a return pass directed through another goal. Players are permitted only two touches to receive and control the ball before dribbling off toward another goal. Partners are penalized 1 point each time a ball passed through a goal is not received and controlled with two touches. Keep track of your pair's penalty points. Continue until you and your partner have made 30 attempted passes through small goals.

*(continued)*

Receiving Ground Balls Drill 5 *(continued)*

### To Increase Difficulty

- Increase required number of attempted passes.
- Reduce goal size to 2 yards.

### To Decrease Difficulty

- Allow target players three touches to receive and control ball.
- Reduce required number of attempted passes.

### *Success Check*

- Provide soft receiving surface.
- Prepare ball with first touch.
- Keep ball within range of control at all times.

### *Score Your Success*

5 or more penalty points = 1 point

3 or 4 penalty points = 3 points

0 to 2 penalty points = 5 points

Your score ___

# Receiving Ground Balls Drill 6  2v2 (+2)

Organize three groups of two players each. Assign groups vests of different colors to differentiate teams. Play within a 12- by 15-yard area. To begin, designate one group as defenders; the two remaining groups join to form a four-player attacking team. The attacking team attempts to keep the ball from the defenders within the area. Attackers are allowed three or fewer touches to receive and pass the ball to one another. Loss of possession occurs when a defending player steals the ball, when an attacker plays the ball outside of the area, or when an attacker uses more than three touches to receive and pass the ball. The group of two whose error causes the loss of possession immediately becomes the defending team, and the original defending team joins the remaining attackers. Play continuously for 10 minutes as teams alternate from attack to defense. A player who uses more than three touches to receive and pass the ball, or loses possession to a defender, is assessed 1 penalty point. Keep track of your individual penalty points.

### To Increase Difficulty for Attackers

- Add one neutral player who always joins defending team, creating a one-player rather than a two-player advantage for attacking team.
- Reduce size of area to 10 by 10 yards to reduce time and space available to receive and pass.

### To Decrease Difficulty for Attackers

- Add two neutral players who always join attacking team, creating a four-player advantage for attacking team.
- Allow attackers three touches to receive, control, and pass ball.
- Increase size of playing area to 15 by 20 yards.

## Success Check

- Withdraw receiving surface as ball arrives.
- Receive and control ball in space away from defender.
- Keep head up to be aware of passing options.
- Move ball quickly from one player to another.

# SUCCESS SUMMARY

Effective passing and receiving skills are the foundation of successful team play, the thread that ties the 10 field players into one cohesive unit. As you master the skills described in step 2, you will gain confidence and become a better all-round soccer player. The game itself will become more enjoyable as you improve your ability to combine with your teammates. As the old adage states, "Perfect practice makes perfect." Begin by rehearsing the correct technique for each skill under minimal pressure. Gradually add the game pressures of movement, restricted space, limited time, and challenging opponents so the drills more closely simulate the actual conditions you will face in the match.

Each of the drills in this step has been assigned a point value to help you evaluate your performance and chart your progress. Enter your score and total the points to get an estimate of your success.

### Passing on the Ground Drills

| | | |
|---|---|---|
| 1. Push Pass Off the Rebound Wall | _____ out of 5 | |
| 2. Rapid Fire | _____ out of 5 | |
| 3. Two-Touch Pass and Support Run | _____ out of 5 | |
| 4. 6v2 Keep-Away | _____ out of 5 | |
| 5. One–Two Combination in the Box | _____ out of 5 | |
| 6. Score Through Multiple Gates | _____ out of 4 | |
| 7. One-Touch Pass to Open Teammate | _____ out of 7 | |
| 8. Moving Targets | _____ out of 5 | |
| 9. Pass and Move to Open Space | _____ out of 5 | |
| 10. Third Player Passing | _____ out of 5 | |

### *Receiving Ground Balls Drills*

1. Dancing Feet　　　　　　　　　　　　　_____ out of 4
2. Turn, Dribble, and Pass On　　　　　　_____ out of 5
3. Two-Touch Keep-Away　　　　　　　　_____ out of 5
4. Bump, Spin, Do It Again　　　　　　　_____ out of 5
5. Receive Through Channels　　　　　　_____ out of 5
6. 2v2 (+2)　　　　　　　　　　　　　　_____ out of 5

**Total**　　　　　　　　　　　　　　　**_____ out of 80**

A combined score of 65 points or greater suggests that you have sufficiently mastered the skills and are prepared to move on to step 3. A score in the range of 45 to 64 is considered adequate. You can move on to step 3 after additional practice on the passing and receiving skills that you find most difficult. A score of 44 or fewer points suggests a lack of sufficient competency in the various passing and receiving techniques. You should review and practice all of the skills discussed in step 2 again before moving on to step 3.

# Passing and Receiving Flighted Balls

In most situations it is to your advantage to pass the ball along the ground. Rolling balls are generally more easily controlled than balls in flight, and can be played with greater accuracy. At times, however, going airborne is your best option. For example, an opponent may be positioned to block the passing lane between you and a teammate who is stationed in a dangerous attacking area, or you may decide to serve the ball over opponents into the open space behind the opponents' back line for a teammate to run to. As modern defenses become more organized and difficult to break down, airborne crosses whipped in from the flanks have assumed a more important role in team attack, as have long, driven diagonal passes that quickly change the point of attack. Finally, on rare occasions you can even score a goal by chipping (lobbing the ball over) an opposing goalkeeper who has drifted too far forward of the goal line.

To make the most of these opportunities, you must become competent at passing the ball through the air over varying distances. Two basic techniques, the *chip pass* and the *flighted instep pass,* are commonly used. The choice of technique depends in large part on how far the ball must travel and how quickly it must achieve height to clear a defending player. Likewise, you must be able to skillfully receive and control balls dropping from above. Step 3 is designed to develop your competence and confidence in passing and receiving balls through the air.

# EXECUTING FLIGHTED PASSES

To send the ball airborne, lean back and drive your foot through the lower third of the ball. It is essential that the ball achieve sufficient height to clear any opponents positioned between you and your target. The basic chip pass technique is generally used for short- to medium-distance passes. The flighted instep pass is the preferred technique for sending the ball over longer distances, as when changing the point of attack from one side of the field to the other.

## Chip Pass

The chip pass technique is used to loft, or pop, the ball up and over an opponent who is blocking the passing lane to a teammate. This situation can occur during the general run of play and also when opponents have formed a wall of players to defend against a free kick. In either case, a properly executed chip pass enables you to exploit the open space behind the defending players.

To execute the chip pass (figure 3.1), begin your approach from behind the ball and at a slight angle. Plant your supporting (nonkicking) foot beside the ball. Draw back your kicking leg with foot extended and firm. Square your shoulders and hips with the target as you drive (wedge) the instep of the kicking foot beneath the ball. Use a short, powerful kicking motion with minimal follow-through to generate immediate height on the pass. Wedging your foot beneath the ball will also impart slight backspin, which makes for a softer pass that is easier to control.

### MISSTEP

The pass does not achieve sufficient height to clear the opponent stationed in the passing lane.

### CORRECTION

Use a short, powerful, snaplike motion of the kicking leg to impart immediate lift on the ball. Wedge your instep underneath the ball to send it over the opponent.

### MISSTEP

The pass does not travel to the intended target.

### CORRECTION

Square your shoulders and hips to the target. Keep your kicking foot firm, and contact the ball on the inner surface of your instep. Execute a short follow-through toward the target.

## Figure 3.1 CHIP PASS

### Approach

1. Approach ball from behind and at a slight angle.
2. Plant supporting foot beside ball with knee bent.
3. Draw back kicking leg with foot extended and firm.
4. Keep arms out to sides for balance.
5. Keep head steady with vision on ball.

### Execution

1. Position knee of kicking leg over ball.
2. Lean forward slightly with hips and shoulders square to target.
3. Drive inside surface of instep beneath ball.
4. Keep kicking foot extended and firm upon contact with ball.
5. Use short, powerful kicking motion.

### Follow-Through

1. Use forward momentum through point of impact.
2. Snap kicking leg straight.
3. Impart slight backspin on ball.
4. Use minimal follow-through.

## Flighted Instep Pass

The instep surface of the foot is used to drive the ball over longer distances. The kicking mechanics are somewhat similar to those used for the instep ground pass, except that you lean back slightly upon contact with the ball and use a longer follow-through of the kicking leg.

For the flighted instep pass (figure 3.2), begin your approach from behind the ball at a slight angle. Plant the supporting foot slightly behind and to the side of the ball. Placing the supporting foot behind the ball allows a greater follow-through motion of the kicking leg and enables you to lean back slightly as you kick the ball. In this position you can generate loft and greater distance on the pass. Extend and firmly position your kicking foot as you drive your instep through the lower third of the ball. Use a complete follow-through motion.

Figure 3.2 **FLIGHTED INSTEP PASS**

*Approach*

1. Approach from behind ball at a slight angle.
2. Plant supporting foot to side and slightly behind ball.
3. Draw back kicking leg.
4. Keep kicking foot extended and firm.
5. Keep arms out to sides for balance.
6. Keep head steady with vision on ball.

*Execution*

1. Position knee of kicking leg slightly behind ball.
2. Lean back and square shoulders with target.
3. Drive instep of kicking foot through lower third of ball.
4. Keep kicking foot firm throughout.

*Follow-Through*

1. Kicking leg snaps straight.
2. Momentum moves forward over ball of supporting foot.
3. Arms move forward.
4. Follow-through motion of kicking leg goes to waist level or higher.

**MISSTEP**

The pass falls short of the target.

**CORRECTION**

Keep the kicking foot firmly positioned as it contacts the ball, and use a complete follow-through motion of the kicking leg. Generate momentum forward through the point of contact.

**MISSTEP**

The pass is inaccurate and off target.

**CORRECTION**

Square your shoulders and hips to the target. Lean back and contact the lower third of the ball with the full instep. Keep your kicking foot firm. The follow-through motion of your kicking leg should generate momentum toward the target.

# Flighted Pass Drill 1  Chip and Catch

Face a partner (server) at a distance of 5 yards. The server rolls the ball slowly toward you. Return the ball by chipping to the server's chest. The server catches the ball in her hands and repeats the sequence. Perform 40 repetitions, 20 chip passes with each foot; then switch roles. Score 1 point each time you chip the ball accurately to the server's chest. Keep track of the points scored.

**To Increase Difficulty**

- Decrease distance to 4 yards so ball must achieve sufficient height more quickly.
- Increase pace of serve.

**To Decrease Difficulty**

- Chip stationary ball.

**Success Check**

- Square shoulders and hips to target.
- Drive instep beneath ball.

- Keep kicking foot extended and firmly positioned.
- Use minimal follow-through.

**Score Your Success**

9 or fewer points = 0 points

10 to 19 points = 2 points

20 to 29 points = 3 points

30 to 34 points = 4 points

35 to 40 points = 5 points

Your score ___

# Flighted Pass Drill 2
## Pass Under and Chip Over

Partner with a teammate. Get in position as the server 10 yards front and center of a regulation goal (without the net). Your partner faces you from the opposite side of the goal, also 10 yards from the goal. You begin as the server by rolling the ball through the goal to your partner, who returns the ball to you by chipping it over the 8-foot-high (2.4 m) crossbar. The kicker may use his favorite foot to chip the ball. Control the ball as it drops to the ground, and repeat the sequence. Kickers earn 1 point for each rolling ball chipped over the goal that drops within 1 yard of the server. Perform 30 repetitions; then switch roles and repeat.

### To Increase Difficulty

- Get in position 7 yards to each side of goal so chip pass must achieve sufficient height more quickly to clear bar.
- Use weaker (nondominant) foot to chip ball.

### To Decrease Difficulty

- Stop ball before chipping over goal.
- Use smaller goal (6 feet, or 1.8 m, high).

### Success Check

- Square shoulders and hips to target.
- Keep head steady with vision on ball.
- Drive instep underneath ball.
- Use short, powerful leg snap.

### Score Your Success

0 to 14 points = 0 points

15 to 19 points = 1 point

20 to 24 points = 3 points

25 to 30 points = 5 points

Your score ___

# Flighted Pass Drill 3   Over the Top

Face a teammate at a distance of 20 yards. A third player (the server) gets in position with the ball midway between the two end players. The server begins the drill by passing a slowly rolling ball toward you. Move forward a step or two and chip the rolling ball over the server's head so that it lands at the feet of the third player standing 20 yards away. Players rotate positions after each chip pass: you follow the ball to the opposite end of the line, the server moves to your original position, and the player who received the ball dribbles it to the server (middle) position. Continue the drill until each player has executed 30 chip passes. Score 1 point for each pass that clears the middle player and lands within 1 yard of the receiving player. Players are permitted to chip the ball with their favorite (stronger) foot.

## To Increase Difficulty

- Increase pace of rolling ball (serve).
- Require players to chip ball with weaker foot.

## To Decrease Difficulty

- Reduce passing distance.
- Allow players to flight stationary ball over middle player.

## Success Check

- Square shoulders and hips to target.

- Drive instep beneath ball.
- Use short, powerful kicking motion.
- Follow through toward target.

## Score Your Success

0 to 14 points = 0 points

15 to 19 points = 1 point

20 to 24 points = 3 points

25 to 30 points = 5 points

Your score ___

# Flighted Pass Drill 4    **Flighted Balls Only**

Organize two equal teams of six to eight players, each with a goalkeeper. Use colored scrimmage vests to differentiate teams. Play on a 75- by 50-yard area. Position markers to outline an 8- by 8-yard goal box at each end of the area. Station a goalkeeper in each goal box. Begin with a kickoff from the center of the field. Teams defend the goal box on their end of the field and score points by flighting the ball into the opponent's goal box so that the goalkeeper can receive the ball directly out of the air. Keepers are not permitted to leave the goal box to receive the ball in their hands, although they can move outside the box to use their feet to control a rolling ball. A ball received directly out of the air is distributed immediately to a teammate, and play continues. The attacking team scores 1 point for each ball flighted into a goal box that the opposing goalkeeper receives out of the air. Regular soccer rules are in effect, other than the method of scoring. Play for 25 minutes. The team scoring more points wins.

## To Increase Difficulty

- Make goal box smaller.

## To Decrease Difficulty

- Make goal box larger.
- Allow goalkeeper to field ball after one bounce.

## Success Check

- Quickly change point of attack (location of ball) to create passing lanes to goal.

- Square shoulders and hips to target.
- Drive instep through lower third of ball.
- Use complete follow-through motion toward target.

## Score Your Success

Member of losing team = 3 points

Member of winning team = 5 points

Your score ___

# Flighted Pass Drill 5   Short-Short-Long

Form groups of four players, one ball per group. Players pass among themselves within an area 30 by 50 yards. Passing combinations must be executed in a short-short-long sequence. For example, players must combine for two consecutive short ground passes (5 to 10 yards) followed by a long flighted ball to the most distant player. Another short-short-long sequence follows immediately. Short passes should be played along the ground; the long pass must be flighted through the air. Perform the drill at game speed, even though there are no opponents to apply pressure on passers. Players are penalized 1 point for each flighted pass that does not drop to the ground within 5 yards of the intended target. Play for 10 minutes and keep track of penalty points.

## To Increase Difficulty

- Place touch restriction on players (such as a two-touch maximum, three-touch maximum).

## To Decrease Difficulty

- Require flighted ball to drop within 10 yards of intended target.

## Success Check

- Square shoulders and hips to target.

- Drive instep though lower third of ball.
- Use complete follow-through toward target.

## Score Your Success

10 or more penalty points = 0 points

6 to 9 penalty points = 3 points

0 to 5 penalty points = 5 points

Your score ___

# Flighted Pass Drill 6
# Switch the Point of Attack

Form a group of six players and mark off an area of 30 by 30 yards. Station one player at each corner (A, B, C, D) of the square, and two players (E, F) in the center of the square. One of the corner players has the ball to begin. Player A in corner A, with the ball, serves a flighted pass to player B in corner B, which is diagonally across the square from corner A. Player B lays the ball off to middle player E, who turns the ball and plays a rolling ball to corner player D. Player D serves a lofted pass diagonally across the square to player C at corner C. Player C lays the ball off to middle player F, who turns and plays to the next player in line at corner A. Repeat the pattern, with players switching positions in the square by following their passes. Players score 1 point for each ball flighted diagonally across the square that can be received directly out of the air by the receiving player. The player totaling the most points after 10 minutes wins the game.

## To Increase Difficulty

- Require players to serve ball with nondominant foot.

## To Decrease Difficulty

- Require flighted ball to drop within 5 yards of intended target.
- Permit players to stop ball and then serve long flighted passes.

## Success Check

- Square shoulders and hips to target.
- Drive instep though lower third of ball.
- Use complete follow-through toward target.

# RECEIVING FLIGHTED BALLS

Four body surfaces—the instep, thigh, chest, and head—are commonly used for receiving and controlling balls arriving through the air. The choice of surface depends on the flight trajectory of the ball and the position of nearby opponents. In all situations you must be able to receive and control the ball skillfully and, if an opponent is nearby, protect the ball as you do so. As is the case when receiving ground passes, your first touch of the ball is critical. You can put yourself at an immediate disadvantage with a poor first touch, or gain a decided edge on your opponent with a great first touch.

## Receiving With the Instep

A ball dropping from above can be collected on the instep surface of the foot (shoelaces) (figure 3.3). Anticipate where the ball will drop and move quickly to that spot. Square your shoulders and hips to the ball and raise the receiving foot approximately 12 inches (30.5 cm) off the ground. At the same time, extend and position the receiving foot parallel to the ground. As the ball arrives, withdraw your foot downward. This action cushions the impact and drops the ball at your feet.

**MISSTEP**

The ball bounces up and away from your control.

**CORRECTION**

This error probably occurred because you elevated your foot as the ball arrived. Raise your receiving foot early, position it parallel to the ground, and then withdraw it downward the instant the ball contacts the instep. This action will cushion the impact and drop the ball within your range of control.

**MISSTEP**

The ball spins back into your body.

**CORRECTION**

This likely occurred because the receiving foot was angled back and improperly positioned, and you were probably leaning back. Extend your receiving foot so that it is parallel to the ground as the ball arrives. Receive the ball on the full instep, with your head down, vision focused on the ball, and upper body erect.

Figure 3.3  **RECEIVING WITH THE INSTEP**

*Preparation*

1. Move into position to receive ball.
2. Raise receiving foot approximately 6 to 12 inches (15.2 to 30.5 cm) off ground.
3. Firmly position receiving foot parallel to ground.
4. Flex knee of supporting leg.
5. Extend arms out to sides for balance.
6. Keep head steady with vision on ball.

*Reception*

1. Collect ball on flat surface of instep.
2. Withdraw receiving foot downward as ball arrives.
3. Drop ball to ground.

*Follow-Through*

1. Maintain close control.
2. Push ball into open space.
3. Position head up with vision on field.

## Receiving With the Thigh

The mid-thigh area can also be used to receive and control a ball dropping from above, or a ball traveling directly at you at approximately waist height (figure 3.4). Anticipate the flight path of the ball and move to intercept it. If you are tightly marked by an opponent, position your body between the defender and the ball as the ball arrives. Raise your receiving leg so that your thigh is nearly parallel to the ground prior to the ball's arrival. Flex the supporting leg at the knee with arms out to the sides for balance. Receive the ball on the large surface of your mid-thigh. To cushion the impact, withdraw the receiving surface downward as the ball arrives. This action will drop the ball to the ground within your range of control.

## Figure 3.4 RECEIVING WITH THE THIGH

### Preparation

1. Move into position to intercept ball's flight path.
2. Raise receiving leg with thigh almost parallel to ground.
3. Bend supporting leg at knee.
4. Keep arms out to sides for balance.
5. Watch ball.

### Reception

1. Receive ball on mid-thigh.
2. Withdraw thigh downward.
3. Drop ball at feet within range of control.

### Follow-Through

1. Control ball into space away from challenging opponent.
2. Keep head up for good field vision.

### MISSTEP

The ball bounces upward off your thigh.

### CORRECTION

Raise your receiving leg and thigh into the proper receiving position just prior to the arrival of the ball. Withdraw your leg downward as the ball contacts your thigh.

### MISSTEP

An opponent tackles the ball away from you as it drops to the ground.

### CORRECTION

Position your body to protect the ball from opponents as it arrives. Your first touch should guide the ball into the space away from a challenging defender.

## Receiving With the Chest

The upper chest area provides an excellent surface with which to control a ball arriving through the air. Two receiving techniques are used depending on the situation: one to control a ball that is bouncing upward off the ground, and the other to control a ball that is descending out of the air. In both cases, you should position your body between the ball and a challenging opponent.

To collect a ball that is dropping directly out of the air, arch back at the waist and receive the ball on the upper central area of your chest, just right or left of center (figure 3.5). As the ball arrives, withdraw your upper body slightly to soften the impact. Control the ball into the space away from a challenging opponent by turning your upper trunk just before the ball contacts your chest.

### MISSTEP

The ball bounces off your chest and out of your range of control.

### CORRECTION

Receive the ball slightly right or left of the center chest where softer muscle tissue provides a more giving receiving surface. Withdraw your upper torso as the ball makes contact.

### MISSTEP

The ball skims off your chest and over your shoulder.

### CORRECTION

This error may occur if you angle your upper body too far back from the vertical. Lean back slightly, but not too far, as the ball arrives.

## Figure 3.5 RECEIVING A FLIGHTED BALL WITH THE CHEST

*Preparation*

1. Get in position to receive oncoming ball.

2. Arch upper body back from waist.

3. Center weight over balls of feet with knees bent slightly.

4. Keep head steady with vision on ball.

*Reception*

1. Receive ball on upper-chest area.

2. Withdraw slightly to cushion impact as ball arrives.

3. Turn upper torso to control ball into space away from opponent.

4. Keep arms out to sides for balance.

*Follow-Through*

1. Position body to protect ball from challenging opponent.

2. Keep head up with good field vision.

3. Push ball into open space and accelerate.

Female players usually are permitted to cross their arms against the chest and receive the ball on the arms, although most high school and college players use the same technique that men do.

Controlling a high-bouncing ball with the chest requires a slightly different technique. Move toward the ball so that you can meet it as it rebounds upward from the ground. Lean forward from the waist, with your upper torso at about a 45 degree angle, with arms extended out to the sides (figure 3.6). Allow the ball to contact your chest as it rebounds up off the ground. This action will direct the ball downward within your range of control.

### MISSTEP

The ball glances sideways off your chest and out of your control.

### CORRECTION

Make sure your upper torso is angled forward and over the ball as it bounces upward off the ground. With your chest in this position, the ball will be directed down to your feet and within your range of control.

**Figure 3.6**  Receiving a bouncing ball with the chest.

## Receiving With the Forehead

Usually, you will use your head to pass the ball to a teammate, make a shot on goal, or clear a flighted ball from the area in front and center of your goal. On rare occasions, you can also use the flat surface of your forehead to control a ball that is dropping from above (figure 3.7). This is a difficult skill to master. Successful execution requires proper technique coupled with precise timing of the jump.

Quickly move into the area where the ball will drop. Use a two-foot takeoff to jump up. Leave the ground early, before the ball's arrival. Angle your forehead back slightly from the vertical, focus on the ball, and allow the ball to contact the flat surface of your forehead. If you've timed the jump properly, you should begin to descend to the ground as the ball arrives. To further cushion the impact, withdraw your head slightly as the ball contacts your forehead. The ball should bounce up off your forehead only a few inches before dropping to the ground at your feet within your range of control.

## Figure 3.7 **RECEIVING WITH THE FOREHEAD**

### Preparation

1. Move into flight path of descending ball.
2. Flex knees with weight centered over balls of feet.
3. Extend arms back and to sides.
4. Focus on ball.

### Reception

1. Jump upward before ball arrives.
2. Square shoulders and hips with ball.
3. Angle forehead back slightly with chin tucked.
4. Keep eyes open and mouth closed.
5. Contact ball at highest point of jump.
6. Receive ball on flat surface of forehead.

### Follow-Through

1. Withdraw head slightly on contact.
2. Drop ball to ground within range of control.
3. Push ball in direction of next movement.

### MISSTEP

The ball rebounds upward off your forehead and out of your range of control.

### CORRECTION

This likely occurred because your body was too rigid or you jumped too late and were still moving up as the ball contacted your forehead. Timing is everything. Leave the ground early so that your body begins to descend as the ball arrives. To further soften the impact, withdraw your head slightly as the ball contacts your forehead.

### MISSTEP

The ball glances sideways off your head.

### CORRECTION

Allow the ball to contact the large, flat surface of your forehead just above your eyebrows. Keep your neck firm and your head steady, and focus on the ball at all times.

# Receiving Flighted Passes Drill 1
## Individual Ball Juggle

Form a group of three players. Players use the instep, thigh, chest, and head to keep the ball airborne while positioned within a 15- by 15-yard area. Players try to keep the ball in the air for as many touches as possible. Beginners can toss the ball up to get started; experienced players must use their feet to lift the ball. Count consecutive touches of the ball without letting it drop to the ground. Perform 10 trials. Count your highest group total of touches as your best score.

### To Increase Difficulty

- Require specific order of touches (e.g., instep to thigh to head to thigh to instep).
- Require players to jog slowly while keeping ball airborne.

### To Decrease Difficulty

- Juggle ball while stationary.

## Success Check

- Select appropriate receiving surface early.
- Withdraw receiving surface to cushion impact.
- Keep ball within range of control.

## Score Your Success

0 to 14 consecutive touches = 1 point

15 to 19 consecutive touches = 3 points

20 or more consecutive touches = 5 points

Your score ___

# Receiving Flighted Passes Drill 2
## Receive and Return With a Supporting Run

Form two teams (A and B) of three players each. Teams face each other at a distance of 5 yards, with players in single file. Team A begins with the ball. The first player in line for team B tosses the ball through the air to the first player in line for team A and then sprints to the end of Team A's line. The player receiving the ball for Team A uses two touches to receive and control the ball out of the air and then returns it (by tossing) to the second (next) player in line for team B. After tossing the ball the player from Team A sprints to the end of line B. Players are penalized 1 point each time they cause the ball to drop to the ground. Continue until each player has received 20 tosses, keeping track of penalty points.

### To Increase Difficulty

- Increase distance between teams.
- Require players to return ball by kicking instead of tossing
- Require teams to move throughout a field area while tossing and receiving.

### To Decrease Difficulty

- Permit three touches to control and return ball.

### *Success Check*

- Select receiving surface early.

- Provide soft target.
- Receive and control ball with two touches.
- Return ball to opposite line (by tossing) with next touch.

### *Score Your Success*

11 or more penalty points = 3 points

7 to 10 penalty points = 4 points

0 to 6 penalty points = 5 points

Your score ___

# Receiving Flighted Passes Drill 3
## Receive, Spin, Do It Again

Two players (servers A and B), each with a ball, face each other at a distance of 10 yards. The third player gets in position midway between the servers. Server A begins the drill by tossing the ball to the middle player. The middle player controls the ball out of the air with the first touch and returns it (by kicking) to the server with the second touch. The ball can be controlled with the instep, thigh, chest, or head. The middle player immediately turns to receive a ball tossed from server B, and then repeats the sequence. After the middle player has received 50 tosses, the players rotate positions and repeat. Continue the drill until each player has taken a turn in the middle. Players earn 1 point for each ball received and returned to the server using only two touches. Keep track of your points.

*(continued)*

Receiving Flighted Passes Drill 3 *(continued)*

### To Increase Difficulty

- Increase height, distance, or velocity of serves.
- Add third server.

### To Decrease Difficulty

- Allow three touches to receive and return ball to server.

## Success Check

- Align body with ball.
- Prepare receiving surface early.

- Withdraw receiving surface as ball arrives.
- Return ball to chest of server.

## Score Your Success

0 to 20 points = 0 points

21 to 34 points = 1 point

35 to 44 points = 3 points

45 to 50 points = 5 points

Your score ___

# Receiving Flighted Passes Drill 4
# Toss, Cushion, and Catch

Organize two equal teams of four to six players and play within an area approximately 30 by 40 yards. Award one team the ball to begin. The team with the ball attempts to play keep-away with the other team. There is one restriction: Teammates must pass to one another by throwing rather than kicking. The receiving player must control the ball out of the air with the instep, thigh, chest, or head, and then catch the ball in the hands before it drops to the ground. Players are permitted only two touches to control the ball: one touch to receive and control it, the second touch to catch it. A player may take up to five steps while in possession of the ball before tossing to a teammate. Loss of possession occurs when an opponent intercepts a pass or when a receiving player fails to control the ball with two touches before it drops to the ground. Defending players are not permitted to wrestle the ball from opponents, but they can intercept passes with their hands. Individual players score 1 point for each ball they receive and control without error (the ball may not touch the ground), and they are penalized 1 point for each ball they fail to receive and control with two touches. Individual players keep a running total of points scored minus points deducted. Play for 15 minutes.

### To Increase Difficulty

- Require all passes to be 10 yards or longer.
- Require players to control ball with specific body part (e.g., thigh only, head only).

### To Decrease Difficulty

- Add two neutral players who play with team in possession of ball.

## Success Check

- Align body with oncoming ball.
- Select receiving surface early.
- Withdraw receiving surface slightly as ball arrives.

## Score Your Success

0 to 5 points = 1 point

6 to 9 points = 3 points

10 or more points = 5 points

Your score ___

# Receiving Flighted Passes Drill 5   **Volleyball**

Play on a regulation volleyball court or an area of similar size. Form two teams of four to six players each. Teams get in position on opposite sides of the net. One team has the serve to begin. To serve, a player must chip a stationary ball over the net from behind the end line. The receiving team must control the ball directly out of the air or after it bounces once. This applies to all plays, not only service returns. If the ball bounces two or more times in the receiving team's court, or if the receiving team fails to return the serve over the net, the serving team scores 1 point and retains service. A player receiving the ball is allowed three touches to control it and play it back over the net or to play it to a teammate who then plays it over the net. Once the ball has been received out of the air, however, it must be returned over the net before it drops to the ground. A fault occurs when the serve or return fails to clear the net, the serve or return lands out of bounds, the ball is allowed to bounce more than once, or a player uses arms or hands to pass or control the ball.

When a member of the serving team commits a fault, the team loses the serve. When the receiving team commits a fault, the serving team scores 1 point. The first team to score 30 points wins the game.

### To Increase Difficulty

- Require server to chip a rolling ball.
- Do not allow ball to bounce before returning it over net.
- Allow players only two touches to receive and return ball.

### To Decrease Difficulty

- Permit server to volley ball out of hands.
- Permit ball to bounce twice before returning it over net.

## Success Check

- Position in line with descending ball.
- Prepare receiving surface early.
- Withdraw receiving surface to cushion impact of ball.

## Score Your Success

Member of losing team = 3 points

Member of winning team = 5 points

Your score ___

# SUCCESS SUMMARY

Successfully executing the skills in passing and receiving flighted balls requires correct technique coupled with confidence in your ability. You can acquire these important assets only through hours of dedicated practice. There are no shortcuts to success. You simply must be willing to put in the time and effort if you want to become an elite player.

Beginners should practice passing and receiving skills in a relatively pressure-free setting. Focus on performing the correct technique without the pressure of opponents' trying to steal the ball from you. Gradually progress to more game-simulating practice situations as your skill level improves and you gain confidence in your abilities. Eventually, you can add the pressure of challenging opponents to your drills. Your ultimate goal should be to execute all of the fundamental passing and receiving skills under match conditions.

Each of the drills in this step has been assigned a point value to enable you to evaluate your performance and chart your progress. Enter your scores in the following chart and then total your points to get an estimate of your overall level of competence.

## Flighted Pass Drills

|   |   |   |
|---|---|---|
| 1. | Chip and Catch | ____ out of 5 |
| 2. | Pass Under and Chip Over | ____ out of 5 |
| 3. | Over the Top | ____ out of 5 |
| 4. | Flighted Balls Only | ____ out of 5 |
| 5. | Short-Short-Long | ____ out of 5 |
| 6. | Switch the Point of Attack | ____ out of 5 |

## Receiving Flighted Passes Drills

|   |   |   |
|---|---|---|
| 1. | Individual Ball Juggle | ____ out of 5 |
| 2. | Receive and Return With a Supporting Run | ____ out of 5 |
| 3. | Receive, Spin, Do It Again | ____ out of 5 |
| 4. | Toss, Cushion, and Catch | ____ out of 5 |
| 5. | Volleyball | ____ out of 5 |
| **Total** | | **____ out of 55** |

A combined score of 48 or more points out of a possible 55 indicates that you have mastered the techniques and are ready to move on to step 4. A score in the range of 35 to 47 is considered adequate. You should move ahead to step 4 after reviewing and practicing the techniques for passing and receiving balls out of the air. A score of 34 or fewer points indicates that you have not sufficiently mastered the skills in step 3. Review and rehearse the techniques a few more times before moving on to step 4.

# Dominating the Air Game

Soccer players most definitely use their head—and not just to make decisions and contemplate game strategies. Using the head to physically propel the ball is unique to the game of soccer. Although younger players (under 10 years) need not focus on heading skills, they should be taught the proper technique. As players get older and advance into more competitive settings, the mastery of heading skills assumes greater importance for both attacking and defending purposes. Three heading techniques are commonly used; each is featured in a specific situation and for a slightly different purpose.

The *jump header* technique is the most often used and is generally used for passing the ball, for striking on goal, and for the defensive purpose of clearing a flighted ball from the goal area. To execute the jump header, use a two-foot takeoff to jump upward, arch back from the waist, and then snap forward to contact the ball with the flat surface of your forehead.

The *dive header* is an exciting and acrobatic skill used only in special situations, such as to score a spectacular goal off a low cross traveling across the goal mouth, or to clear low-driven balls out of the goal area. To execute the dive header, dive parallel to the ground with your head tilted back and neck firm. Contact the ball on the flat surface of your forehead. Extend your arms down to break your fall to the ground. Use good judgment when executing the dive header. It's not an appropriate choice when in the midst of a crowd of players; an opponent (or even a teammate) may try to kick the ball away and, in doing so, inadvertently kick you in the head. Recent research emphasizing the dangers of concussions and their aftereffects makes it more important than ever for players to employ proper heading technique so as to minimize situations conducive to sustaining head trauma.

The *flicked header* alters the flight path of the ball slightly while allowing it to continue in the same direction. This technique is generally used in an attacking situation to deflect an airborne ball into the path of a rushing teammate. To execute the flicked header, you must move into a position to intercept the ball's flight path, angle your forehead back, and allow the ball to glance off the top or side of your forehead. This action creates a sudden change in the ball's flight trajectory, which can unbalance defending players and create scoring opportunities.

Some teams rely on heading skills much more than others do. For example, the national teams from Norway, Ireland, and to a lesser extent England have traditionally based their attacking games on their forwards' ability to go up and win air balls. From a tactical point of view, these teams have traditionally favored a style of play that emphasizes long-driven balls played through the air direct from the defenders to the forwards. The midfielders then push forward to collect the balls nodded down to the ground by the target forwards. In contrast, many South American and Central American teams, as well as European powers such as Spain and Portugal, have traditionally embraced a shorter-pass, ball-control style of play with the ball on the ground much of the time.

Regardless of the team's philosophy of play, however, it is inevitable that the ball will be airborne at various times during a game. Goal kicks, corner kicks, free kicks, flighted passes, throw-ins, and defensive clearances must in many cases be played directly out of the air with the head. To become a complete soccer player, you must develop competence in performing the various heading skills.

# JUMP HEADER

To perform the jump header, face the ball with your shoulders square (figure 4.1). Judge the ball's flight, bend your knees slightly, and prepare to spring upward into the air to meet it. Use a two-foot takeoff to jump straight up. While airborne, arch back from the waist and tuck your chin to your chest. Keep your neck and upper body firm. As the ball arrives, snap your upper trunk forward from the waist and contact the ball on the flat surface of your forehead at the highest point of the jump.

Timing your takeoff is probably the most difficult element of the jump header. Beginners have a tendency to jump either too late or too early. If you jump late, you will still be moving up as the ball arrives. If you jump too early, you will descend as the ball sails over your head. The key is to jump at the correct time, hang suspended in the air for a moment or two, and then snap your upper trunk and head forward to meet the oncoming ball with power and confidence.

You must attack the ball; do not simply allow the ball to hit your head and bounce off. When attempting to score, strike through the top half of the ball to send it on a downward plane toward the goal line. The same form applies when passing to a teammate's feet.

Conversely, for defensive clearances you should contact the lower half of the ball to send it high, far, and wide, away from the danger area and preferably toward the flank area of the field. In all cases, keep your eyes open and mouth closed as the ball contacts your forehead. Heading with the mouth open invites injury because you may inadvertently bite your tongue if an opponent who is also jumping for the ball collides with you.

Figure 4.1   **JUMP HEADER**

*Preparation*

1. Face oncoming ball with shoulders square.
2. Flex knees with weight centered over balls of feet.
3. Draw arms back, preparing to jump.
4. Focus on ball.

*Execution*

1. Use two-foot take-off to jump up.
2. Simultaneously raise arms for upward momentum.
3. Arch upper trunk back from vertical with chin tucked.
4. Keep neck and upper trunk firm.
5. Snap upper trunk forward to meet ball.
6. Contact ball on flat surface of forehead.
7. Keep eyes open and mouth closed.

*Follow-Through*

1. Drive forehead through point of contact with ball.
2. Keep arms out to sides for balance.
3. Descend to ground.

### MISSTEP

The header lacks power.

### CORRECTION

Attack the ball. Jump early and maintain the arched position from the waist until the last possible moment before snapping your upper trunk forward. Keep your head steady and neck firm. Proper timing and correct technique are essential.

### MISSTEP

The ball hits you in the face or nose or skips off the top of your head.

### CORRECTION

Keep your eyes open with your vision on the ball as it contacts your forehead. Do not be distracted by nearby opponents.

# Jump Header Drill 1   Group Head Juggle

The first step in heading is to become comfortable with the skill. Form groups of three or four players; each group stations within a 10- by 10-yard square. To begin, toss a head-high ball upward toward one of your teammates. With your teammates, attempt to keep the ball airborne for as many touches as possible before it drops to the ground, using only your head to contact the ball. Keep track of the number of combined headers with teammates before the ball drops to the ground. Record the best of 10 trials.

## To Increase Difficulty

- Require two-touch heading (receive with first touch, return ball with second touch).
- Head juggle with teammates while jogging slowly around large field area.

## To Decrease Difficulty

- Keep ball airborne on your own (individual head juggle).

## Success Check

- Flex knees for balance and body control.
- Tilt head back.
- Contact ball on upper forehead.
- Keep arms out to sides for balance.

## Score Your Success

0 to 19 consecutive headers = 1 point

20 to 29 consecutive headers = 3 points

30 or more consecutive headers = 5 points

Your score ___

# Jump Header Drill 2    Jump Header Technique

Stand facing a partner who holds the ball about 12 inches (30.5 cm) above and to the front of his head. Step forward, jump straight up with your upper trunk arched back, and snap forward from the waist to contact the ball on your forehead. Combine all elements of the jump header technique. Repeat 30 times; then switch roles with your partner.

### To Increase Difficulty

- Increase number of repetitions.
- Increase speed of repetition.
- Require partner to slowly back-pedal while holding ball.

### To Decrease Difficulty

- Reduce number of repetitions.

## Success Check

- Jump straight up.
- Arch upper body back from vertical.
- Tuck chin with neck firm.

- Keep eyes open and mouth closed.
- Snap upper trunk forward from waist.
- Contact ball on forehead.

## Score Your Success

0 to 14 correct jump headers = 0 points

15 to 19 correct jump headers = 1 point

20 to 24 correct jump headers = 3 points

25 to 30 correct jump headers = 5 points

   Your score ___

# Jump Header Drill 3    Jack in the Box

Face a teammate (server) standing 5 yards away. The server tosses a ball to a spot 12 to 18 inches (30.5 to 45.7 cm) above your head. Use a two-foot takeoff to jump up and head the ball back to the server. Contact the ball on your forehead at the highest point of the jump and direct it toward the server's chest. Execute 30 jump headers; then switch roles with your partner and repeat.

### To Increase Difficulty

- Increase distance from server.
- Perform as many repetitions as possible in 60 seconds.
- Use two servers tossing from different angles.

### To Decrease Difficulty

- Reduce distance to server.
- Slow speed of repetitions.
- Reduce number of repetitions.

## Success Check

- Use two-foot takeoff.

- Arch upper trunk back from waist.
- Keep eyes open and mouth closed.
- Snap forward to meet ball.

## Score Your Success

0 to 14 headers directed to server's chest = 0 points

15 to 19 headers directed to server's chest = 1 point

20 to 24 headers directed to server's chest = 3 points

25 to 30 headers directed to server's chest = 5 points

   Your score ___

## Jump Header Drill 4   Jump, Head, Do It Again

Two players (servers), each with a ball, face each other at a distance of 8 yards. A third player stands midway between the servers. The servers take turns tossing a ball up toward the middle player, who jumps up and heads the ball directly back to the server who tossed it. After each header the middle player immediately turns 180 degrees to jump up and head a ball tossed by the opposite server. The middle player continues for 40 jump headers. Score 1 point for each ball headed back to the server so that she can catch it directly out of the air. Each player takes a turn as the middle player.

### To Increase Difficulty

- Increase distance between servers to 12 yards.
- Increase number of repetitions.
- Increase speed of repetitions.

### To Decrease Difficulty

- Head ball without jumping.
- Decrease number of repetitions.

### *Success Check*

- Square shoulders to target.

- Use two-foot takeoff.
- Snap upper trunk forward.
- Contact ball on forehead.
- Keep head steady and neck firm.

### *Score Your Success*

0 to 19 points = 0 points

20 to 27 points = 1 point

28 to 34 points = 3 points

35 to 40 points = 5 points

Your score ____

## Jump Header Drill 5
## Toss, Head, and Catch to Score

Three teammates form a triangle with about 10 yards between players. One player (A) has the ball to begin. Player A tosses the ball to player B, who jumps up and heads the ball to player C. Player C catches the ball and tosses it to player A, who jumps up and heads the ball to player B, who catches and tosses it to player C. Continue the toss-head-catch routine until each player has executed 30 jump headers. Score 1 point for each ball headed directly to a teammate so that it does not hit the ground.

### To Increase Difficulty

- Increase distance between players to 12 yards.
- Perform drill with all three players moving slowly through field area.

### To Decrease Difficulty

- Reduce distance between players to 6 yards.
- Execute headers without jumping.

### *Success Check*

- Use two-foot takeoff to jump up.
- Square shoulders to target.
- Contact ball on forehead.
- Keep eyes open and mouth closed.

## Score Your Success

0 to 14 tosses headed directly to teammate = 0 points

15 to 19 tosses headed directly to teammate = 1 point

20 to 24 tosses headed directly to teammate = 3 points

25 to 30 tosses headed directly to teammate = 5 points

Your score ___

# Jump Header Drill 6
## Heading Race Front to Back to Front

Divide the group into equal-sized teams of four to six players. Teams stand side by side in single file with 3 yards between teams. One player from each team functions as the server and holds a ball and faces the first person in that team's line at a distance of 3 yards. On the signal "Go," the server tosses a ball up to the first player in line. That player jumps up and heads the ball back to the server and then drops to his knees. The server immediately tosses to the next player in line, who also heads the ball and then kneels. Servers continue through their lines until they reach the last player, at which point all team members have headed the ball and are kneeling. The last player in line heads two consecutive tosses to the server. The next to the last in line immediately stands to jump up and head a ball back to the server; then the player in front of him stands to head, and so on. The race continues, from front to back to front, until all players are again standing and the server has control of the ball.

Individual players are assessed 1 penalty point each time they fail to head the ball directly back to the server so that the server can catch it directly out of the air. The team whose server goes through the entire line of players, front to back to front, in the shortest time wins the race. Repeat with a different player as server. The first team to win five races wins the competition.

### To Increase Difficulty

- Add more players to each team.
- Repeat for two consecutive repetitions through entire line.

### To Decrease Difficulty

- Do not require players to jump.

### Success Check

- Jump up with shoulders square.
- Arch upper body back.
- Keep neck stiff and chin tucked.
- Eyes open and mouth closed.
- Thrust forward from waist.
- Contact ball on forehead.

### Score Your Success

3 or more penalty points = 0 points

1 or 2 penalty points = 2 points

0 penalty points = 4 points

Your score ___

## Jump Header Drill 7    Headers End to End

Use markers to represent two 5-yard-wide goals positioned 15 yards apart. Get in one goal with a ball; an opponent gets in the opposite goal. Toss the ball up so that it drops near the center of the area. Your opponent moves forward and attempts to score by heading the ball past you through the goal. Alternate turns, attempting to score from jump headers. Return to your respective goals after each attempt. Score 2 points for a goal scored and 1 point for a ball headed on goal but saved. Perform 30 headers each. The player scoring more points wins the game.

### To Increase Difficulty

- Reduce width of goal to 3 yards.

### To Decrease Difficulty

- Increase width of goal to 7 yards.
- Do not require player to jump when heading.

### Success Check

- Square shoulders to ball.
- Jump straight up.
- Snap upper trunk forward.
- Contact ball on forehead.
- Head ball on downward angle toward goal line.

### Score Your Success

0 to 19 points = 0 points

20 to 29 points = 2 points

30 to 44 points = 4 points

45 to 60 points = 6 points

Your score ___

## Jump Header Drill 8    Defensive Clearances

Four players compete to execute the technique of defensive heading (clearing a ball high and far). A neutral server tosses the balls. Use markers to designate two parallel lines approximately 15 yards apart. One player positions between the lines, in the middle zone; one player stations in each end zone; the server stations with a supply of balls to the side of the field. To begin, the server tosses a lofted ball toward one of the end zone players, who attempts to jump and head (clear) the ball over the middle zone to the player in the opposite end zone. Players then rotate zones and repeat. Continue until each player has performed 30 headers. A ball headed completely over the middle zone so that the player in the opposite end zone can receive it out of the air scores 1 point. The player who scores the most points wins the competition.

### To Increase Difficulty

- Increase width of middle zone to 20 yards.
- Increase number of repetitions.

### To Decrease Difficulty

- Decrease width of middle zone to 10 yards.

## Success Check

- Square shoulders to goal.
- Use two-foot takeoff to jump up.
- Contact ball on upper surface of forehead.
- Snap upper trunk forward with power.
- Head ball high and as far as you can.

## Score Your Success

Third-place finish = 1 point

Second-place finish = 3 points

First-place finish = 5 points

Your score ___

# Jump Header Drill 9
## Score by Headers Only (With Neutrals)

Organize two teams of three to five players each. Designate two additional players as neutrals; these players always play with the team in possession of the ball. Play within a 25- by 35-yard area with a small goal (4 yards wide) at the center of each end line. Award one team the ball to begin. Passing is accomplished by throwing and catching rather than kicking. Players score by heading a ball tossed by a teammate through the opponent's goal. Players may take a maximum of five steps with the ball before passing to a teammate. Neutral players join with the attacking team to create a two-player advantage. Do not use goalkeepers.

Field players can use their hands to intercept opponents' passes and block headers directed at goal. The defending team is awarded the ball when an opponent takes more than five steps with the ball without releasing it, after an opponent's score, when a defending player intercepts a pass, when an opponent drops the ball to the ground, or when the ball that goes out of bounds was last touched by a member of the opposing team. Players are not permitted to wrestle the ball from an opponent. Play for 15 minutes. The team scoring more goals wins the game.

## To Increase Difficulty

- Decrease size of goal.
- Play with goalkeepers.

## To Decrease Difficulty

- Increase size of goal.
- Play with four neutrals.

## Success Check

- Square shoulders to goal.
- Use two-foot takeoff to jump up.
- Contact ball on forehead.
- Head ball down toward goal line.

## Score Your Success

Member of losing team = 0 points

Member of winning team = 1 point

Your score ___

# DIVE HEADER

The dive header technique is used to head a ball that is traveling parallel to the ground at waist level or lower. This situation may occur with a ball driven directly at you, but more often than not the dive header skill is used to head a ball crossed from the flank and traveling across the goal mouth. Defenders use this skill to clear balls out of the danger zone front and center of the goal, whereas attackers employ the dive header to score spectacular goals. In preparation to head the ball, square your shoulders, when possible, to the oncoming ball and assume a slightly crouched position (figure 4.2). Move toward the ball, anticipate its trajectory, and dive parallel to the ground to meet it. Tilt your head back with eyes open, mouth closed, and neck firm. Contact the ball on the flat surface of your forehead, just above your eyebrows. Extend your arms downward to break your fall to the ground.

## MISSTEP

The header lacks power or accuracy, or both.

## CORRECTION

Lack of power or poor accuracy means that you either mistimed the dive or failed to keep your head and neck firmly positioned as you contacted the ball. Tilt your head back, keep your neck firm, and contact the ball on the flat surface of your forehead.

## MISSTEP

The ball pops upward off your head.

## CORRECTION

When the ball pops up, it means that you have either contacted the ball too high on your forehead or dipped your head as the ball arrived. Keep your eyes on the ball, keep your head and neck firmly positioned, and contact the ball on the central area of your forehead, just above your eyebrows.

## Figure 4.2 **DIVE HEADER**

*Preparation*

1. Square shoulders to oncoming ball if possible.
2. Flex knees with weight centered over balls of feet.
3. Draw arms back and to sides.
4. Focus vision on the ball.

*Execution*

1. Move forward to intercept ball.
2. Propel body toward ball parallel to ground.
3. Tilt head back with neck firm.
4. Extend arms forward and angled down.
5. Keep eyes open and mouth closed.
6. Contact ball on forehead.

*Follow-Through*

1. Maintain momentum forward through point of contact.
2. Break fall with arms.
3. Jump to feet.

# Dive Header Drill 1    **Fundamental Dive Headers**

Perform this drill on a soft field surface or a gymnastic mat if training indoors. Face a server standing 10 yards away. The server tosses a ball toward you at approximately waist height. Flex your knees slightly, dive forward parallel to the ground, and contact the ball on the flat surface of your forehead. Extend your arms down to break your fall. Score 1 point for heading the ball directly back to the server so that he does not have to move more than one step in any direction to collect it. After each header, jump to your feet and prepare to head again. Head 10 tosses in succession; then switch roles with the server.

## To Increase Difficulty

- Increase number of repetitions.
- Change angle of delivery of service.

## To Decrease Difficulty

- Start on all fours rather than diving from standing position.
- Move closer to server.
- Decrease number of repetitions.

## Success Check

- Dive parallel to ground.

- Tilt head back with neck rigid.
- Keep eyes open and mouth closed.
- Contact ball on flat surface of forehead.

## Score Your Success

0 to 4 points = 0 points

5 to 7 points = 1 point

8 to 10 points = 3 points

Your score ___

# Dive Header Drill 2    **Score Off Dive Headers**

Play with two teammates within a 10- by 15-yard area. Place two flags to represent a goal 4 yards apart on one end of the area. One player stands in goal as the goalkeeper. One player, the server, stands to the side of the field, about 6 yards out from the end line. You get in position 10 yards front and center of the goal. The drill begins as the server tosses a ball across the goal mouth to simulate a crossed ball, at about waist height. Judge the flight of the ball and attempt to score using the dive header technique. Score 2 points for a goal scored and 1 point for a ball headed on goal but saved by the goalkeeper. Players rotate positions after each attempt on goal. Continue until each player has performed 20 dive headers.

## To Increase Difficulty

- Reduce size of goal.
- Increase number of repetitions.

## To Decrease Difficulty

- Increase width of goal to 6 yards.
- Do not use goalkeeper.

## Success Check

- Dive parallel to ground.
- Tilt head back with neck rigid.
- Extend arms down to break fall to ground.
- Contact ball on forehead.

## Score Your Success

0 to 14 points = 0 points

15 to 19 points = 1 point

20 to 29 points = 3 points

30 to 40 points = 5 points

Your score ___

# Dive Header Drill 3
## Dive Header Team Competition

Form two equal teams of four to six players each. Teams stand side by side in single file 15 yards front and center of a regulation-size goal. Station a neutral goalkeeper in the goal and a server 5 yards to each side of the goal. Servers alternate tossing balls into the area front and center of the goal. Players from each team take turns attempting to score off dive headers. The goalkeeper tries to save all shots. Score 2 points for a goal scored and 1 point for a ball headed on goal but saved by the goalkeeper. The first team to score 50 points wins.

### To Increase Difficulty

- Decrease width of goal to 6 yards.

### To Decrease Difficulty

- Increase width of goal to 10 yards.

## Success Check

- Dive parallel to ground.
- Tilt head back with neck stiff.
- Contact ball on forehead.
- Extend arms to cushion fall.

## Score Your Success

Member of losing team = 3 points

Member of winning team = 5 points

Your score ___

# Dive Header Drill 4   Dive Headers Only

Three players participate in this drill. One player (server) stands 10 yards behind a regulation goal with a supply of balls. A second player (attacker) stands on the top edge of the penalty area, facing the goal. The third player gets in position as the goalkeeper. The server chips a ball over the crossbar of the goal so that it drops within the penalty area. The attacker rushes forward and attempts to score off a first-time dive header. Make sure the ground in the penalty area is soft and free of rocks, sharp objects, or other hazards. A ball headed on goal saved by the keeper earns 1 point; a goal scored earns 2 points. The attacker performs 20 dive headers, after which players switch positions and repeat. Players keep track of their points. (*Note:* This drill is most appropriate for older, experienced players.)

*(continued)*

Dive Header Drill 4 *(continued)*

## To Increase Difficulty

- Reduce width of goal.

## To Decrease Difficulty

- Do not use goalkeeper.

## Success Check

- Dive parallel to ground.
- Tilt head back with neck rigid.
- Contact ball on forehead.

- Keep eyes open and mouth closed.
- Break fall to ground with arms.

## Score Your Success

0 to 11 points = 0 points

12 to 19 points = 1 point

20 to 29 points = 3 points

30 to 40 points = 5 points

Your score ___

# Dive Header Drill 5
# Multiple Goal Scoring Game

Play on a 40-yard-square field area. Position markers to represent six mini-goals, each 3 yards wide, spaced randomly within the field area. Organize two teams of equal numbers differentiated by colored vests. Award one team the ball to begin. Do not use goalkeepers. Teams can score through either side of all six goals, and must defend all six goals. Passing and receiving among teammates is accomplished by tossing and catching, rather than kicking, the ball. Players on the team with possession of the ball are restricted to four or fewer steps before releasing the ball to a teammate. Loss of possession to the opposition occurs if a player takes more than five steps with the ball, if the ball drops to the ground, or if a defending player intercepts a pass. All goals must be scored from dive headers, so the tosses must be accurate and the final pass must be at a height that requires the dive header technique. Play for 20 minutes. Score 1 team point for each goal scored.

## To Increase Difficulty

- Reduce width of goals.

## To Decrease Difficulty

- Increase width of goals.

## Success Check

- Dive parallel to ground.
- Tilt head back with neck rigid.

- Contact ball on forehead.
- Keep eyes open and mouth closed.
- Break fall to ground with arms.

## Score Your Success

Member of losing team = 3 points

Member of winning team = 5 points

Your score ___

# FLICKED HEADER

The flicked header can be used in any area of the field, although it is most often used by attacking players attempting to direct the path of flighted balls into gaps of space within the opponent's defense. This technique differs to some extent from other types of heading, because the objective is merely to alter the original flight path of the ball as opposed to heading it with power and accuracy in a specific direction. To perform a flicked header (figure 4.3), move toward the oncoming ball and allow it to glance off your forehead as it travels past. The sudden change in trajectory can cause opposing players to misjudge the flight of the ball and create confusion within the defense.

## Figure 4.3   FLICKED HEADER

*Preparation*

1. Move into position to intercept oncoming ball.

2. Tilt head back with neck firm.

3. Keep eyes open and mouth closed.

*Execution*

1. Jump upward (if need be) to align with the flight path of oncoming ball

2. Keep arms out to sides for balance.

3. Angle head to deflect ball in desired direction.

4. Allow ball to glance off forehead.

*(continued)*

Figure 4.3 *(continued)*

*Follow-Through*

1. Flick forehead slightly in direction ball is traveling.

2. Descend to ground.

**MISSTEP**

You fail to alter the flight path of the ball.

**CORRECTION**

Be sure to make contact with enough surface area of the ball to alter the trajectory. Move toward the ball, angle your forehead back, and allow the ball to glance off your upper forehead.

# Flicked Header Drill 1
## Flicked Headers End to End

Two players (servers A and B) face each another at a distance of 20 yards. Server A has the ball to begin. A third player (player C) gets in position midway between the servers. Server A tosses a head-high ball at player C, who moves toward the ball and flicks it to server B. Server B collects the ball and repeats the sequence in the opposite direction. Player C executes 30 flicked headers, after which the players rotate positions. Continue until each player has executed 30 flicked headers. Score 1 point for each header flicked to the opposite server. (*Note:* Accurate tosses from servers are essential for this drill to flow smoothly.)

**To Increase Difficulty**

- Increase distance and velocity of serve.

**To Decrease Difficulty**

- Decrease distance of serve.
- Do not require players to leave ground to head ball.

## Success Check

- Tilt head back.
- Keep eyes open and mouth closed.
- Allow ball to glance off top of forehead.

## Score Your Success

0 to 9 points = 0 points

10 to 17 points = 1 point

18 to 24 points = 3 points

25 to 30 points = 5 points

Your score ___

# Flicked Header Drill 2
## Flicked Headers to Open Space

Play on one end of a regulation field. Position two mini-goals (3 to 4 yards wide) on the end line of the field, 15 yards apart. A server gets in position 40 yards from the end line with a supply of balls. A second player (header) stands at the penalty spot with her back to the goal. The server kicks a flighted ball toward the player stationed at the penalty spot. The header moves to intercept the flight of the ball and flick it into one of the small goals. After 30 repetitions, players switch roles and repeat the drill. Score 1 point for each flicked header directed into an open goal for a possible maximum of 30 points. (*Note:* Accurate service is required for this drill to work effectively, so this drill is appropriate for higher-level players.)

### To Increase Difficulty

- Reduce width of goal to 2 yards.

### To Decrease Difficulty

- Position header closer to goals.
- Have server toss ball with hands.

## Success Check

- Move toward ball.
- Angle head back with neck firm.
- Allow ball to glance off top of forehead.
- Flick head in direction you want ball to travel.

## Score Your Success

0 to 9 points = 0 points

10 to 19 points = 2 points

20 to 30 points = 4 points

Your score ___

# SUCCESS SUMMARY

To compete successfully at higher levels of competition, you must become competent in executing the various heading techniques. Focus on the following key points.

When performing the jump header, contact the ball at the highest point of your jump. Jump early, hold the arched position until the last possible moment, and then snap forward from the waist to contact the ball on your forehead. Keep your head and neck firmly positioned.

When executing a dive header, fully extend your body parallel to the ground as you dive to meet the ball. Tilt your head back, keep your neck firm, and contact the ball on your forehead. Use your arms and hands to break your fall to the ground.

To execute the flicked header, allow the ball to glance off the upper surface of your forehead and go past you, rather than heading it back in the direction from which it came. Because it's difficult to visualize whether you are heading the ball correctly, have a coach or teammate observe or videotape you performing the various heading techniques. The observer can evaluate your performance and, if necessary, offer helpful feedback.

Each of the drills in step 4 has been assigned a point value so that you can evaluate your performance and chart your progress. Record your score in the following chart, and then total your points to get an estimate of your overall level of competence.

## Jump Header Drills

1. Group Head Juggle                                    _____ out of 5
2. Jump Header Technique                                _____ out of 5
3. Jack in the Box                                      _____ out of 5
4. Jump, Head, Do It Again                              _____ out of 5
5. Toss, Head, and Catch to Score                       _____ out of 5
6. Heading Race Front to Back to Front                  _____ out of 4
7. Headers End to End                                   _____ out of 6
8. Defensive Clearances                                 _____ out of 5
9. Score by Headers Only (With Neutrals)                _____ out of 1

## Dive Header Drills

1. Fundamental Dive Headers                             _____ out of 3
2. Score Off Dive Headers                               _____ out of 5
3. Dive Header Team Competition                         _____ out of 5
4. Dive Headers Only                                    _____ out of 5
5. Multiple Goal Scoring Game                           _____ out of 5

## Flicked Header Drills

1. Flicked Headers End to End                           _____ out of 5
2. Flicked Headers to Open Space                        _____ out of 4

**Total**                                               **_____ out of 73**

A combined score of 55 or more points indicates that you have sufficiently mastered heading skills and are ready to move on to step 5. A score in the range of 40 to 54 is considered adequate. You can move on to step 5 after reviewing and rehearsing each of the heading skills one more time. A score of 39 or fewer points indicates that you have not sufficiently mastered the heading skills described in step 4. You should review the material and rehearse each of the skills several times before moving on to step 5.

# Shooting to Finish the Attack

Scoring goals remains the single most difficult task in soccer. As a consequence the player who can consistently put the ball in the back of the opponent's net, the so-called "game changer," is a rare and valuable commodity to the team. It should be no surprise, then, that the most widely recognized players throughout the soccer world are the elite goal scorers, players who can determine the outcome of a game with one strike of the ball. The most famous of them all, the incomparable Brazilian Edson Arantes do Nascimento (Pelé), scored more than 1,200 goals during his illustrious professional career. Although Pelé has been retired as a player for more than three decades, soccer players worldwide still revere him and recognize his place in soccer history. As I write this chapter, the ultimate marksmen on the international scene include players such as Mario Gomez (Bayern Munich, Bundesliga), Lionel Messi (Barcelona, La Liga) and Robin Van Persie (Manchester United, Premier League), strikers who lead their respective leagues in scoring. On the women's side there is Marta Vieira da Silva, commonly known as Marta, of the Brazilian National team (FIFA World Player of the Year five consecutive times) and Abby Wambach, top striker of the US Women's National team. These players and a handful of others make up an elite group of world-class marksmen and are paid handsomely for their efforts.

The great goal scorers possess a rare and special gift—the ability to create and finish scoring opportunities that most others typically squander. Their success depends on several factors. The ability to shoot powerfully and accurately with either foot is essential if you are to finish your scoring opportunities. Physical assets such as speed, quickness, and strength are definite benefits. Intangibles such as anticipation and composure under pressure are also important—simply being in the right place at the right time to tap in a rebound or redirect a ball driven across the front of the goal. A bit of luck doesn't hurt either, although scoring goals on a regular basis surely isn't the result of blind luck. As the old coaching adage so aptly states, "Good luck generally occurs where preparation meets opportunity." The key word here is *preparation*.

You can prepare to take advantage of scoring opportunities by practicing the various shooting techniques in exercises that mirror actual game conditions.

The *instep drive* technique is used for striking a stationary or rolling ball. The *full-volley*, *half-volley*, and *side-volley* techniques are used for striking a bouncing ball or a ball that drops from above. A *swerving shot* bends the ball's trajectory of flight and is particularly effective when taking free kicks and corner kicks, but also can be effective when striking a rolling ball.

# INSTEP DRIVE SHOT

In most situations players use the instep drive technique when striking a rolling or stationary ball. The kicking mechanics are similar to those used when passing with the instep except that there is greater follow-through of the kicking leg to generate velocity on the shot.

Approach the ball from behind and at a slight angle (figure 5.1). Plant your supporting foot beside the ball with your knee slightly flexed. Keep your head steady and focus on the ball. Draw your kicking leg back with your foot extended and firm. At this point, the knee of the kicking leg should be directly over the ball. Snap the leg straight and contact the center of the ball with the full instep (laces) of your foot. Keep your kicking foot firm and pointed down as it strikes the ball. This will ensure that your knee is over the ball at the moment of contact and will keep the trajectory of the shot low. As you follow through, square your shoulders and hips to the target, and use a complete follow-through motion to generate maximum power on the shot.

### MISSTEP
The ball travels up and over the goal.

### CORRECTION
This occurs when you lean back as your foot strikes the ball. Plant your supporting foot beside, not behind, the ball. From this position, lean forward slightly, with the knee of the kicking leg positioned directly over the ball. Keep your kicking foot fully extended and pointed down as the instep contacts the center of the ball. Generate forward momentum through the point of contact.

### MISSTEP
The shot lacks power and velocity.

### CORRECTION
A weak shot is usually due to an inadequate follow-through motion of the kicking leg, failure to transfer weight forward as the kicking foot contacts the ball, or failure to keep the kicking foot firm. Generate forward momentum as you drive your foot through the ball. The kicking leg should continue forward and upward to waist level or above during the follow-through.

## Figure 5.1   INSTEP DRIVE SHOT

### Preparation

1. Approach from behind and at a slight angle.
2. Lean forward and plant supporting foot beside ball.
3. Flex supporting leg and keep arms out to sides for balance.
4. Draw back kicking leg with foot extended.
5. Keep head steady with vision on ball.

### Execution

1. Point supporting (plant) foot toward target.
2. Square shoulders and hips to target.
3. Snap kicking leg straight.
4. Keep kicking foot pointed downward and diagonally across ball.
5. Contact center of ball with instep.
6. Keep kicking foot firm throughout.

### Follow-Through

1. Keep momentum forward through point of contact.
2. Allow supporting foot to leave ground.
3. Complete follow-through kicking motion toward target.

# Instep Drive Shot Drill 1   Hit the Target

Face a teammate (server) standing 10 yards away. The server plays a slowly rolling ball toward you. Shoot the ball first time (without stopping it) directly back at the server using the instep drive technique. Perform 40 shots, alternating between the use of your right and left feet. Award yourself 1 point for each shot that permits the server to collect the ball without moving more than one step to either side.

## To Increase Difficulty

- Increase distance from server.
- Increase velocity of serve.

## To Decrease Difficulty

- Reduce distance to server.
- Take all shots with dominant foot.
- Shoot stationary ball to server.

## Success Check

- Square shoulders and hips to target.

- Position knee of kicking leg over ball.
- Keep kicking foot extended and firm.
- Keep head steady.
- Follow through toward target.

## Score Your Success

0 to 25 points = 1 point

26 to 34 points = 3 points

35 to 40 points = 5 points

Your score ___

# Instep Drive Shot Drill 2
# Shoot Through the Central Goal

Place two markers 8 yards apart to represent a regulation-width goal. Partner with a teammate. You get in position with a ball 25 yards from the goal. Your partner (target) stands 5 yards behind the goal, facing you. Dribble forward a couple of yards and attempt to shoot the ball through the goal (at the target) using the instep drive technique. The target immediately retrieves the ball and returns it to you. Perform 30 shots, alternating between using your left and right feet, and then switch roles with the target player. All shots must be taken from a distance of at least 20 yards. Score 1 point for each shot that travels through the goal below the target's head height.

## To Increase Difficulty

- Increase shooting distance to 30 yards.
- Reduce width of goal.

## To Decrease Difficulty

- Decrease shooting distance to 15 yards.
- Increase width of goal.
- Shoot stationary ball.

## Success Check

- Square shoulders and hips to goal.
- Position knee of kicking leg over ball.
- Keep kicking foot extended down and firm.
- Follow through toward target.

## Score Your Success

0 to 19 points = 1 point

20 to 24 points = 3 points

25 to 30 points = 5 points

Your score ___

# Instep Drive Shot Drill 3
## Combine With the Target and Score

Join with two teammates and get in position on one end of a regulation field. One player is the goalkeeper. A second player (target) gets in position with her back to the goal at the top of the penalty area. You stand 30 yards from the goal with a supply of balls, facing the target. To begin the drill, dribble forward a couple of yards and play a firm pass to the feet of the target, who is checking toward you. She deflects the ball sideways a couple of feet, just outside the top of the penalty area. Immediately after passing, sprint forward and strike the ball first time on goal (without controlling it) using the instep drive technique. The goalkeeper tries to save all shots. Sprint back to your original position and repeat for 10 shots. Award yourself 1 point for a shot on goal saved by the goalkeeper and 2 points for a goal scored. All shots must be taken from a distance of 18 yards or greater. After 10 shots, players rotate positions and repeat the drill. Continue until each player has taken a turn as the shooter.

### To Increase Difficulty

- Increase shooting distance.
- Increase number of repetitions.

### To Decrease Difficulty

- Reduce shooting distance to 15 yards.
- Allow two-touch shooting.

## Success Check

- Square shoulders and hips to goal.
- Position knee of kicking leg over ball.
- Keep kicking foot extended down and firm.
- Keep head steady with vision on ball.
- Follow through toward target.

## Score Your Success

0 to 8 points = 1 point

9 to 13 points = 3 points

14 to 20 points = 5 points

Your score ___

# Instep Drive Shot Drill 4  **Pressure Shooting**

Play with two teammates on one end of a regulation field with a regulation goal on the end line. One player is a goalkeeper. A second player (server) stands 25 yards from the goal with a dozen soccer balls. You get in position directly in front of the server with your back to the goal, facing the server. The drill begins as the server rolls a ball past you a couple of yards into the penalty area. Turn and sprint to the ball, shoot first time using the instep drive, and sprint immediately back to your original spot. The server rolls a second ball past you to the opposite side. Again, turn, sprint to the ball, and shoot to score. You must strike each ball first time, without stopping or controlling it. The server alternates rolling balls to your left and right. Continue until the supply of balls is depleted; then switch positions with the server and repeat. (The goalkeeper remains the goalkeeper.) Score 2 points for each goal scored and 1 point for each shot on goal saved by the goalkeeper. Play two rounds as shooter for a total of 24 shots.

### To Increase Difficulty

- Increase shooting distance.
- Increase number of shots to induce physical fatigue.

### To Decrease Difficulty

- Reduce shooting distance.
- Decrease speed of repetitions.
- Allow shooter two touches to control and shoot ball.

### *Success Check*

- Turn and sprint to ball.
- Square shoulders and hips to goal.
- Position knee of kicking leg over ball.
- Keep kicking foot extended and firm.
- Keep head steady.
- Follow through toward target.

### *Score Your Success*

0 to 21 points = 1 point

22 to 32 points = 3 points

33 to 48 points = 5 points

Your score ___

# Instep Drive Shot Drill 5
## Two-Touch Shoot to Score

Play on one end of a regulation field. Position a server beside the goal with a supply of balls and the goalkeeper in goal. You get in position 25 yards front and center of the goal. To begin the drill, the server kicks a ball toward you, either along the ground or through the air. Move toward the oncoming ball, control and prepare it with your first touch, and shoot on goal with your second touch. All shots must be two-touch shots only and must be taken from a distance of 15 yards or greater from goal. After each shot, return immediately to your starting position and repeat the sequence for a total of 10 shots on goal. The goalkeeper attempts to save all shots. Score 1 point for a shot on goal and 2 points for a goal scored. Keep a tally of points scored. After completing 10 shots, switch positions with the server and repeat the drill. The goalkeeper remains the goalkeeper. Play two rounds of shots for each player, for a total of 20 shots at goal.

### To Increase Difficulty

- Have a defending player sprint off end line to challenge shooter.
- Reduce width of goal to 6 yards.
- Increase number of shots.

### To Decrease Difficulty

- Allow three touches to control, prepare, and shoot ball on goal.
- Shoot stationary ball placed 15 yards from goal.

## Success Check

- Move forward to receive ball.

- Push ball toward goal with first touch.
- Strike ball on goal with second touch.
- Keep shoulders and hips square to goal.
- Keep knee of kicking leg over ball.
- Keep kicking foot extended and firm.

### Score Your Success

0 to 21 points = 1 point

22 to 29 points = 3 points

30 to 40 points = 5 points

Your score ___

# Instep Drive Shot Drill 6
## Shoot to Score Off the Dribble

Form two teams of three to five players each. Teams stand side by side in two single-file lines facing the goal 25 yards away. A neutral goalkeeper positions in goal. The first player in each line alternately dribbles forward at top speed and shoots on goal from a distance of 15 yards or greater. After each shot, the shooter quickly retrieves the ball and returns to the end of the line. Continue the drill until each player has attempted 15 shots. Score 1 point for each shot on goal and 2 points for each goal scored. Players keep tallies of their own points. (**Note:** Rotate two or three goalkeepers in goal because of the large number of shots taken.)

### To Increase Difficulty

- Increase shooting distance.
- Have defender chase dribbler.
- Increase number of repetitions.

### To Decrease Difficulty

- Reduce dribbling speed.
- Reduce shooting distance.
- Reduce number of repetitions.

## Success Check

- Dribble at top speed toward goal.
- Square shoulders and hips to target.

- Position knee of kicking leg over ball.
- Keep kicking foot pointed down and firm.
- Completely follow through toward target.

### Score Your Success

0 to 14 points = 1 point

15 to 21 points = 3 points

22 to 30 points = 5 points

Your score ___

# Instep Drive Shot Drill 7   2v2 Scoring Derby

Play at one end of a regulation soccer field. Six players are required; one is the goalkeeper and one is the server. The remaining players are divided into two teams of two players each. Both teams take positions in the 18- by 44-yard penalty area. The server stands at the top of the penalty arc with a dozen soccer balls and initiates play by rolling a ball into the penalty area. Both teams vie for possession. The team that wins the ball attempts to score while the other team defends. If a player steals the ball, that player's team immediately goes on the attack and tries to score. The goalkeeper is neutral and attempts to save all shots. The server immediately rolls another ball into the area after the goalkeeper makes a save, when the ball is kicked out of play, or when a goal is scored. Play nonstop until the supply of balls is depleted. The team scoring more goals wins the game. Play five games. Award yourself 1 point for each goal scored.

## To Increase Difficulty

- Use markers to designate smaller goal.
- Add one player who always plays with defending team, creating a one-player advantage for defense.
- Require that all goals be scored off first-time shots.

## To Decrease Difficulty

- Use markers to represent enlarged goal.
- Add one player who always plays with attacking team, creating a one-player advantage for offense.

## *Success Check*

- Combine with teammate to create scoring opportunities.
- Recognize scoring opportunities and take the shot.
- Favor accuracy over power.

## *Score Your Success*

Average 1 goal scored per game = 1 point

Average 2 or more goals scored per game = 3 points

Your score ___

# Instep Drive Shot Drill 8
## World Cup Scoring Game

Organize four to six teams of two players each. All teams take positions within the penalty area. Each team chooses a country to represent (e.g., United States, England, Germany, Spain). A neutral goalkeeper stands in goal. A server positions beside the goal with a supply of balls. The game begins when the server tosses a couple of balls toward the outer edge of the penalty area. All teams vie for possession. Teams gaining possession of a ball attempt to score in the full-size goal; all other teams defend. The offside rule is not in effect. A team that loses possession immediately goes on defense; a team gaining possession immediately attacks. The server returns a ball into play after each save or goal by tossing the ball toward the outer edge of the penalty area. Two balls are kept in play at all times.

A team that scores on the goalkeeper advances to the next round of play. After scoring, the players shout their team name and sprint off the field behind the goal to wait for the next round. The round ends when all but one team has scored. That team is eliminated from the World Cup competition. Remaining teams advance to the next round, which is organized in the same manner as the first.

Play a sufficient number of rounds until only one team remains—the World Cup champion. Eliminated teams practice ball juggling behind the goal until the game is repeated. Play five games.

## To Increase Scoring Difficulty

- Increase number of teams to reduce available time and space.
- Position two goalkeepers in goal.

## To Decrease Scoring Difficulty

- Increase width of goal.

## Success Check

- Turn and shoot at any half chance.
- Square shoulders and hips to goal.

- Keep kicking foot down and firm.
- Shoot low and hard.

## Score Your Success

Win 0 or 1 World Cup competitions = 1 point

Win 2 or 3 World Cup competitions = 2 points

Win 4 or 5 World Cup competitions = 3 points

Your score ___

# Instep Drive Shot Drill 9    Empty Net

Play on one end of a regulation field with a full-size goal on the end line. Divide the group into two teams. Team 1 players position next to one goalpost; team 2 players station at the other goal post. Place a marker 18 yards front and center of goal. Each team has a supply of soccer balls nearby.

To begin, one player from team 1 positions in goal. The first player in line for team 2 sprints out from the goalpost, around the marker 18 yards from goal, and then turns toward goal. At that moment the second player in line for team 2 plays a rolling ball toward the penalty spot for his teammate to finish with a one-time shot. After the player shoots to score, he immediately sprints to the goal line and becomes the goalkeeper. Team 1 attempts to score in the same manner. If the shooter, after shooting, fails to get to the goal in time, the opposing shooter has an "empty net" to shoot at (hence the drill name). Teams compete for a predetermined amount of time or number of goals scored. Each goal scored earns 1 point. The team scoring more goals wins the game. Play three rounds.

*Note:* The server can vary the type of service (rolling balls, bouncing balls, angled passes, etc) depending on the focus of the scoring session.

*(continued)*

Instep Drive Shot Drill 9 *(continued)*

### To Increase Scoring Difficulty

- All shots must be taken from 18 yards or farther.

### To Decrease Scoring Difficulty

- Use markers to increase width of goal.

## *Success Check*

- Square shoulders and hips to goal.

- Keep kicking foot down and firm.
- Shoot with full follow-through motion toward goal.
- Shoot low and hard.

## *Score Your Success*

Win 0 or 1 round (team) = 1 point

Win 2 rounds (team) = 3 points

Win all 3 rounds (team) = 5 points

Your score ___

# Instep Drive Shot Drill 10
## 4v4 With Sideline and End Line Targets

Play on a 60-yard-long by 50-yard-wide field area, divided in half by a midline, with a full-size goal centered on each end line. Organize two teams of eight players each. A neutral goalkeeper stations in each goal.

To begin, each team positions four players within the field area to compete with four players from the opposing team. Each team defends a goal and can score in the opponent's goal. The remaining four players from each team position as targets in their opponent's half of the field—one target on each sideline and one target on the end line on each side of the opponent's goal. The sideline targets are limited to two touches to receive and pass a ball; the end line targets are restricted to one-touch passing. Targets may not enter the field area, but can receive and return passes from their teammates competing within the field.

Players on the four-player team in possession within the field area can pass among themselves or to their targets, who can return passes or serve balls into the goal area for attempted scores. The use of targets creates an 8v4 situation, a four-player advantage for the team in possession, although the targets are not permitted to enter the field area. The first team to score two goals wins the round; target players then immediately switch places with teammates on the field to play the next round. The first team to win three rounds wins the game.

### To Increase Scoring Difficulty

- All scores must originate off first-time shots.
- All targets must play one-touch.

### To Decrease Scoring Difficulty

- Targets may enter field area to create four-player advantage for attacking team.

## Success Check

- Combine with teammates to create scoring opportunities.
- Penetrate opposing defense by playing balls into targets.
- Square up with goal when shooting.
- Keep kicking foot down and firm.
- Use full follow-through motion toward goal.

## Score Your Success

Win 1 round (team) = 1 point

Win 2 rounds (team) = 3 points

Win 3 rounds (team) = 5 points

Your score ___

# VOLLEY SHOTS

There will be situations in which you won't have time to bring the ball to the ground before shooting on goal. In those instances your best option is to volley it directly out of the air. Successfully executing a volley shot requires precise timing and proper form. If you perform a volley shot correctly, you can generate tremendous velocity. Some of the most spectacular goals I've witnessed during my long career as a player and coach have been scored off volleys.

## Full-Volley Shot

Use the full-volley technique to strike a bouncing ball or a ball that drops from above. Approach the ball with shoulders square to the target (figure 5.2). Flex your supporting leg slightly at the knee to maximize balance and body control. Draw your kicking leg back with the foot extended and firm. Keep your head steady with your vision focused on the ball. As the ball descends, snap your kicking leg straight and contact the center of the ball with your full instep. Strike the ball when it is as low to the ground as possible. At the moment of contact, the knee of your kicking leg should be directly above the ball and your kicking foot should be pointed down. Use a short, powerful kicking motion, rather than a sweeping follow-through, as the leg snaps straight.

### MISSTEP

The ball travels up and over the goal.

### CORRECTION

This common error happens when you lean back and reach for the ball as you kick it. Timing of the kick is everything. Allow the ball to drop as close to the ground as possible before striking it with your instep. The kicking foot should be pointed down with the knee over the ball at the moment of contact.

Figure 5.2   **FULL-VOLLEY SHOT**

### Preparation

1. Move to spot where ball will drop.
2. Approach ball with shoulders square.
3. Flex supporting leg at knee.
4. Draw back kicking leg with foot extended.
5. Hold arms out to sides for balance.
6. Keep head steady and focus on ball.

### Execution

1. Square hips to target.
2. Position knee of kicking leg over ball.
3. Keep kicking foot firm and pointed down.
4. Contact center of ball with instep.

### Follow-Through

1. Kicking leg snaps straight.
2. Momentum is forward toward target.

# Half-Volley Shot

The half-volley technique is similar in many ways to the full-volley technique. The primary difference is that the ball is kicked the instant it hits the ground rather than directly out of the air. Anticipate where the ball will drop; then move to that spot (figure 5.3). Draw your kicking leg back with your foot extended and firm. Square your shoulders and hips to the target as you snap your kicking leg straight. Strike the center of the ball with the full instep the instant the ball hits the ground. The knee of the kicking leg should be above the ball at the moment of contact, and the foot should be pointed down and firmly positioned. Use a short, powerful snaplike motion of the kicking leg.

## Figure 5.3 HALF-VOLLEY SHOT

*Preparation*

1. Anticipate where ball will drop and move to that spot.
2. Flex supporting leg at knee.
3. Draw back kicking leg with foot extended and firm.
4. Hold arms out to sides for balance.
5. Keep head steady and eyes on ball.

*Execution*

1. Square shoulders and hips to target.
2. Position knee of kicking leg over ball.
3. Snap kicking leg straight.
4. Keep kicking foot extended and firm.
5. Strike through center of ball as it hits the ground.

*Follow-Through*

1. Kicking leg follows through toward target.
2. Momentum is forward through point of contact.

**MISSTEP**

The shot slices right or left of the target.

**CORRECTION**

Precise timing and proper technique are essential. It's too late to contact the ball once it has begun to rebound upward off the ground. Move into position early, judge the descent of the ball, and strike the ball at the exact instant it hits the ground. Square up with the target at the moment of contact with the ball.

**MISSTEP**

The shot travels up and over the goal.

**CORRECTION**

This error occurs when you lean back as your foot contacts the ball. Time your shot release so that your body is moving forward with your knee above the ball as you kick it. Your kicking foot should be pointed down at the moment of contact.

## Side-Volley Shot

Use the side-volley technique to shoot a ball that bounces or drops to your side or to redirect a ball directly out of the air that crosses into the goal area. Face the ball as it approaches (figure 5.4). As the ball arrives, turn your body sideways so that your lead (front) shoulder is pointing in the direction in which you want the ball to travel. Raise your kicking leg to the side so that it is almost parallel to the ground. Draw back your kicking foot with the leg bent at the knee. Keep your head steady with eyes focused on the ball. Snap the kicking leg straight and contact the top half of the ball with your instep. Follow through by rotating your body toward the target. The kicking leg should travel on a slightly downward plane.

The shot will lack power if you swing your kicking leg at the ball rather than powerfully snap the lower leg through the point of contact. Keep your leg in the cocked position until the last possible moment; then snap it straight and drive the kicking foot through the upper half of the ball with a short, explosive motion.

**MISSTEP**

The ball travels up and over the goal.

**CORRECTION**

The knee of the kicking leg must be on an even plane with or slightly above the ball as you kick it. The kicking leg should travel on a downward plane through the top half of the ball.

**MISSTEP**

The shot travels wide of the goal.

**CORRECTION**

Rotate your body toward the target as you kick the ball. At the completion of the follow-through kicking motion, you should be square to the goal.

## Figure 5.4  **SIDE-VOLLEY SHOT**

### *Preparation*

1. Face oncoming ball.
2. Raise kicking leg to side, parallel to ground.
3. Draw back kicking foot with knee bent.
4. Balance weight on supporting leg.
5. Keep arms out to sides for balance.
6. Keep head steady.

### *Execution*

1. Rotate half turn toward ball on balance foot.
2. Point front shoulder toward target.
3. Snap kicking leg straight.
4. Contact top half of ball with instep.

### *Follow-Through*

1. Rotate body square to target.
2. Angle kicking motion slightly downward.
3. Generate momentum forward in direction of shot.
4. Drop kicking foot to ground.

# Volley Shot Drill 1   Volley to Partner

Face a partner from 6 yards away. Hold the ball in your hands at waist level. Drop the ball, step forward, and kick a full-volley shot to your partner's chest. Your partner catches the ball and volleys it back to you in the same manner. Continue for 30 full volleys each, alternating between your left and right feet. Repeat the drill for 30 half-volley shots each, alternating feet with every shot. Score 1 point for each ball volleyed directly at your partner that she can catch out of the air. Keep track of points scored.

### To Increase Difficulty

- Increase distance to 10 yards.
- Volley and half-volley a ball tossed to you by your partner.
- Return tosses to partner by volley while jogging around field.

### To Decrease Difficulty

- Decrease distance to 5 yards.

*(continued)*

Volley Shot Drill 1 *(continued)*

### Success Check

- Square shoulders and hips to target.
- Keep head steady with vision on ball.
- Extend foot down and firm.
- Contact vertical midline of ball on full instep.

- Use short, powerful snap of kicking leg.

### Score Your Success

0 to 39 points = 1 point

40 to 49 points = 3 points

50 to 60 points = 5 points

Your score ___

---

# Volley Shot Drill 2   Round the Flag and Volley

Play on one end of a field with a regulation goal and two teammates (servers). Position a flag post (or similar marker) 10 yards front and center of goal. You stand at the marker; station a server at each goal post, each with a supply of balls. Begin with one server tossing a ball into the area front of the goal so that it drops about 5 yards from goal. You sprint forward and volley the ball out of the air into the open goal. Immediately sprint back to the flag; then repeat to the opposite side with the other server. Continue the exercise for 20 full volleys, alternating between your left and right feet. Score 1 point for each ball volleyed directly into the goal. Keep track of points scored.

### To Increase Difficulty

- Increase shooting distance to 10 yards.
- Increase number of repetitions.

### To Decrease Difficulty

- Allow ball to bounce once before shooting.

### Success Check

- Square shoulders and hips to target.
- Keep head steady and vision on ball.

- Keep foot extended down and firm.
- Contact vertical midline of ball on full instep.
- Use short, powerful snap of kicking leg.

### Score Your Success

0 to 10 points = 1 point

11 to 15 points = 3 points

16 to 20 points = 5 points

Your score ___

# Volley Shot Drill 3    Toss and Volley to Score

Get in position 20 yards front and center of a regulation goal with a supply of balls. A goalkeeper plays in goal. Toss a ball into the air so that it drops 3 to 4 yards in front of you. Move forward, allow the ball to bounce once, and execute a full-volley shot on goal. Take 20 full-volley shots followed by 20 half-volley shots for a total of 40 volleys. Alternate left- and right-foot volley shots. Score 1 point for each shot on goal, even if the goalkeeper saves the shot.

**To Increase Difficulty**

- Increase shooting distance.
- Volley ball tossed by server.
- Volley only with weaker (nondominant) foot.

**To Decrease Difficulty**

- Reduce shooting distance.
- Increase size of goal.
- Volley the ball directly out of your hands.

**Success Check**

- Square shoulders and hips to goal.

- Keep head steady.
- Allow ball to drop until it is only a few inches off ground.
- Position kicking foot down and firm.
- Contact vertical midline of ball with instep.
- Use short, powerful follow-through.

**Score Your Success**

0 to 19 points = 1 point

20 to 34 points = 3 points

35 to 40 points = 5 points

Your score ___

# Volley Shot Drill 4    Side Volley to Score

Get in position 6 to 8 yards front and center of a regulation goal. A server stands on the flank 20 to 25 yards away with a supply of balls. The server crosses or tosses a ball for you to side volley into the goal. Do not use a goalkeeper. Perform 20 side volleys from the right side; then 20 from the left side. Score 1 point for each side volley kicked into the open goal.

**To Increase Difficulty**

- Increase shooting distance to 15 yards.

**To Decrease Difficulty**

- Toss ball to yourself to side volley on goal.

**Success Check**

- Face server.
- Raise and cock kicking leg with foot extended and firm.

- Rotate on supporting foot as ball arrives.
- Turn lead shoulder to goal.
- Kick on downward plane through top half of ball.

**Score Your Success**

0 to 19 points = 1 point

20 to 29 points = 3 points

30 to 40 points = 5 points

Your score ___

# Volley Shot Drill 5    Score by Volleys Only

Form two equal teams of four to six players each. Use markers to outline a rectangular playing area 40 by 60 yards. Center a full-size goal on each end line. Do not use goalkeepers. Each team defends a goal and can score in the opponent's goal. Passing among teammates is accomplished by throwing and catching rather than kicking the ball. A player may take no more than four steps with the ball before releasing it to a teammate. Change of possession occurs when a defending player intercepts a pass, when an out-of-bounds ball was last touched by an attacking player, when the ball is dropped to the ground, when a player takes more than four steps with the ball, and after a goal is scored.

Points are scored by volleying a ball tossed by a teammate directly out of the air into the opponent's goal. Players are not permitted to toss the ball to themselves to volley on goal. Although goalkeepers are not designated, all players are permitted to use the hands to catch the ball and to block passes or shots on goal. Play for 15 minutes. The team scoring more goals wins.

*Note:* Successful execution of full-volley shots requires precise timing and correct technique, so this game may not be appropriate for younger players.

## To Increase Difficulty

- Use goalkeepers.

## To Decrease Difficulty

- Allow players to volley directly out of hands.

## Success Check

- Square shoulders and hips to target.
- Allow ball to drop as low to the ground as possible.

- Position knee over ball at moment of contact.
- Keep kicking foot extended and firm.
- Use short, powerful snap of kicking leg.

## Score Your Success

Member of losing team = 0 points

Member of winning team = 1 point

Your score ___

# SWERVING (BENDING) SHOT

Sometimes the most direct path to goal is not always the best route. This is particularly true on corner kicks and free kicks, during which you may attempt to bend the ball around or over a wall of players. You can cause the ball to swerve and dip in flight by imparting spin to it. Striking the outer half of the ball with the inside of the right instep causes the ball to bend from right to left. Striking the outer half of the ball with the inside of the left instep bends the ball from left to right. These types of swerving shots are commonly referred to as *inswingers* and can create goal-scoring opportunities.

To swerve the ball, begin your approach from behind the ball at a slight angle (figure 5.5). Plant your supporting foot beside or slightly behind the ball. Keep your head steady and eyes focused on the ball. Draw back your kicking leg with the foot extended and firm. Lean slightly back and away from the ball as you strike it. Use an outside-in follow-through motion as you contact the ball with the inside area of the instep.

You can swerve the ball in the opposite direction using the outside surface of the instep. Contact the inside half of the ball with the outside of your right instep to make the shot bend from left to right. Contact the inside half of the ball with the outside of your left instep to make the shot bend from right to left. These types of shots are often referred to as *outswingers*. Use an inside-out follow-through motion of the kicking leg. Position the kicking foot down and diagonally inward as it contacts the ball. A complete follow-through motion will generate greater power and swerve.

## Figure 5.5  SWERVING SHOT

### Preparation

1. Approach ball from behind at slight angle.

2. Plant supporting foot beside or slightly behind ball.

3. Draw back kicking leg with foot extended and firm.

4. Keep arms out to sides for balance.

5. Keep head steady and eyes on ball.

### Execution

1. Lean back slightly and away from ball.

2. Contact ball left or right of vertical midline with inside or outside surface of instep.

3. Keep kicking foot firm and angled down.

### Follow-Through

1. Keep momentum forward through point of contact.

2. Use inside-out kicking motion for outside-of-the-instep shot.

3. Use outside-in kicking motion for inside-of-the-instep shot.

4. Follow through to waist level or higher.

### MISSTEP

The ball fails to curve in flight.

### CORRECTION

The shot will not swerve in flight unless you impart sufficient velocity and spin to the ball. Contact the ball left or right of its vertical midline, not directly through its center. Lean away from the ball as you kick it. Use an inside-out kicking motion for an outside-of-the-instep shot, and use an outside-in kicking motion for an inside-of-the-instep shot.

### MISSTEP

The shot lacks power.

### CORRECTION

A weak shot usually occurs for one of the following reasons: the kicking foot contacts the ball too close to its outer edge, the kicking foot is not firm as it contacts the ball, or follow-through is insufficient. Contact the ball just right or left of center, not along its outer edge. Get as much surface area of your instep on the ball as possible while still imparting sufficient spin. Extend and firmly position your kicking foot. A complete follow-through motion coupled with proper kicking mechanics will generate sufficient velocity and spin on the ball to bend the flight path of the shot.

## Swerving Shot Drill 1   Target Practice

Use masking tape to outline a 4- by 4-yard target on a wall or kickboard. Shoot (swerve) stationary balls to hit the target from a distance of 20 yards or greater. Take 30 shots using your favorite (dominant) foot. Award yourself 1 point for each shot that bends in flight and hits inside the square.

### To Increase Difficulty

- Reduce size of target to 3 by 3 yards.

### To Decrease Difficulty

- Reduce shooting distance.
- Increase size of square to 5 by 5 yards.

### Success Check

- Approach ball from behind at slight angle.
- Square hips to target.
- Keep kicking foot extended down and firm.

- Contact ball right or left of vertical midline.
- Impart sufficient spin and velocity to the ball.

### Score Your Success

4 or fewer points = 0 points

5 to 8 points = 2 points

9 to 14 points = 3 points

15 to 19 points = 4 points

20 to 30 points = 5 points

Your score ___

# Swerving Shot Drill 2   Scoring From Set Pieces

Place a dozen soccer balls at various spots just outside of the penalty area. A goal-keeper positions in the regulation goal. Practice scoring from direct free kicks. Attempt to swerve each shot with the inside or outside surface of the instep. After 12 shots, repo-sition the balls at different spots and repeat the drill for a total of 24 free-kick attempts. Award yourself 1 point for each shot on goal that bends in flight, and award yourself 2 points for a goal scored. The goalkeeper collects and returns each shot on goal.

## To Increase Difficulty

- Shoot from greater distance.
- Make goal smaller.
- Position portable (movable) kick wall 10 yards in front of ball.

## To Decrease Difficulty

- Shoot from 15 yards.

## Success Check

- Approach ball from behind at slight angle.
- Square shoulders and hips to goal.

- Lean back slightly and away from ball.
- Keep kicking foot extended and firm.
- Use complete follow-through motion.

### Score Your Success

0 to 24 points = 1 point

25 to 34 points = 3 points

35 to 48 points = 5 points

Your score ___

# Swerving Shot Drill 3
# Bending Balls From the Run of Play

This drill requires seven players, one a neutral goalkeeper. Play within a 50- by 50-yard field area. Mark off a 25-yard square within the larger field. Position two cones or flags in the center of the 25-yard square to represent an 8-yard-wide goal. The neutral goalkeeper stands in goal and attempts to save all shots. The remaining players divide into two teams of three players each.

Teams compete 3v3 within the larger area. One team begins with possession of the ball; the other team defends. Players score by shooting the ball through either side of the central goal below the height of the goalkeeper. The goalkeeper must readjust position (side of the goal) depending on the location of the ball. Players are not permitted to enter the 25-yard square. All shots must be taken from outside the 25-yard square and must be swerved with the inside or outside surface of the instep. A ball that goes out of play is returned by a throw-in. If the defending team gains possession of the ball, it immediately switches to the attack and tries to score. After making a save, the goalkeeper tosses the ball to a corner of the playing area where both teams compete for possession. Play for 15 minutes. Players keep their own tallies of the number of swerving shots they kick on goal. (*Note:* This drill is most appropriate for older, experienced players.)

*(continued)*

Swerving Shot Drill 3 *(continued)*

## To Increase Difficulty for Attacking Team

- Reduce size of goal.
- Limit players to three or fewer touches to pass or shoot the ball.
- Add neutral player who always plays with defending team to create one-player advantage.

## To Decrease Difficulty for Attacking Team

- Enlarge goal.
- Add neutral player who always plays with attacking team to create one-player advantage.

## Success Check

- Square shoulders and hips to goal.
- Keep head steady and kicking foot firm at ball contact.
- Impart spin and velocity to the ball.
- Shoot at every opportunity.

## Score Your Success

4 or fewer shots on goal = 1 point

5 to 9 shots on goal = 2 points

10 or more shots on goal = 3 points

Your score ___

# SUCCESS SUMMARY

Developing your ability to shoot with power and accuracy is the first step toward becoming a proficient goal scorer. Once you're able to shoot consistently with power and accuracy in a low-pressure practice-type environment, move on to more gamelike situations that involve the pressures of limited time and space and physical fatigue as well as the challenge of determined opponents. If necessary, you can modify the drills in step 5 to match your level of expertise.

Each of the drills in step 5 has been assigned a point value so that you can evaluate your performance and chart your progress. Record your scores in the following chart and then total the points to get a rough estimate of your overall level of success.

### Instep Drive Shot Drills

| | | |
|---|---|---|
| 1. | Hit the Target | ____ out of 5 |
| 2. | Shoot Through the Central Goal | ____ out of 5 |
| 3. | Combine With the Target and Score | ____ out of 5 |
| 4. | Pressure Shooting | ____ out of 5 |
| 5. | Two-Touch Shoot to Score | ____ out of 5 |
| 6. | Shoot to Score Off the Dribble | ____ out of 5 |
| 7. | 2v2 Scoring Derby | ____ out of 3 |
| 8. | World Cup Scoring Game | ____ out of 3 |
| 9. | Empty Net | ____ out of 5 |
| 10. | 4v4 With Sideline and End Line Targets | ____ out of 5 |

### *Volley Shot Drills*

1. Volley to Partner             _____ out of 5
2. Round the Flag and Volley      _____ out of 5
3. Toss and Volley to Score       _____ out of 5
4. Side Volley to Score           _____ out of 5
5. Score by Volleys Only          _____ out of 1

### *Swerving Shot Drills*

1. Target Practice                _____ out of 5
2. Scoring From Set Pieces       _____ out of 5
3. Bending Balls From the Run of Play   _____ out of 3

**Total**                             **_____ out of 80**

A combined score of 63 or more points indicates that you have sufficiently mastered the shooting skills and are prepared to move on to step 6. A total score in the range of 45 to 62 is considered adequate. Move on to step 6 after you have reviewed and rehearsed each of the shooting techniques one more time. If you had fewer than 45 points, you need to polish your shooting skills. Review all of the material in step 5, practice each of the shooting techniques, and then progress through each of the drills at least one more time to improve your overall score before moving on to step 6.

# Goalkeeping

**G**oalkeeper is a difficult and demanding position to play, one that requires a special type of athlete. Action in and around the goal mouth is usually fast, furious, and physical. Courage is a key component of the keeper makeup, because this player can expect to be involved in a number of physical challenges during a match. As a keeper, you may be required to dive at the feet of an onrushing opponent to smother a loose ball, or fearlessly sacrifice your body to block a point-blank shot—whatever it takes to keep the ball out of the back of the net. Given that a single error in judgment can cost the team a win, a high degree of mental toughness is equally as important as, if not more important than, physical toughness. You must be prepared to make split-second decisions in the heat of competition, and then be able to deal with the consequences—good and bad. When an error in judgment does occur, and invariably that will happen to every goalkeeper at one time or another, you cannot allow it to affect your confidence or concentration. You must put the mistake behind you and immediately move on. *Never allow your last play to affect your next play.*

Because keepers perform a different set of skills than typical field players, they have different equipment needs. Most keepers wear specialized goalkeeper gloves that aid in holding hard shots and also soften the impact of powerfully driven balls. Goalkeeper jerseys are often padded at the elbows, because the keeper must dive to save on many occasions, and goalkeeper shorts typically have thin padding to protect the hips and hip joints.

Equipment aside, to consistently perform at a high level, top-flight netminders combine a high degree of mental toughness with outstanding physical ability and sound decision-making abilities. Most elite goalkeepers, although not all, are tall and rangy and have excellent jumping ability. They possess the ability to catch and hold powerful shots that arrive from various trajectories and distances. When required, they can propel their bodies through the air to make acrobatic saves or courageously dive at the feet of rushing opponents to smother the ball on a breakaway. Superior levels of agility, balance, and body control enable goalkeepers to react instantly to rapidly changing situations that occur in the goal mouth. Powerful legs and upper bodies enable them to leap up to catch balls served into the goal mouth and, when necessary, fend off the determined challenge of opponents attempting to win the ball.

In addition to mastering fundamental handling skills, the modern keeper must also be proficient at receiving, preparing, and passing the ball with the feet, because defenders will often pass back to the goalkeeper when under pressure. With the advent of the back-pass rule, a ball deliberately passed back to the keeper by a teammate must be played with the feet, and not the hands.

Despite the expanded role of the modern keeper, this player can still be considered the one true specialist on the soccer team. Assigned the task of protecting a goal

8 feet (2.4 m) high and 24 feet (7.3 m) wide, the keeper stands as the final obstacle opponents must bypass to score. Important goalkeeping skills include the basic goalkeeper stance, commonly referred to as the *starting, or ready, position*; the ability to receive low (ground-level), medium-high, chest-high, and high balls; diving skills; and the ability to distribute the ball by rolling, throwing, dropkicking, and punting.

# STARTING, OR READY, POSITION

As goalkeeper, you must maintain good balance and body control at all times. All movements begin in the standard goalkeeper posture, commonly referred to as the starting, or ready, position (figure 6.1). Assume the starting position whenever an opponent has the ball within shooting distance of your goal. Face the ball with your shoulders square and feet approximately shoulder-width apart. Keep your head and upper body erect with your knees slightly flexed. Center your body weight forward over the balls of your feet so that your heels elevate slightly off the ground. Carry your hands at approximately waist level with palms forward and fingers pointing up. Keep your head steady with your focus on the ball. From this position you will be able to move quickly in any direction to receive a ball or save a shot at goal.

## Figure 6.1 **STARTING POSITION**

### Preparation

1. Position forward (off) goal line.
2. Align body with ball.
3. Keep head steady and eyes on ball.
4. Square shoulders and hips to ball.
5. Keep upper body erect.
6. Keep weight forward over balls of feet.
7. Keep hands at waist level with palms forward and fingers pointing up.
8. Flex knees slightly for maximum balance.
9. Set feet before shot.
10. Reposition in response to location of ball.

**MISSTEP**

You are unable to quickly move laterally to make the save.

**CORRECTION**

Set your feet just before the shot to ensure maximum balance and body control.

# RECEIVING GROUND BALLS

Consistency is a common characteristic of top-flight netminders. Therefore, making the routine play on a regular basis is equally as important as, if not more important than, the occasional spectacular save. If you position correctly, most of your saves should be of the routine variety, unless your teammates fail to provide much of a defense in front of you. Three techniques are used to receive ground balls, depending on the nature of the shot. You must become competent at performing each technique.

## Standing "Scoop" Save

A ball rolling directly at the goalkeeper is received using the scoop technique. This is commonly referred to as the *standing save* (figure 6.2). Quickly shuffle sideways to a position between the ball and the goal. (*Note:* Do not cross your legs when moving sideways.) Come to the set position with legs straight and feet planted a few inches apart. As the ball arrives, bend forward at the waist and extend your arms down, palms facing forward, hands slightly cupped. Forearms are parallel to each another, and fingertips should almost touch the ground. Allow the ball to roll up onto your wrists and forearms and then return to an upright position with the ball clutched securely against your chest. Do not attempt to catch a rolling ball directly in your hands.

**MISSTEP**

The ball rebounds off your hands into the path of a rushing opponent.

**CORRECTION**

Do not attempt to catch a rolling ball directly in your hands. Instead, allow the ball to roll up onto your wrists and forearms, and clutch it to your chest as you return to a standing position.

**MISSTEP**

The ball rolls between your legs and into the goal.

**CORRECTION**

If possible, always position your body behind the ball with your feet only a few inches apart. If the ball should inadvertently slip between your hands, it will rebound off your legs rather than roll past you into the goal.

## Figure 6.2 STANDING "SCOOP" SAVE

### Preparation

1. Set feet and body in starting position between ball and goal.
2. Focus on ball.
3. Bend forward at waist.
4. Extend arms down.
5. Turn palms forward and cup palms.

### Execution

1. Allow ball to roll onto wrists and forearms.
2. Keep legs straight with feet only a few inches apart.
3. Withdraw body slightly on impact.
4. Curl arms around ball.

### Follow-Through

1. Clutch ball against chest with forearms.
2. Return to standing position.
3. Distribute ball to teammate.

## Kneeling, or Tweener, Save

A rolling ball arriving to the goalkeeper's side is commonly referred to as a *tweener* and is usually received using the *kneeling*, or *tweener, save* technique. This shot is far enough away to make the standing save impossible but not so far as to require a diving save. The kneeling save technique also can be used to block a close-in shot that is bouncing, skipping, or arriving with some velocity.

To make the kneeling save (figure 6.3), shuffle sideways (laterally) across the goal. Extend your lead foot in the direction in which you are moving with your leg flexed at the knee. Kneel on the trailing leg and position it parallel to the goal line. To prevent the ball from squirting through your legs, allow only a few inches of open space between the heel of your lead foot and the knee of the trailing leg. From the kneeling position, bend your upper body forward with your shoulders square to the oncoming ball. Allow the ball to roll up onto your wrists and forearms before clutching it to your chest.

Figure 6.3 **KNEELING, OR TWEENER, SAVE**

*Preparation*

1. Set shoulders and hips square in starting position.
2. Keep feet shoulder-width apart.
3. Keep hands at waist level with palms forward.
4. Focus on ball.

*Execution*

1. Shuffle sideways to intercept oncoming ball.
2. Kneel on trailing leg and position it parallel to goal line.
3. Lean forward at waist.
4. Keep shoulders forward and square to ball.
5. Keep palms forward and fingers extended.
6. Allow ball to roll onto wrists and forearms.

*Follow-Through*

1. Clutch ball to chest with fore-arms.
2. Return to upright position.
3. Distribute ball.

## MISSTEP

The ball rebounds off your hands into the area in front of the goal.

## CORRECTION

This can occur if you try to catch the ball directly in your hands rather than allowing it to roll up onto your wrists and forearms. Use a scooping motion of the arms to receive the ball, and clutch the ball to your chest before you return to a standing position.

# Forward Vault

The conventional standing save is not appropriate when fielding a low, powerfully driven shot coming directly at you or a ball that skips off the ground immediately in front of you. This is especially true when playing on a slippery field (i.e., the ball accelerates when it hits standing water or wet grass). To compensate for the added velocity of such shots and to prevent rebounds, use the *forward vault* technique (figure 6.4) to receive the ball.

Face the oncoming ball with your shoulders square. Bend forward at the waist, flex your knees, and vault forward toward the ball and down to the ground. Extend your forearms and hands beneath the ball with your palms facing up. Allow the ball to contact your wrists and forearms rather than your hands. Fall forward and trap the ball between your forearms and chest. Extend and slightly spread your legs behind you for balance and support.

## MISSTEP

The ball slips through your arms, between your legs, and into the goal.

## CORRECTION

This error can occur even with experienced keepers if they lose focus and use improper technique. To avoid this misstep, position your forearms close together beneath the ball as you vault forward. Keep your arms extended and parallel to one another with your forearms a few inches apart as you receive the ball. Scoop the ball and clutch it between your chest and forearms.

Figure 6.4   **FORWARD VAULT**

### Preparation

1. Begin in basic starting, or ready, position.
2. Square shoulders and hips to ball.
3. Bend forward slightly at waist with knees bent.
4. Focus on ball.

### Execution

1. Vault forward and down to ground.
2. Extend forearms beneath ball with palms facing up.
3. Allow ball to contact wrists and forearms.

### Follow-Through

1. Fall forward onto forearms.
2. Trap ball between forearms and chest.
3. Extend legs behind and spread slightly.
4. Scramble to feet and distribute ball.

# Receiving Ground Balls Drill 1 Scoop Save

Servers (A and B), each with a ball, face each other 20 yards apart. You get in position midway between the servers. Server A begins the drill by rolling a ball toward you at moderate pace. Receive the ball using the standing (scoop) save technique and toss it back to server A. Immediately turn to receive a rolling ball from server B. Continue until you have received 30 balls using the scoop save technique. Score 1 point for each ball received and held without rebound.

## To Increase Difficulty

- Increase velocity of serves.
- Increase number of repetitions.

## To Decrease Difficulty

- Scoop a slowly rolling ball.

## Success Check

- Bend forward at waist.
- Keep legs together and straight.

- Allow ball to roll onto wrists and forearms.
- Scoop ball to chest.
- Return to upright position.

## Score Your Success

0 to 24 points = 1 point

25 to 27 points = 3 points

28 to 30 points = 5 points

Your score ___

# Receiving Ground Balls Drill 2
# Shooter and Keeper

A goalkeeper positions to defend the goal. A shooter faces him from just inside the top of the penalty area, with a supply of balls. The shooter touches the ball toward goal and then strikes a rolling ball directly at the keeper. The keeper collects the ball using the standing save technique, returns the ball to the shooter, and repeats. Continue the drill until the goalkeeper has received 30 rolling balls. Score 1 point for each ball received and held (no rebound) using the standing (scoop) save.

## To Increase Difficulty

- Increase velocity of serves.
- Have several servers stationed at various angles within penalty area.

## To Decrease Difficulty

- Reduce velocity of serves.

## Success Check

- Square shoulders and hips to ball.
- Bend forward at waist.

- Keep legs together and straight.
- Allow ball to roll onto wrists and forearms.
- Scoop ball to chest.
- Return to upright position.

## Score Your Success

0 to 24 points = 1 point

25 to 27 points = 3 points

28 to 30 points = 5 points

Your score ___

# Receiving Ground Balls Drill 3
## Kneeling, or Tweener, Save

A goalkeeper positions in goal next to the right goalpost. A server positions in line with each goalpost, 10 yards out from the goal line. Server A (directly in front of the keeper) rolls a ball to the keeper's left toward the center of the goal. The keeper moves laterally to receive the ball using the kneeling save technique, immediately returns the ball to server B, and continues to shuffle sideways across the goal to the left goalpost. At that point, server B rolls the ball to the keeper's right toward the center of the goal. The keeper moves laterally toward the ball, receives it using the kneeling save, and returns the ball to server A. Continue shuffling sideways from post to post for a total of 20 kneeling saves. Score 1 point for each properly executed save.

### To Increase Difficulty

- Increase velocity of serves.
- Increase speed of repetitions.
- Increase number of repetitions.

### To Decrease Difficulty

- Decrease speed of repetitions.
- Decrease number of repetitions.

### Success Check

- Extend lead foot toward ball.
- Kneel on trailing leg.
- Align trailing leg parallel to goal line.
- Allow ball to roll up onto wrists and forearms.
- Clutch ball to chest.

### Score Your Success

0 to 14 points = 1 point

15 to 17 points = 3 points

18 to 20 points = 5 points

Your score ___

# Receiving Ground Balls Drill 4
## Forward Vault to Save Skippers

Perform this drill on soft ground outdoors or on a gymnastic mat indoors. Kneel facing a partner who is also kneeling 5 yards away. Toss a ball so that it skips immediately in front of your partner, who falls forward to receive the ball using the forward vault technique. Your partner returns the ball in a similar manner for you to receive using the forward vault technique. Continue the drill until each player has executed 20 saves using the forward vault. Score 1 point for each ball received with proper technique and held without a rebound.

### To Increase Difficulty

- Vary trajectory and velocity of serves.
- Execute forward vault from squat position.
- Execute forward vault from standing position.

### To Decrease Difficulty

- Reduce velocity of serve.

## Success Check

- Square shoulders with ball.
- Flex knees.

- Fall forward.
- Scoop ball with palms up and forearms underneath ball.
- Keep forearms parallel to each other.
- Clutch ball to chest.

## Score Your Success

0 to 14 points = 1 point

15 to 17 points = 3 points

18 to 20 points = 5 points

Your score ___

# Receiving Ground Balls Drill 5
## Collecting the Through Ball

Goalkeeper A positions in a regulation goal on one end of the field. Goalkeeper B stands at the top of the penalty area, facing the goal. A server positions 25 yards front and center of goal with a supply of balls. To begin, the server plays a ball forward into the penalty area, past goalkeeper B, who sprints forward to get the ball. Goalkeeper A quickly advances from the goal and uses the forward vault technique to collect and secure the ball before goalkeeper B can get to it. Players then return to their original positions and repeat. Goalkeepers switch positions after 20 forward vault saves. Score 1 point for each ball received without rebound.

### To Increase Difficulty

- Increase velocity of serves.
- Increase number of repetitions.

### To Decrease Difficulty

- Decrease velocity of serves.

## Success Check

- Move forward quickly toward ball.
- Dive forward and down to ground.

- Keep palms up and forearms parallel.
- Slip forearms beneath ball.
- Clutch ball to chest.

## Score Your Success

0 to 13 points = 1 point

14 to 16 points = 3 points

17 to 20 points = 5 points

Your score ___

# Receiving Ground Balls Drill 6
## Ground Ball Keeper Wars

Place two full-size goals with nets 20 yards apart. Station a goalkeeper (A and B) in each goal. Goalkeeper A begins with the ball and attempts to score on goalkeeper B by rolling or dropkicking the ball past goalkeeper B and into the goal. Goalkeeper B attempts to save the shot and then tries to score on goalkeeper A in a similar manner. Keepers are permitted only one step before shooting on goal. All shots must be driven along the ground and aimed directly at the opposing goalkeeper if possible. Goalkeepers should use the standing save, kneeling save, or forward vault, depending on the nature of the shot. Score 1 point for each goal scored. Play for 15 minutes and keep track of the score. The keeper conceding fewer points (goals) wins the game.

### To Increase Difficulty for Defending Goalkeeper

- Decrease distance of shot and increase velocity.

### To Decrease Difficulty for Defending Goalkeeper

- Increase distance of shot.

### Success Check

- Square up with oncoming ball.
- Choose appropriate receiving technique.
- Clutch ball to chest.
- Do not give up rebounds.

### Score Your Success

Losing goalkeeper = 0 points

Winning goalkeeper = 2 points

Your score ___

# RECEIVING AIR BALLS

To dominate the goal box, you must be able to receive and control driven balls that arrive through the air as well as balls traveling along the ground. The space front and center of the goal is considered the goalkeeper's personal domain, an area that she must control to be successful. Powerful shots from outside the penalty area and balls crossed or lofted into the goal mouth pose definite challenges. The technique used for receiving the ball depends on the height, velocity, and trajectory of the ball.

## Receiving Medium-High Balls

A medium-high ball is defined as one that arrives between the ankles and waist. Use a scoop technique similar to the standing save to receive a ball out of the air that is arriving at approximately ankle height. Position your body between the ball and the goal with legs straight and feet a few inches apart. Bend forward at the waist with arms extended down, fingers pointing forward, and palms turned up. Receive the ball on your wrists and forearms and then secure it by cupping it against your chest. Do not attempt to catch a medium-high ball directly in the palms of your hands, because securing the ball in this way is difficult.

Receive a ball arriving at waist height by bending forward at the waist with forearms parallel and extended down (figure 6.5). Receive the ball on the insides of your forearms, just below your elbows. As the ball arrives, jump back a few inches to absorb its impact. The greater the velocity of the shot, the more cushion you must provide to prevent the ball from bouncing away from you.

## Figure 6.5 RECEIVING A MEDIUM-HIGH BALL

### Preparation

1. Get in line with oncoming ball.
2. Keep legs straight with feet planted a few inches apart.
3. Extend arms down and keep forearms parallel.
4. Point fingers forward and turn palms up.
5. Focus on ball.

### Execution

1. Bend forward at waist.
2. Flex knees.
3. Allow ball to contact wrists and forearms.

### Follow-Through

1. Jump back a few inches to cushion shot.
2. Allow ball to roll up onto forearms.
3. Clutch ball against chest with forearms.
4. Distribute ball.

**MISSTEP**

The ball rebounds off your hands.

**CORRECTION**

Do not attempt to catch the ball in your hands. Instead, allow the ball to contact your wrists and forearms first before clutching it to your chest.

# Receiving Medium-High Balls Drill 1
## Collecting Medium-High Balls

You and another goalkeeper (A and B) face each other at a distance of 8 yards. Toss the ball at approximately waist level to goalkeeper B, who receives it using the proper receiving technique. Goalkeeper B returns the ball to you in a similar manner. Position your body behind the ball. Lean forward with forearms extended beneath the ball and palms up. Allow the ball to contact your wrists and forearms; then secure the ball against your body. Perform 30 repetitions each. Score 1 point for each ball received and held without rebounding.

### To Increase Difficulty

- Vary serve.
- Increase velocity of serve.
- Play for time (perform as many reps as possible in specified time limit).

### To Decrease Difficulty

- Decease velocity of serve.

### Success Check

- Align body with oncoming ball.
- Keep legs straight with feet planted a few inches apart.

- Extend arms down and keep forearms parallel.
- Bend forward at waist.
- Allow ball to contact wrists and forearms.
- Secure ball to chest.

### Score Your Success

0 to 19 points = 1 point

20 to 25 points = 3 points

26 to 30 points = 5 points

Your score ___

# Receiving Medium-High Balls Drill 2
## Save, Turn, and Save Again

Goalkeepers A and B, each with a ball, get in position 20 yards apart. Goalkeeper C stands midway between them. Goalkeeper A tosses or kicks a medium-high ball to goalkeeper B, who receives the ball and returns it to goalkeeper A. Goalkeeper B immediately turns to receive a medium-high ball from goalkeeper C. Repeat for 20 repetitions, after which players rotate positions and repeat. Score 1 point for each ball received and held without rebound. Serves should be aimed directly at the goalkeeper.

## To Increase Difficulty

- Increase velocity of serve.
- Increase number of serves.

## To Decrease Difficulty

- Decease velocity of serve.

## Success Check

- Align with oncoming ball.
- Keep legs straight with feet planted a few inches apart.

- Extend arms down and keep forearms parallel.
- Bend forward at waist.
- Contact ball on wrists and forearms.

## Score Your Success

0 to 13 points = 1 point

14 to 17 points = 3 points

18 to 20 points = 5 points

Your score ___

# Receiving Medium-High Balls Drill 3
## Repetition Training

Play with one goalkeeper and six or eight field players within an area approximately 30 yards square. Position flags to represent a regulation-width goal at one end of the area. The goalkeeper takes position in goal. The field players pass four balls among themselves while moving throughout the area. On the goalkeeper's command (shouts a player's name), that player with a ball serves a medium-height shot directly to the keeper, who receives the ball and immediately distributes it to the nearest open player. The keeper then demands a ball from a different field player by shouting his or her name. All serves must be from a distance of 15 yards or greater from the goal. The goalkeeper continuously receives and distributes the ball for 15 minutes. Players are assessed 1 penalty point for each ball not secured and held.

## To Increase Difficulty

- Increase velocity of serves.

## To Decrease Difficulty

- Reduce number of repetitions.

## Success Check

- Square up with server.
- Keep legs straight with feet planted a few inches apart.
- Extend arms down and keep forearms parallel.

- Bend forward at waist.
- Contact ball on wrists and forearms and secure to chest.

## Score Your Success

6 or more penalty points = 1 point

4 or 5 penalty points = 3 points

0 to 3 penalty points = 5 points

Your score ___

## Receiving Chest-High and Head-High Balls

A shot arriving at chest or head height is received with shoulders square to the oncoming ball. Position your hands in what is generally referred to as the *W (window) position* (figure 6.6). Fingers are spread and extended toward the oncoming ball with thumbs almost touching behind. Always try to catch the ball with your hands on top (upper half). Position your forearms behind the ball and parallel to each other. Extend your arms toward the ball with slight flexion at the elbow. Attempt to catch the chest-high and head-high shot on your fingertips. As the ball arrives, withdraw your arms to cushion the impact and then secure the ball to your chest.

**Figure 6.6** W position of the hands.

When possible, follow the *hands-eyes-head (HEH) principle* when receiving a chest-high or head-high ball (figure 6.7). Position your hands, eyes, and head in a direct line with the ball as you receive it. Watch the ball into your hands by looking through the window formed by your thumbs and index fingers. There should be little or no sound as the ball contacts your fingertips. Keepers often refer to this as having soft hands.

### MISSTEP

The ball slips through your hands.

### CORRECTION

Position your hands close together to form the window. Thumbs and forefingers should almost touch behind the ball as you receive it. Catch with your hands on top of the ball.

### MISSTEP

The ball bounces off your hands.

### CORRECTION

Receive the ball on your fingertips, not your palms. To soften the impact, withdraw your arms and hands slightly as the ball arrives.

## Figure 6.7 RECEIVING THE CHEST-HIGH OR HEAD-HIGH BALL

*Preparation*

1. Square shoulders and hips to oncoming ball.
2. Position feet approximately shoulder-width apart.
3. Carry hands at chest level with palms forward.
4. Extend fingers.
5. Keep head steady with vision on ball.

*Execution*

1. Place hands in W position.
2. Flex slightly at elbows.
3. Look through window as ball arrives.
4. Catch with hands on upper half of ball.
5. Receive ball on fingertips.

*Follow-Through*

1. Withdraw hands and arms.
2. Secure ball to chest.
3. Distribute ball.

# Receiving Chest- and Head-High Balls Drill 1
## The W Catch Warm-Up

Hold a ball with both hands at approximately chest level. Bounce the ball hard off the ground and receive it with hands in the W position before the ball rises above your waist. Repeat 50 times. Score 1 point for each ball received and held.

### To Increase Difficulty

- Bounce and catch ball while walking at fast pace.

### To Decrease Difficulty

- Bounce ball more softly off ground.

*(continued)*

Receiving Chest- and Head-High Balls Drill 1 *(continued)*

### *Success Check*

- Catch ball on fingertips.
- Keep thumbs behind ball.
- Withdraw hands to cushion impact.

### *Score Your Success*

0 to 39 points = 1 point

40 to 44 points = 3 points

45 to 50 points = 5 points

Your score ___

# Receiving Chest- and Head-High Balls Drill 2
## Toss and Catch

Goalkeepers A and B face each other at a distance of 8 yards. Goalkeeper A tosses a ball to the right or left of goalkeeper B's head. Goalkeeper B receives the ball on the fingertips with hands on the top half of the ball. Goalkeeper B then tosses the ball to goalkeeper A, who receives it in the same manner. Repeat for 40 tosses each. Score 1 point for each ball caught and held with proper technique.

### To Increase Difficulty

- Increase velocity of tosses.
- Perform drill while shuffling sideways.

### To Decrease Difficulty

- Reduce distance between keepers.
- Toss ball very softly.

### *Success Check*

- Keep head steady and focus on ball.
- Align hands, eyes, and head with ball.
- Place hands in W position.
- Receive ball on fingertips.
- Position hands on top half of ball.

### *Score Your Success*

0 to 35 points = 0 points

36 to 39 points = 1 point

40 points = 3 points

Your score ___

# Receiving Chest- and Head-High Balls Drill 3
## Saving Chest- and Head-High Shots

A goalkeeper positions in goal, and a server with a supply of balls faces the keeper from the top of the penalty area. The server drives a chest-high or head-high ball toward the keeper, who receives it with proper form (hands in the W position, forearms parallel, and elbows tucked in slightly). The goalkeeper immediately returns the ball to the server and sets up to receive another head-high shot. Continue for 60 repetitions. Score 1 point for each ball caught and held with proper form.

## To Increase Difficulty

- Increase velocity of serves.
- Increase number of repetitions.

## To Decrease Difficulty

- Decrease number of repetitions.
- Soft toss the ball from shorter distance.

## *Success Check*

- Square up with server.
- Carry hands at chest level with palms turned forward.

- Extend fingers toward ball.
- Place hands in W position with elbows bent.
- Look through window as ball arrives.
- Receive ball on fingertips.
- Position hands on top half of ball.

## *Score Your Success*

0 to 49 points = 1 point

50 to 54 points = 3 points

55 to 60 points = 5 points

Your score ___

# Receiving High Balls and Crosses

A high ball is any ball arriving into the goal area above head height. Crosses are driven balls directed into the goal mouth from a flank area of the field. Both high balls and crosses present a difficult challenge for goalkeepers. In some instances you will have to get airborne to receive and control the ball and at the same time fend off the challenge of an opponent trying to head the ball into the goal.

As a general rule, try to catch the high ball or cross rather than box or parry it away (push or deflect the ball wide of or over the goal). That said, if you are not confident that you can hold the ball, maybe because of wet conditions or wind, use the alternative technique discussed later in this step (uncatchable high balls). In preparation to receive the high ball or cross, face the ball with your shoulders square. Take a moment to judge the ball's trajectory before moving toward it. Your running path to the ball should end a couple of yards from the point at which you actually expect to catch it. At that point you initiate your movement upward. If you have to get airborne to receive the ball, use a *one-leg takeoff* to generate maximum upward momentum. The jumping technique looks similar to that used when shooting a layup in basketball. Try to catch the ball at the highest point possible by extending your arms overhead and toward the ball.

It's important to leap up off the correct foot. To receive a high ball arriving from the flank (figure 6.8), move toward the ball and thrust your arms and outside leg (the leg toward the field) up in one fluid movement with your knee pointed toward the oncoming ball. Shoulders and hips are square to the oncoming ball. The inside leg (the leg closer to the goal) remains straight and serves as the balance leg. Hold your hands in the W position, watch the ball into your hands, and then secure it to your chest. Drop to the ground on your balance leg.

## Figure 6.8 RECEIVING HIGH BALLS AND CROSSES

**Preparation**

1. Face ball with shoulders square.
2. Move toward ball.
3. Keep head steady and vision on ball.

**Execution**

1. Use one-leg takeoff to jump up.
2. Thrust arms and outside leg up in one fluid motion.
3. Extend arms up; keep hands in W position.
4. Receive ball at highest point of jump on fingers and palms.

**Follow-Through**

1. Withdraw arms and hands.
2. Secure ball to chest.
3. Descend to ground.
4. Distribute ball.

**MISSTEP**

An opponent cuts in front of you and heads the ball into the goal.

**CORRECTION**

Move toward the ball, jump early, and catch the ball at the highest point of your jump. Thrust your arms and takeoff leg up in one fluid motion.

# Receiving High Balls and Crosses Drill 1
## High Ball Technique Training

Toss a ball high in the air as you jog slowly across the field. Use a one-leg takeoff to jump up and catch the ball at the highest point of your jump. Toss and receive 40 high balls. Alternate using right- and left-leg takeoffs when jumping. Score 1 point for each high ball received with proper form at the highest possible point.

**To Increase Difficulty**

- Compete against teammate who is also jumping to catch ball.

**To Decrease Difficulty**

- Rehearse one-leg takeoff movement without catching high ball.
- Don't leave ground when receiving ball.

**Success Check**

- Square shoulders and hips to ball.

- Thrust arms and leg up in one smooth motion.
- Hold hands in W position.
- Catch ball at highest point of jump.

**Score Your Success**

24 or fewer points = 1 point

25 to 34 points = 2 points

35 to 39 points = 3 points

40 points = 5 points

Your score ___

# Receiving High Balls and Crosses Drill 2
## High Balls Angled Away From Keeper

Set up three cones in the shape of a triangle, with approximately 10 yards between them. The goalkeeper gets in position at the apex of the triangle. The server stands 10 yards in front of the base of the triangle, facing the goalkeeper. The server tosses or volleys a ball up into the air so that it drops near one of the cones at the base of the triangle. The goalkeeper moves forward, catches the ball at the highest possible point, and returns it to the server. The goalkeeper quickly backpedals to the starting point and repeats the drill to the opposite side. The goalkeeper receives 30 high balls, 15 to each base cone. Score 1 point for each high ball received using the proper technique.

*(continued)*

Receiving High Balls and Crosses Drill 2 *(continued)*

### To Increase Difficulty

- Add opponent who contests goal-keeper for ball.
- Increase velocity of serves.

### To Decrease Difficulty

- Rehearse jumping movement without actually leaving ground.

## Success Check

- Use one-leg takeoff to jump.
- Thrust arms and outside leg up in one fluid motion.

- Keep inside leg straight.
- Extend arms with hands in W position.
- Receive ball on fingers and palms at highest point of jump.

## Score Your Success

17 or fewer points = 1 point

18 to 23 points = 2 points

24 to 27 points = 3 points

28 to 30 points = 5 points

Your score ___

# Receiving High Balls and Crosses Drill 3
## High Ball Repetition Training

Four servers position an equal distance apart around the center circle of a regulation field; the goalkeeper positions in the center of the circle. Each server in turn tosses a high ball that drops near the center of the circle. The goalkeeper moves toward the ball, squares shoulders and hips, jumps up using the correct takeoff leg, and catches the ball at the highest possible point. Continue for 40 tosses. The goalkeeper alternates between left and right legs for takeoff. Score 1 point for each ball received with proper technique.

### To Increase Difficulty

- Increase number of repetitions.
- Station two goalkeepers within circle who compete for high ball.

### To Decrease Difficulty

- Reduce number of repetitions.
- Do not require goalkeeper to leave ground.

## Success Check

- Use one-leg takeoff to jump.

- Point knee of takeoff leg toward ball.
- Extend arms and hands above head.
- Hold hands in W position.

## Score Your Success

21 or fewer points = 1 point

22 to 29 points = 2 points

30 to 35 points = 3 points

36 to 40 points = 5 points

Your score ___

# Receiving High Balls and Crosses Drill 4
## Receiving Crossed Balls

Set up two regulation-size goals opposite each other, one on the end line of the field and the other at the top edge of the penalty area. Two players (servers) get in position, one on each flank, in the space between the edge of the penalty area and the touch-line. Goalkeepers A and B take position in each goal. Goalkeeper A starts the drill by rolling a ball to one of the flank players. The flank player controls the ball and serves a cross to goalkeeper B. Goalkeeper B receives the ball at the highest possible point and distributes it to a flank player on the opposite side of the field. That player controls the ball and crosses it into the goal for goalkeeper A to collect and distribute. Continue until each goalkeeper has the opportunity to receive 40 crossed balls, 20 from each flank. Score 1 point for each cross received and held using the proper technique.

### To Increase Difficulty

- Station attacking player in goal area to contest goalkeeper for crossed ball.

### To Decrease Difficulty

- Flank players toss soft crosses to goalkeeper.

### Success Check

- Square up with oncoming ball.
- Move toward ball and initiate upward movement.
- Thrust arms and outside leg up in one fluid motion.

- Extend arms and hands toward ball.
- Receive ball on fingers and palms at highest point of jump.
- Withdraw arms and hands.
- Secure ball to chest.

### Score Your Success

0 to 28 points = 1 point

29 to 34 points = 3 points

35 to 40 points = 5 points

Your score ___

# Receiving High Balls and Crosses Drill 5
## Game Situation: Controlling the Goal Area

Play on a 70-yard-wide by 80-yard-long field area divided by a halfway line. Position a regulation goal on each end line. Place a line of markers a few yards in from each sideline to create a channel for unopposed flank players. Organize two teams of seven field players and a goalkeeper. Use colored vests to differentiate teams. Each team stations one player within each flank channel, three players (attackers) in the opponent's half of the field, and two players (defenders) in its own half. The goalkeepers position in their respective goals, each with a supply of balls. One goalkeeper (A) has the ball to begin. To begin the game, goalkeeper A tosses the ball to a teammate stationed in either flank channel. That player immediately dribbles unopposed the length of the channel and serves the ball into the opponent's goal area. The three teammates in that half of the field attempt to finish the cross, while

*(continued)*

Receiving High Balls and Crosses Drill 5 *(continued)*

the two opponents in that half attempt to clear the ball out of the goal area. Once goalkeeper B secures the ball, or after a goal is scored, the goalkeeper distributes the ball to the teammate in the opposite flank channel of the field, and the game continues toward the opposite goal. A crossed ball not secured by the goalkeeper is considered a live ball and can be finished by the attacking team. Play continues for 20 minutes. The team (goalkeeper) who concedes fewer goals wins the game.

**To Increase Difficulty**

- Station an attacking player inside the 6-yard goal area to contest goalkeeper for every crossed ball.

**To Decrease Difficulty**

- Do not permit opponents to challenge keeper for crossed ball.

*Success Check*

- Square up with oncoming ball.
- Initiate path toward ball and begin upward movement.

- Thrust arms and outside leg up in one fluid motion.
- Extend arms and hands toward ball.
- Receive ball on fingers and palms at highest point of jump.
- Withdraw arms and hands.
- Secure ball to chest.
- Distribute ball to a teammate.

*Score Your Success*

Losing goalkeeper = 1 point

Winning goalkeeper = 3 points

Your score ___

# Uncatchable High Balls

You should attempt to catch a high or crossed ball as opposed to boxing it away from the goal area. However, you may have difficulty gauging the flight of a ball that dips or swerves as it enters the goal mouth, adverse weather conditions may cause you to wonder whether you can hold the ball, or opposing players may challenge for the ball as you attempt to catch it. If you have any doubts about your ability to catch and hold the ball, it's best to choose safety first. Rather than trying to catch the ball, you can box, or punch, it away from the goal mouth. This decision is a critical one that you must make swiftly and decisively. Poor decisions ultimately result in goals scored against you.

As a general rule, you should box the ball rather than catch it if one or more of the following conditions are present:

- The goal mouth is crowded with players and you do not have a clear path to the ball.

- There is a strong likelihood that you will collide with an opponent who is also challenging for the ball.

- You are knocked off balance as you jump up to receive the ball.

- The ball is hard to handle because of rain, snow, or sleet.

- Footing is poor and you are not sure you can get to the ball.

Once you have made the decision, you have the option of boxing the high ball with one or two hands. Your choice of technique depends on the angle of the ball's approach, your position in relation to the ball and opponents, and your degree of confidence in boxing.

## TWO-FIST BOXING TECHNIQUE

Use the *two-fist boxing technique* when you can move directly toward the oncoming ball with shoulders square. The objective is to direct the ball away from the goal mouth toward a less dangerous scoring area. You accomplish this by boxing the ball high, far, and wide toward a flank area of the field. Boxing the ball upward gives teammates precious moments to regroup and reorganize. Boxing the ball as far as possible reduces the likelihood of an opponent's volleying the ball back at the goal as it drops to the ground. Boxing the ball toward the flank area removes the ball from the dangerous scoring zone immediately front and center of the goal.

To execute the two-fist boxing technique (figure 6.9), form two solid fists with your knuckles facing forward and thumbs on top. Position your hands side by side with wrists firm and arms tightly against your sides. Bend your elbows at approximately 90 degrees. As the ball arrives, thrust your arms forward in unison using a short, compact, powerful movement. Keep your wrists firm and fists together, and contact the ball just below its horizontal midline. Box the ball at the highest possible point.

## Figure 6.9 TWO-FIST BOXING

**Preparation**

1. Square shoulders and hips to ball.

2. Position fists side by side with wrists firm.

3. Bend elbows and hold them tightly to sides.

**Execution**

1. Extend arms toward ball in short, powerful movement.

2. Keep fists together with wrists firm.

3. Contact ball below its horizontal midline.

4. Contact ball at highest possible point.

**Follow-Through**

1. Follow through in direction in which you want ball to go.

2. Box ball high, far, and wide of goal area.

### MISSTEP

The clearance lacks height and distance.

### CORRECTION

Generate maximum power by keeping your arms tight to your sides with elbows bent at 90 degrees. Thrust your arms and fists forward to meet the ball as it arrives. Keep your wrists firmly positioned. Use a short, compact extension of your arms rather than a looping movement.

## ONE-FIST BOXING TECHNIQUE

A ball driven from a flank area that travels across the goal mouth poses a different challenge. Because the ball is moving at a high velocity and is not coming directly at goal, it is easier to continue the ball's flight toward the opposite flank than to box it back in the direction it is coming from. In this situation, box the ball across your body using a *one-fist technique* (figure 6.10). A ball crossed from the opponent's right flank (your left) is boxed with the left hand to continue its flight toward the opponent's left flank (your right). A ball served from the opponent's left flank is boxed with the right hand toward the opponent's right flank. The boxing motion is short and compact. A powerful extension of your arm angled across your body provides the greatest degree of control. Avoid a wide, looping-type arm motion. Keep your fist tight and wrist firm.

You also can use a slight variation of the one-fist boxing technique in those rare instances when you are caught off the goal line with a high ball dropping behind you. If you cannot backpedal and catch the ball cleanly, use the one-fist boxing technique to punch the ball over the crossbar and out of play. Take a deep drop step with the foot farther from the ball, angle your body sideways to the ball, and box the ball over the bar with a short, powerful extension of your arm. When boxing a ball that is dropping over your left shoulder near the crossbar, take a drop step left and box across your body with your right hand. To box a ball dropping over your right shoulder, take a drop step right and box across your body with your left hand.

### MISSTEP

You mis-hit the ball and box it straight up into the air so that it drops in the goal area.

### CORRECTION

Box the ball across your body to keep it traveling toward the opposite flank. The boxing motion should be compact and powerful.

## Figure 6.10 **ONE-FIST BOXING**

*Preparation*

1. Judge flight of ball.

2. Form solid fist with arm held against chest.

3. Keep head steady and vision focused on ball.

*Execution*

1. Move toward ball.

2. Punch ball toward opposite flank with short, compact extension of arm across chest.

3. Keep wrist firm.

*Follow-Through*

1. Direct ball toward opposite flank with follow-through motion of arm.

2. Extend arms downward to break your fall to the ground.

There is an alternative method you can use to handle a high ball dropping behind you. In many cases the *open-palm technique* (figure 6.11) is actually preferable to one-fist boxing because it provides a greater degree of control. Rather than boxing with your fist, simply guide the ball over the crossbar with your open hand. This is commonly referred to as turning, or palming, the ball over the bar.

Begin by executing a drop step with the foot farther from the ball. For example, do a drop step with the left foot when preparing to palm a ball crossed from your right side (the opponent's left) that is dropping over your left shoulder. As the ball arrives, extend your right arm and hand up and across your body to guide the ball over the crossbar. After turning the ball over the bar, rotate your body to face the ground as you fall. Arms and hands contact the ground first. Tuck your shoulder and roll to further cushion the impact.

Figure 6.11 **ONE-HAND PALMING OVER THE BAR**

*Preparation*

1. Judge flight of ball.
2. Do drop step with foot farther from ball.
3. Turn body sideways to ball.

*Execution*

1. Extend arm up and across body.
2. Guide ball over bar with palm of hand.
3. Watch ball travel over crossbar.

*Follow-Through*

1. Rotate body to face ground.
2. Tuck shoulder to roll as you contact ground.

**MISSTEP**

You slap at the ball rather than guide it, and it drops behind you into the goal.

**CORRECTION**

You should virtually carry the ball over the bar with your palm and fingers. Don't slap it.

# Uncatchable High Balls Drill 1
## Two-Fist Boxing

Goalkeepers A, B, and C get in line about 6 yards apart. Goalkeeper A kneels and faces goalkeepers B and C, who are standing. Goalkeeper B, stationed between goalkeepers A and C, has the ball to begin. Goalkeeper B tosses a high ball toward goalkeeper A. Goalkeeper A, while kneeling, uses a two-fist technique to box the ball over goalkeeper B's head to goalkeeper C. Goalkeeper A performs 15 repetitions; then players rotate positions and repeat. Keep track of the number of balls boxed directly to the target.

### To Increase Difficulty

- Increase distance between goalkeepers.
- Increase velocity of service.

### To Decrease Difficulty

- Decrease distance between goalkeepers.

### *Success Check*

- Position fists side by side.
- Hold elbows tight to sides.
- Extend arms in short, explosive motion.

- Contact ball below its horizontal midline.
- Follow through in direction in which you want ball to go.

### *Score Your Success*

0 to 9 balls boxed directly to target = 1 point

10 to 13 balls boxed directly to target = 3 points

14 or 15 balls boxed directly to target = 5 points

Your score ___

# Uncatchable High Balls Drill 2
## One-Fist Boxing

Goalkeepers A, B, and C get in line 8 yards from each other. Goalkeeper B, stationed between goalkeepers A and C, kneels sideways to the other goalkeepers. Goalkeeper A begins the drill by tossing a ball about 2 feet (61 cm) above goalkeeper B's head. Goalkeeper B continues the flight of the ball to goalkeeper C by boxing the ball across his body. Goalkeeper C catches the ball and tosses it back at goalkeeper B, who continues the ball's flight to goalkeeper A by boxing it across his body with the opposite arm. Goalkeeper B boxes 20 tosses (10 with each fist), after which players rotate positions and repeat. Keep track of the number of balls boxed directly to the target. (*Note:* It's important that serves be accurate.)

### To Increase Difficulty

- Increase distance between goalkeepers.
- Box from standing position.

- Increase speed or number of repetitions.

### To Decrease Difficulty

- Reduce distance between players to 5 yards.

*(continued)*

Uncatchable High Balls Drill 2 *(continued)*

### Success Check

- Use short, compact extension of arm across chest.
- Keep wrist firm.
- Contact underside of ball.
- Follow through to continue ball's flight.

### Score Your Success

0 to 10 balls boxed directly to target = 1 point

11 to 15 balls boxed directly to target = 3 points

16 to 20 balls boxed directly to target = 5 points

Your score ___

# Uncatchable High Balls Drill 3
## Two-Fist Boxing Under Pressure

Two pairs of goalkeepers (A and B, C and D) participate in this drill. Goalkeepers A and B stand between goalkeepers C and D, who get in position 15 yards apart and act as servers. Each server has a ball. Goalkeeper A stands about 1 yard directly behind goalkeeper B. Both players face goalkeeper C to begin. Goalkeeper C tosses a high ball toward goalkeeper A, who steps forward, jumps above goalkeeper B (stationary obstacle), and boxes the ball back to goalkeeper C. Goalkeepers A and B then turn and face goalkeeper D, who serves a high ball to goalkeeper B. Goalkeeper B jumps upward and boxes the ball over goalkeeper A and back to goalkeeper D. Each goalkeeper performs 15 repetitions, after which goalkeepers A and B switch positions with the servers and repeat the drill. Keep track of the number of serves boxed directly to the target. Serves should be of sufficient height to allow the goalkeeper an opportunity to time the approach, jump up, and box the ball.

### To Increase Difficulty

- Box as many balls as possible in 60 seconds.
- Add second player who challenges for ball.

### To Decrease Difficulty

- Do not require keeper to box over opponent.

### Success Check

- Put fists together to form solid block.
- Keep wrists firm.
- Extend arms in short, explosive motion.
- Contact lower half of ball.
- Follow through toward target.

### Score Your Success

0 to 9 balls boxed directly to target = 1 point

10 to 12 balls boxed directly to target = 3 points

13 to 15 balls boxed directly to target = 5 points

Your score ___

# Uncatchable High Balls Drill 4
## Fundamental Palming

Three goalkeepers (A, B, and C) are in a straight line 5 yards apart. Goalkeepers A and C face each other, and goalkeeper B is in the middle facing goalkeeper A. Goalkeeper A tosses a high ball over goalkeeper B's right shoulder. Goalkeeper B should take a drop step with the right foot and palm the ball to goalkeeper C using the left hand. Goalkeeper C then serves over goalkeeper B's left shoulder and takes a left-foot drop step and turns the ball to goalkeeper A using the right hand. Goalkeeper B takes five serves with each hand and then switches. Score 1 point for each serve that is properly palmed over an imaginary crossbar. *The serves must be accurate.* Serves should have sufficient height, which will give the goalkeeper the opportunity to take a drop step and palm the ball across the body.

### To Increase Difficulty

- Increase number of repetitions.
- Add additional player who challenges goalkeeper for ball.

### To Decrease Difficulty

- Soft toss from short distance.

### Success Check

- Cup palm slightly.
- No slapping sound (soft hands).
- Place palm under bottom half of ball.
- Keep head steady and follow ball with eyes.

### Score Your Success

1 to 6 balls palmed directly to target = 1 point

7 or 8 balls palmed directly to target = 3 points

9 or 10 balls palmed directly to target = 5 points

Your score ___

# Uncatchable High Balls Drill 5
## Turning Over the Bar

Three servers and one goalkeeper play on one end of a field with a full-size goal. Servers A and C are positioned at the intersection of the goal area and the end line. Server B is 10 yards out facing the goal. Each server has two or three balls. Server A tosses a high ball above the crossbar. The goalkeeper must turn the ball safely out of play with the open palm. The goalkeeper then faces server C, who tosses the same type of serve. The goalkeeper turns this ball over with the other hand and then moves forward toward server B. Server B tosses a high ball behind the goalkeeper near to the crossbar. The goalkeeper must take a drop step and correctly turn the ball over the bar. Continue so the goalkeeper receives 10 tosses from each server (i.e., 30 tosses).

*(continued)*

Uncatchable High Balls Drill 5 *(continued)*

### To Increase Difficulty

- Increase number of repetitions.
- Add additional player who challenges goalkeeper for ball.

### To Decrease Difficulty

- Soft toss from short distance.
- Reduce number of repetitions.

## *Success Check*

- Drop step to initiate movement.
- Keep head steady and vision on ball.
- Cup palm slightly.

- No slapping sound (soft hands).
- Place palm under bottom half of ball.
- Eyes watch ball go over bar.

## *Score Your Success*

15 to 20 balls turned over the bar = 1 point

21 to 25 balls turned over the bar = 3 points

26 to 30 balls turned over the bar = 5 points

Your score ___

# DIVING TO SAVE

Diving to save (figure 6.12) is probably the most acrobatic of all goalkeeping skills. It's used in situations in which you must leave your feet and propel your body sideways through the air to make the save. The initial movement begins from the starting position. Take a step in the direction of the dive with the foot nearer the ball, and then push off that foot to initiate the dive. For example, step sideways and push off your right foot when diving to your right. The opposite leg and arm follow to generate additional momentum in the direction of the dive. Extend both arms toward the ball with hands in a sideways version of the W position. Receive the ball on your fingertips and palms with the lower hand behind the ball and elbow tucked to your side. Contact the ground on your side, not your belly.

Rebounds in the goal area most often lead to goals against, so if you are unsure about being able to hold the ball, follow this basic rule of goalkeeping: *When in doubt, parry it out.* Rather than try to catch the ball in your hands, simply parry (deflect) the ball past the goalpost with the open palm of your lower hand. Angle your hand slightly back with the wrist firm. Contact the inside half of the ball.

### MISSTEP

You dive and land flat on your belly.

### CORRECTION

Contacting the ground on your side will protect your lower back from a rushing opponent and enable you to receive the ball using the HEH (hand-eyes-head) principle.

## Figure 6.12  DIVING TO SAVE

### Preparation

1. Begin in basic starting, or ready, position.
2. Step in direction of dive with foot nearer ball.

### Execution

1. Vault toward ball.
2. Thrust opposite arm and leg in direction of dive.
3. Extend arms and hands toward ball.
4. Position hands in sideways W.
5. Receive ball on fingertips and palms.

### Follow-Through

1. Descend to ground.
2. Ball contacts ground first, then forearm, shoulder, hip, and finally legs.
3. Regain footing and distribute ball.

# Diving Drill 1   Fundamental Diving Technique

Kneel on both knees with a ball placed within reach to each side. Fall sideways and pin the stationary ball to the ground. Emphasize the proper diving form. Contact the ground on your side while placing one hand behind the ball and one on top to pin it to the ground. Repeat 10 times to each side.

## To Increase Difficulty

- Move balls farther away.
- Increase number of repetitions.
- Increase speed of repetitions.
- Pin slowly rolling ball.

## To Decrease Difficulty

- Decrease number of repetitions.

## Success Check

- Tuck elbow of lower arm to side.

- Contact ground on side and hip.
- Pin ball with one hand on top of ball and one behind.

## Score Your Success

14 or fewer dives using correct form = 1 point

15 to 18 dives using correct form = 2 points

19 or 20 dives using correct form = 3 points

Your score ___

# Diving Drill 2   Save a Rolling Ball

Stand in the goal facing a server who is 8 yards away. The server rolls a ball 3 to 4 yards to your side. Dive sideways to pin the ball, jump to your feet, and return the ball to the server. Repeat the drill to the opposite side. Attempt 10 saves to each side. As a variation, have the server toss the ball at waist height. (*Note:* Perform this drill on a soft field surface.)

## To Increase Difficulty

- Increase velocity of serves.
- Increase speed of repetitions.
- Increase number of repetitions.

## To Decrease Difficulty

- Dive to pin stationary ball.

## Success Check

- Step sideways with foot nearer ball.

- Vault toward ball.
- Extend arms and hands.
- Contact ground on side.
- Pin ball to ground.

## Score Your Success

0 to 14 successful dives = 1 point

15 to 17 successful dives = 3 points

18 to 20 successful dives = 5 points

Your score ___

# Diving Drill 3   Flying Side to Side

Begin in a squat position facing a server 8 yards away. The server tosses a chest-high ball 3 to 4 yards to your side. Step toward the ball, vault through the air, and make the save. The ball should contact the ground first, followed by your forearms, shoulders, hips, and legs. Quickly jump to your feet and return the ball to the server. Repeat, diving to the other side. Repeat the exercise at maximum speed for 30 seconds; then rest for 30 seconds and repeat.

### To Increase Difficulty

- Place obstacle (ball, cone, small hurdle) to goalkeeper's side that goalkeeper must dive over to save ball.

### To Decrease Difficulty

- Reduce diving distance.

## Success Check

- Step sideways toward ball.

- Thrust opposite arm and leg in direction of dive.
- Extend arms and hands.
- Position hands in sideways W.
- Receive ball on fingertips and palms.

## Score Your Success

Fail to hold all tosses = 3 points

Hold all tosses = 5 points

Your score ___

# Diving Drill 4   Keeper Wars

Set up two full-size goals 20 yards apart. Station a goalkeeper in each goal. One goalkeeper has the ball to begin. Goalkeepers take turns trying to score on each other. The shooting goalkeeper may take three steps forward from the goal before releasing the shot. The defending goalkeeper may advance off the line to narrow the shooting angle. Score 2 points for a ball saved and held without rebound and 1 point for a shot saved but not held. Play to a predetermined number of points or a time limit.

### To Increase Difficulty

- Reduce shooting distance.

### To Decrease Difficulty

- Increase shooting distance.
- Decrease width of goal.

## Success Check

- Begin in ready position.
- Move forward of goal line to narrow shooting angle.
- Initiate dive toward ball.

- Extend arms and hands toward ball.
- Receive ball on fingertips and palms.
- Ball contacts ground first followed by forearm, shoulder, hip, and legs.
- Parry wide of goal if you can't hold ball.

## Score Your Success

Losing goalkeeper = 1 point

Winning goalkeeper = 3 points

Your score ___

# Diving Drill 5   Parry It Wide

The goalkeeper begins in a squatting position. A server holds a ball in each hand with arms outstretched facing the goalkeeper at a distance of 2 or 3 yards. A third player keeps the server supplied with balls. To begin, the server tosses one of the balls at approximately chest height 2 to 3 yards to the goalkeeper's side. The keeper must quickly react to deflect the ball with the open palm of the upper hand. As soon as the keeper gets to his feet, the server repeats to the opposite side. Repeat tosses to the keeper's right and left for about 30 to 40 seconds, rest, and repeat. It is essential that the keeper quickly push off and explode to the ball. Tosses should be out of the keeper's reach. The keeper should use the open palm of the upper hand to direct the ball out and away from the server.

## To Increase Difficulty

- Place obstacle (ball, cone, small hurdle) to goalkeeper's side that goalkeeper must dive over to save ball.

## To Decrease Difficulty

- Reduce diving distance.

## Success Check

- Step sideways toward ball.

- Thrust opposite arm and leg in direction of dive.
- Extend arms and hands.
- Parry ball wide with open palm of upper hand.

## Score Your Success

Fail to parry all tosses = 3 points

Parry all tosses with correct form = 5 points

Your score ___

# Diving Drill 6   Reaction Saves

Play on one end of a regulation field. The goalkeeper positions in the full-size goal, facing a shooter who stands about 10 yards front and center of the goal. A server with a supply of 10 to 12 balls positions about 8 yards out from the end line, to the side of the goal. To begin, the server tosses a ball to the shooter, who strikes a volley first time to the goal. The goalkeeper must make a reaction save on the first-time, point-blank volley, either holding or parrying the ball wide of the goal. Continue for 10 repetitions; then rest and repeat.

After each save, the goalkeeper should reposition immediately and be set to explode to the ball. The keeper should try to hold the ball if possible, but deflect wide of the goal if unable to hold it. As a variation the server plays a ground ball to the shooter to give the keeper a different look and reaction. The shooter can head the ball as well as volley it.

## To Increase Difficulty

- Place obstacle (ball, cone, small hurdle) to goalkeeper's side that goalkeeper must dive over to save ball.

## To Decrease Difficulty

- Reduce number of repetitions.

## Success Check

- Take explosive step toward ball.
- Thrust opposite arm and leg in direction of dive.
- Extend arms and hands.
- Parry ball wide with open palm of upper hand.

## Score Your Success

Save 5 to 7 out of 10 point-blank shots = 3 points

Save 8 or more point-blank shots = 5 points

Your score ___

# SAVING PENALTY KICKS

The penalty kick provides the ultimate one-on-one test for the goalkeeper. The ball is spotted 12 yards front and center of the goal. Only the designated kicker and the goalkeeper are permitted to position within the penalty area and penalty arc until after the ball has been kicked. The goalkeeper must position with both feet on the goal line. He is permitted to move laterally along the line prior to the kick, but may not move forward off of the goal line until the ball has been played.

There is not a general consensus as to the best method of defending a penalty kick. Anticipating which way the shooter will go is half the battle. Some goalkeepers prefer to focus on subtle cues that may reveal the kicker's intentions, such as the position of the player's hips when approaching the ball. Others simply pick one side of the goal and dive in that direction in hope that the kicker has decided to shoot to that side. Through practice and experience you will learn what works best for you.

In preparation to make the big save, assume a posture similar to the basic ready position with both feet on the goal line. Lean slightly forward with weight evenly distributed and centered over the balls of the feet. As designated kicker kicks the shot, vault sideways parallel to or slightly forward of the goal line to narrow the shooting angle. If you get your hands to the ball but cannot hold it, box or deflect it wide of the goal. Rebounds in front of the goal must be avoided at all costs, as the kicker is permitted to move forward after taking the penalty kick to finish a shot that rebounds off of the keeper.

To maximize your chances of saving the penalty shot, be alert for subtle cues inadvertently provided by the kicker just prior to and during the approach to the ball. Picking up on the following bits of information (based upon a right-footed kicker) may reveal the shooter's intentions.

- **Angle of approach.** A kicker who approaches the ball at a sharp angle will most likely aim the shot to the goalkeeper's left. From an angled approach it is difficult for the kicker to pull the ball back toward the right corner of the goal. A kicker who approaches the ball from directly behind is more likely to shoot the ball to the goalkeeper's right—usually!

- **Position of the kicking foot**. When the kicking foot is positioned sideways-on the shooter will most likely attempt to push the ball to the goalkeeper's left with the inside surface of the instep. If the kicking foot is extended down and pointed inward, the kicker will probably strike the ball with the full instep and attempt to drive it to the goalkeeper's right.

- **Position of shoulders and hips**. Body position can be a very revealing cue. In most cases the shooter's hips and shoulders will square with the intended target (area of the goal) at the moment the ball is contacted. In this situation the goalkeeper must be able to make a last-second decision and adjustment.

Making the big save in a penalty kick situation can change the momentum of the game and ultimately determine the outcome. A combination of factors—anticipation, athleticism, technique, and sometimes just plain good luck—interact to determine a goalkeeper's success or lack thereof in penalty kick situations. Like virtually all other types of goalkeeper skills, the ability to save penalty kicks can be improved through repetitive practice situations. It is, therefore, important to set aside adequate practice time to perfect technique.

# DISTRIBUTING THE BALL

As goalkeeper, you are much more than a shot stopper! Once you have secured the ball, you must initiate your team's attack by quickly and accurately distributing the ball to a teammate. You can do this by rolling, throwing, or kicking the ball. The rolling technique is generally used to release the ball to a nearby teammate (defender) who is not under immediate pressure from an opponent. Throwing is an effective means of distributing the ball over greater distances, typically to teammates positioned in the middle third of the field or in flank areas along the touchlines. Kicking is the optimal choice when the objective is to quickly send the ball down the field into the opponent's half. In most cases, distributing the ball by kicking sacrifices accuracy for greater distance.

## Rolling

Rolling, or bowling, the ball is an effective way to distribute the ball quickly and accurately over a short distance. After making the save, cup the ball in the palm of your hand, step toward the target, and release the ball with a bowling-type motion (figure 6.13). Release the ball at ground level to prevent bouncing.

**MISSTEP**

The ball bounces toward the target.

**CORRECTION**

Release the ball at ground level with a smooth motion.

## Figure 6.13 ROLLING THE BALL

### Preparation

1. Square shoulders.
2. Hold ball securely in hands.
3. Select target.

### Execution

1. Cup ball in palm of hand.
2. Draw back arm and ball.
3. Step toward target with leg opposite throwing arm.

### Follow-Through

1. Release ball at ground level with bowling-type motion.
2. Follow through with arm toward target.
3. Resume erect posture.

## Throwing

You can distribute the ball over longer distances by throwing or kicking it. Throwing has the advantage of greater accuracy and quicker delivery. Use the *baseball throw* (figure 6.14) to distribute the ball over distances of 20 to 35 yards. Hold the ball in the palm of your hand next to your ear, as you would when throwing a baseball. Step toward the target and use a three-quarter or overhand throwing motion to release the ball. Snap your wrist toward the target to add velocity to the throw.

Figure 6.14  **BASEBALL THROW**

1. Face target.
2. Hold ball in palm of hand.
3. Cock arm behind ear.
4. Step toward target with foot opposite throwing arm.
5. Using three-quarter throwing motion, snap wrist toward target.
6. Follow through toward target with momentum moving forward.
7. Throw to target's feet.

Use the *javelin throw* (figure 6.15) to deliver the ball over distances of 40 yards or greater. Curl your hand around the ball, encasing it with the fingers, palm, and wrist. Bring the throwing arm back with the ball at approximately waist level. Arch back, step toward the target, and snap your upper body forward from the waist. The throwing motion moves along an upward arc and ends with a whiplike action above your head. You can release the ball at any point along the throwing arc. The sooner you release the ball along the throwing arc, the higher the trajectory.

## Figure 6.15 **JAVELIN THROW**

1. Encase ball in fingers, palm, and wrist.
2. Bring back throwing arm.
3. Point opposite arm toward target.
4. Arch upper body back.
5. Hold ball at waist level.

6. Step toward target with foot opposite throwing arm.
7. Whip throwing arm along upward arc, releasing ball.
8. Follow through with throwing arm, with momentum moving forward.

---

### MISSTEP

The throw is off target.

### CORRECTION

Step toward the target as you release the ball. When using the baseball throw, snap your wrist toward the target as you release the ball. When using the javelin throw, point your nonthrowing arm toward the target as you prepare to deliver the ball. The follow-through motion should be directed at the target.

### MISSTEP

The throw lacks distance.

### CORRECTION

When executing the baseball throw, use a complete follow-through motion of the throwing arm. When using the javelin throw, fully extend the throwing arm behind and employ a whiplike motion of the arm along an upward arc to propel the ball toward the target. Generate momentum forward toward the target.

# Kicking

Kicking is a less accurate means of distribution than throwing, but it is a viable option if your objective is to deliver the ball quickly into the opponent's end of the field. Kicking is also a good choice in adverse weather conditions. By immediately sending the ball far down the field, you eliminate the risk of possession loss in your end of the field. The most common kicking techniques used for distributing the ball are the full-volley punt and the dropkick.

For the *full-volley punt* (figure 6.16), hold the ball in the palm of the hand opposite the kicking foot. Extend your arm forward with the ball held at approximately waist level. Step forward with your nonkicking foot, release the ball, and volley it directly out of the air. Square your shoulders and hips to the target and contact the center of the ball with the instep. Keep your kicking foot fully extended and firmly positioned. Use a complete follow-through motion of the kicking leg to generate distance and height on the punt. The *side-volley punt* has also become popular for goalkeeper distribution in recent years, because it results in a trajectory of the ball that is generally lower and more direct than that of the full-volley punt.

## Figure 6.16 **FULL-VOLLEY PUNT**

1. Keep head steady and vision on ball.

2. Step toward target with nonkicking foot and release ball.

3. Swing kicking leg forward and drive instep through lower half of ball.

4. Keep foot extended and firm.

5. Square shoulders and hips to target.

6. Follow through to waist level or higher.

The *dropkick* (figure 6.17), or half volley, is a good choice on windy days because the ball's trajectory is generally lower than that of a full-volley punt. A lower trajectory means the ball's flight path will not be affected as much by swirling and gusty winds. The lower trajectory also makes it easier for teammates to receive and control the ball. The kicking mechanics for a dropkick are similar to those for a full volley except that the ball is contacted just as it hits the ground rather than directly out of the air. Hold the ball in the palm of the hand opposite the kicking foot with the arm fully extended. Step forward and release the ball. Drive the instep of the kicking foot through the ball the moment the ball contacts the ground. Square your shoulders and hips to the target as your foot contacts the ball.

## Figure 6.17   DROPKICK

1. Face target.
2. Extend arm opposite kicking foot with ball in palm of hand.
3. Lean forward, step toward target, and release ball.
4. Drive instep through center of ball as soon as ball hits ground.

5. Keep kicking foot extended and firm.
6. Square hips and shoulders to target.
7. Bring momentum forward through point of contact.
8. Follow through to waist level or higher.

**MISSTEP**

The punt or dropkick travels to the right or left of the target.

**CORRECTION**

Square your shoulders and hips to the target as you kick the ball. Contact the vertical midline of the ball with the full instep.

**MISSTEP**

The punt or dropkick lacks distance.

**CORRECTION**

Keep your kicking foot firm as it contacts the ball. Use a complete follow-through motion of the kicking leg to waist level or higher.

# Keeper Distribution Drill 1    Target Practice

Play on half of a regulation-size field. Four servers, each with a ball, stand at various distances from the goal. Three additional players, designated as targets, take positions at various distances from the goal. A goalkeeper stands in goal. Servers take turns kicking a ball into the goal area for the goalkeeper to receive and control. After collecting the ball, the goalkeeper immediately distributes the ball by throwing it to one of the targets, who change their locations (distance from goal) and positions with every repetition. The goalkeeper chooses the method of distribution appropriate for the distance the ball must travel, as follows:

- Roll the ball when the target is 15 to 20 yards from goal.
- Use a baseball throw when the target is 21 to 40 yards from goal.
- Use a javelin throw when the target is 40 yards or more from goal.

A throw is considered accurate if the target does not have to move more than three steps in any direction to receive the ball. Goalkeepers perform 15 repetitions of each type of throw. Score 1 point for each accurate toss for a maximum of 45 points.

### To Increase Difficulty

- Define as accurate any throw that drops within two steps of target player.

### To Decrease Difficulty

- Define as accurate any throw that drops within five steps of target player.

### Success Check

- Step toward target.

- Use appropriate throwing technique.
- Use complete follow-through motion.

## Score Your Success

0 to 24 points = 0 points

25 to 29 points = 1 point

30 to 34 points = 3 points

35 to 45 points = 5 points

Your score \_\_\_

# Keeper Distribution Drill 2    Volley to the Midline

Get in position within the penalty area with a supply of balls. Attempt to full-volley punt or half-volley punt the ball so that it lands within the center circle of the field. Score 2 points for each ball that drops within the circle on the fly and 1 point for a ball that bounces into the circle. Execute 20 full-volley punts and 20 half-volley punts. Keep track of points scored.

### To Increase Difficulty

- Decrease size of target area.
- Increase distance to target area.

### To Decrease Difficulty

- Increase size of target area.

## Success Check

- Square shoulders to target.
- Extend arms with ball held at approximately waist height.

- Keep head steady and vision on ball.
- Contact ball through center.
- Follow through toward target.

## Score Your Success

0 to 39 points = 0 points

40 to 49 points = 1 point

50 to 59 points = 3 points

60 to 80 points = 5 points

Your score ___

# Keeper Distribution Drill 3   Distribution Circuit

Goalkeepers A, B, C, and D get in position at various locations on the playing field. Goalkeeper A stands in one penalty area. Goalkeeper B assumes a position on the flank outside the penalty area near the touchline. Goalkeeper C gets in position within the center circle, and goalkeeper D stands in the opposite penalty area. The drill begins as goalkeeper A distributes the ball to goalkeeper B by rolling it. Goalkeeper B receives the ball and delivers it to goalkeeper C using the baseball throw. Goalkeeper C receives the ball and delivers it to goalkeeper D using the javelin throw. Goalkeeper D completes the circuit by returning the ball to goalkeeper A via a dropkick or punt. Repeat the circuit five times, after which goalkeepers rotate positions and repeat the drill. Continue the drill until each keeper has performed five repetitions of each distribution technique for a total of 20 attempts. Score 1 point for each repetition performed with correct technique.

### To Increase Difficulty

- Require keeper to distribute ball to moving targets.

### To Decrease Difficulty

- Reduce distance to targets.

## Success Check

- Step toward target.

- Use appropriate throwing or kicking technique.
- Use complete follow-through motion.

## Score Your Success

14 or fewer points = 1 point

15 to 17 points = 2 points

18 to 20 points = 3 points

Your score ___

# Keeper Distribution Drill 4   Baseball Toss

Use tape to mark several target areas on a wall or kickboard. One target area should be in the lower left corner, one in the lower right corner, and one in the center. The target areas should be a 4- by 4-yard square. The goalkeeper throws the ball to hit the target areas from various angles and distances of more than 20 yards. Attempt 30 tosses to hit the targets. Award yourself 1 point each time you hit the target.

Choose a specific technique and focus at first on accuracy; then gradually attempt to increase the velocity. After demonstrating proficiency from the center of the goal, move to wider angles and then longer distances.

### To Increase Difficulty

- Increase throwing distance.

### To Decrease Difficulty

- Define as accurate any throw that hits within 2 yards of designated target.

## Success Check

- Step toward target.

- Use proper throwing technique.
- Use complete follow-through motion.

## Score Your Success

0 to 20 points = 1 point

21 to 25 points = 3 points

26 to 30 points = 5 points

Your score ___

---

# SUCCESS SUMMARY

If you are a novice and new to the goalkeeper position, you should begin by slowly rehearsing each technique until you feel comfortable with the movements. As you gain confidence, increase the speed and intensity of your training. Eventually, you will be able to progress to more challenging game-simulation situations.

Each of the drills in step 6 has been assigned a point value to help you evaluate your performance and chart your progress. Record your score in the following chart. Total your points to get an estimate of your overall mastery of goalkeeping skills.

### Receiving Ground Balls Drills

1. Scoop Save      ___ out of 5
2. Shooter and Keeper      ___ out of 5
3. Kneeling, or Tweener, Save      ___ out of 5
4. Forward Vault to Save Skippers      ___ out of 5
5. Collecting the Through Ball      ___ out of 5
6. Ground Ball Keeper Wars      ___ out of 2

### Receiving Medium-High Balls Drills

1. Collecting Medium-High Balls      ___ out of 5
2. Save, Turn, and Save Again      ___ out of 5
3. Repetition Training      ___ out of 5

### Receiving Chest- and Head-High Balls Drills

1. The W Catch Warm-Up           \_\_\_\_ out of 5
2. Toss and Catch           \_\_\_\_ out of 3
3. Saving Chest- and Head-High Shots           \_\_\_\_ out of 5

### Receiving High Balls and Crosses Drills

1. High Ball Technique Training           \_\_\_\_ out of 5
2. High Balls Angled Away From Keeper           \_\_\_\_ out of 5
3. High Ball Repetition Training           \_\_\_\_ out of 5
4. Receiving Crossed Balls           \_\_\_\_ out of 5
5. Game Situation: Controlling the Goal Area           \_\_\_\_ out of 3

### Uncatchable High Balls Drills

1. Two-Fist Boxing           \_\_\_\_ out of 5
2. One-Fist Boxing           \_\_\_\_ out of 5
3. Two-Fist Boxing Under Pressure           \_\_\_\_ out of 5
4. Fundamental Palming           \_\_\_\_ out of 5
5. Turning Over the Bar           \_\_\_\_ out of 5

### Diving Drills

1. Fundamental Diving Technique           \_\_\_\_ out of 3
2. Save a Rolling Ball           \_\_\_\_ out of 5
3. Flying Side to Side           \_\_\_\_ out of 5
4. Keeper Wars           \_\_\_\_ out of 3
5. Parry It Wide           \_\_\_\_ out of 5
6. Reaction Saves           \_\_\_\_ out of 5

### Keeper Distribution Drills

1. Target Practice           \_\_\_\_ out of 5
2. Volley to the Midline           \_\_\_\_ out of 5
3. Distribution Circuit           \_\_\_\_ out of 3
4. Baseball Toss           \_\_\_\_ out of 5

**Total**           **\_\_\_\_ out of 147**

A combined score of 120 or more points indicates that you have achieved competency in performing fundamental goalkeeping skills and are prepared to move on to step 7. A score in the range of 100 to 119 is considered adequate, but you still need to polish some of the techniques. Before moving on, review the skills that are giving you the most difficulty. A score of 99 or fewer points suggests that you have not sufficiently mastered the goalkeeping skills described in step 6. Rehearse and practice each of the skills several more times before moving on to step 7. (*Note:* If you are primarily a field player, feel free to move on to step 7 at your discretion. You need not master all of the goalkeeping skills.)

# Winning One-on-One Matchups

A soccer game is an interconnected series of constantly changing situations, each lasting only a few moments before flowing into the next. Your ability to make good decisions, to quickly choose the most appropriate action in a given situation, will in large part determine your performance on the soccer pitch. In short, you must be able to assess each situation as it develops, consider possible options, and react accordingly. This is commonly referred to as "game sense," or the ability to figure things out, so to speak. From a more technical point of view, this ability is referred to as *tactical speed*—the ability to consistently make good decisions under the game pressures of limited time and space. All elite players and elite teams demonstrate a high level of tactical speed.

You can improve your tactical speed by developing a thorough understanding of the principles on which players' decisions and subsequent actions are based. Soccer tactics provide a frame of reference for decision making, problem solving, and playing cooperatively with teammates. Tactics are applied on three levels: individual, group, and team. Individual tactics deal with the principles of attack and defense applicable in one-on-one (1v1) situations. Group tactics involve two or more players (2v1, 2v2, 3v2, and so on) working in combination. Team tactics are applied to the group as a whole with the ultimate goal of maximizing team performance above and beyond the ability of the individual players.

To improve your tactical speed, you should start with the most fundamental tactical unit, the individual player-versus-player (1v1) confrontation. Although soccer is in the purest sense a team game, virtually every situation in some manner or another involves a one-on-one matchup—the player with the ball versus the opponent responsible for defending against that player. It is not uncommon to hear coaches say, "We lost the game because we lost the majority of the one-on-ones," and that observation is very true. These minibattles waged between opposing players are links in the chain of events that collectively determine the outcome of the game. Step 7 provides information that will improve your ability to win the one-on-one matchup.

# INDIVIDUAL ATTACK TACTICS

Unlike in American football, there are no offensive or defensive specialists in international football (soccer). All players, including the goalkeeper, must be prepared to defend when the opponents have the ball and contribute to the attack when their team has the ball. More important, players must be willing and able to make an immediate transition from one role to another.

In this discussion of soccer tactics, we speak of the first, second, and third attacker and the first, second, and third defender. Individual tactics deal primarily with the first attacker and the first defender. The player with possession of the ball, the first attacker, is the focal point of individual attack tactics. When in the role of first attacker, you should base your decisions and subsequent actions in accordance with the objectives discussed in the following sections.

## Keep the Ball

It's pretty simple. Your team cannot score without the ball. Likewise, the opposing team cannot score when your team has the ball. So the first order of business is to maintain possession of the ball once you have it. Use the dribbling and shielding skills discussed in step 1 to protect the ball from opponents trying to steal it from you (figure 7.1).

## Turn to the Goal

Possession of the ball in and of itself won't necessarily result in goals scored. The defending team, and the opponent marking you, is still in good shape as long as you are not in a position to penetrate with the ball. You can shift the advantage to your favor by turning with the ball to face

**Figure 7.1** Protect the ball by positioning your body between the ball and the opponent.

the opponent's goal, a position from which you can penetrate the opposing defense by dribbling, passing, or shooting. Before attempting to turn with the ball, however, you must first separate from the defender who is marking you.

In soccer an important equation always holds true: *Space equals time.* That is, the more space you can create between yourself and the opponent marking you, the more time you will have to maneuver with the ball and make plays. In essence, you become a better player simply by creating more space and time for yourself.

You can free yourself from a marking defender through the use of *body feints.* Body feints are deceptive body and foot movements designed to mislead, or unbalance, an opponent. A slight dip of the shoulder or a quick step over the ball may be all you need to get your opponent leaning the wrong way (figure 7.2). Sudden changes of speed and direction can also create distance between you and the defender, and provide the opportunity to turn with the ball to face the opponent's goal. Actions such as sharply cutting the ball right or left with the inside or outside surface of the foot, stopovers and scissors movements, and explosive bursts into open space all serve to separate you from an opponent.

**Figure 7.2**    Body feints are one way to create space for yourself: *(a)* step over the ball; *(b)* dribble away with the outside of the other foot.

## Attack the Defense

Once you have turned with the ball to face the opponent's goal, you should immediately attack (dribble at) the nearest defender. The objective here is to commit the defender to you, and then bypass that defender by dribbling past him or passing the ball into the space behind him. Your choice of action will in part be determined by your location on the field at that time.

## Penetrate via Pass or Dribble

When attempting to penetrate the opposing defense, consider your position on the field, the risk of losing possession versus the potential reward of pressing forward in that area, and your technical strengths and weaknesses.

Practice safety first when in your defending half of the field, an area where possession loss can be very costly. Passing the ball forward to a teammate stationed in a more advanced position, as opposed to dribbling, is the optimal choice of penetration when you're positioned in your own half. Even if the pass is cut off, your team will still have a sufficient number of players behind the ball to thwart an immediate counterattack by the opponents. Conversely, loss of possession on the dribble in your own half of the field may prove more costly because many of your teammates will already be ahead of the ball, a situation that gives the opposing team an opportunity to mount an immediate counterattack on your goal.

Penetration via the dribble is used to best advantage in the attacking third of the field nearest the opponent's goal. In this area defending players are usually positioned to close down space and eliminate passing lanes. The player who can take on and beat defenders on the dribble becomes a valuable asset to the attack. Likewise, the risk of possession loss via the dribble in this area is overshadowed by the potential reward of bypassing a defender to create a scoring opportunity.

When attempting to penetrate on the dribble, take the most direct route toward the goal, an action that will draw the first (nearest) defender to you. This tactic is commonly referred to as *taking on* the defender because it forces that player to either step forward to tackle the ball from you or withdraw to delay your forward penetration.

If the defender commits to the tackle, it may open up passing lanes to teammates in more forward positions, or it may provide an opportunity for you to dribble past the defender to create a numbers-up situation (numerical advantage) on the attack. Once you have beaten a defender on the dribble, continue at speed directly at the goal. You should never have to pass the same defender twice.

### MISSTEP

The defender kicks the ball away as you attempt to turn with the ball.

### CORRECTION

Separate yourself from the marking defender before attempting to turn with the ball. Use body feints coupled with sudden changes of speed and direction to create space in which to turn with the ball.

### MISSTEP

You turn with the ball to face the opponent's goal but then dribble east-west instead of north-south.

### CORRECTION

Once you have turned with the ball, dribble immediately toward goal to commit the nearest defender. Depending on how that player reacts, you can then penetrate by passing to a teammate in a more forward position or by dribbling past the defender.

# Individual Attack Drill 1   1v1

Play against an opponent within a 10- by 20-yard area. You begin with the ball. Try to keep the ball from your opponent through close control of the ball coupled with sudden changes of speed and direction. Play for 30 seconds, rest for 30 seconds, and repeat. Score 1 point each time you can maintain possession of the ball for a 30-second round. You are not permitted to leave the playing field area to elude the defender. Play 10 rounds as the attacker; then switch roles and play 10 rounds as the defender.

### To Increase Difficulty

- Add second defender.
- Decrease size of playing area.

### To Decrease Difficulty

- Score 1 point for 15-second possession time.
- Increase size of playing area.

### Success Check

- Position body to shield ball.

- Maintain space between ball and defender.
- Use sudden changes of speed and direction.
- Use deceptive body feints and foot movements.

### Score Your Success

0 to 3 points = 1 point

4 to 6 points = 3 points

7 to 10 points = 5 points

Your score ___

# Individual Attack Drill 2   **Turn and Play On**

Form two teams (A and B) of two players each. Play within a 10- by 20-yard field area. One player from each team acts as a target. Targets, each with a ball, get in position on opposite end lines while their partners take positions in the middle of the field area. Target A begins by passing the ball to a teammate, who attempts to turn and play the ball forward to target B. The middle player on team B attempts to prevent the turn and deny penetration via the pass or dribble. The middle player for team A scores 1 point for turning with the ball to face the defender and 1 additional point for eluding the opponent and playing the ball accurately to target B. Target players are free to move anywhere (side-to-side) along the 10-yard-wide end line. The middle player has 15 seconds once she receives the ball to turn and play the ball to the opposite target. After a score or 15 seconds, whichever comes first, the round ends, and target B serves a ball to her teammate. Each middle player plays 10 rounds as the attacker for a possible maximum of 20 points.

## To Increase Difficulty

- Reduce size of playing area to limit attacking space.
- Allow only 10 seconds to turn and penetrate opposite end line.

## To Decrease Difficulty

- Reduce number of rounds.

## *Success Check*

- Check toward ball to receive it.

- Control and shield ball from defender.
- Create separation from defender.
- Turn to face defender.
- Take on defender.

## *Score Your Success*

0 to 7 points as attacker = 1 point

8 to 11 points as attacker = 3 points

12 to 20 points as attacker = 5 points

Your score ___

# Individual Attack Drill 3   **1v1 to a Common Goal**

Play 1v1 within a 20- by 20-yard area. Place flags 3 yards apart near the center of the area to represent a common goal. You begin with possession of the ball; your opponent plays as the defender. The objective is to beat your opponent and pass or dribble the ball through either side of the common goal. Award yourself 1 point for each goal scored. Change of possession occurs when the defender steals the ball, when the ball travels outside of the area, and when a goal is scored. Players alternate from attack to defense with each change of possession. Play two 5-minute halves with a short rest between. The player scoring more points wins the game.

### To Increase Difficulty for Attacker

- Decrease width of goal to 2 yards.

### To Decrease Difficulty for Attacker

- Increase width of goal to 4 yards.

## Success Check

- Protect ball from defender.

- Turn with ball when possible.
- Take on defender via pass or dribble.

## Score Your Success

Lose the game = 0 points

Win the game = 3 points

Your score ___

---

# Individual Attack Drill 4
# 1(+1) v 1(+1) to Mini-Goals

Organize teams of two players each. Use markers to create a 15-yard-wide by 20-yard-long playing area for each game with a goal 4 yards wide at the center of each end line. One player on each team positions in the goal as a target. The remaining two players station in the center of the area. One has the ball to begin; the other defends. The middle players compete 1v1. Points are scored by passing the ball to the feet of the opponent who is standing in the goal. If the defending player steals the ball, he immediately becomes the attacker and attempts to score in the opponent's goal. Central players are permitted to play the ball back to their teammates (in the goal) to alleviate pressure, and can receive a return pass from their goal players. However, goal players are not permitted to move forward off the end line in support of their teammates. Change of possession occurs when the defender steals the ball, when the ball travels out of play, and after each score. Play three-minute rounds, after which teammates switch positions; the goal player becomes the field player and vice versa. The player scoring more goals wins the round and is awarded 1 point. The first team to score 5 points wins the game.

### To Increase Difficulty for Attacker

- Decrease width of goal to 2 yards.

### To Decrease Difficulty for Attacker

- Increase width of goal to 6 yards.

## Success Check

- Protect ball from defender.

- Turn with ball when possible.
- Take on defender via pass or dribble.
- Penetrate to goal.

## Score Your Success

Member of losing team = 1 point

Member of winning team = 3 points

Your score ___

## Individual Attack Drill 5    **Four-Goal Game**

Use markers to outline a 25- by 25-yard field area. Position flags to represent a 3-yard-wide goal at the midpoint of each sideline. Form two teams of four players each; number players on each team 1 through 4. Teams take positions on opposite sidelines. To begin, the coach calls a number (e.g., 2) and kicks a ball into the field. The number 2 players from each team sprint into the area to compete 1v1. The player who wins the ball can score by dribbling through any of the four goals; the other player defends. Player roles reverse on change of possession. After each score, or when the ball goes out of the area, the coach immediately kicks another ball into the field area and the same pair continues the competition. Play continuously for 60 seconds, after which the coach signals a different pair into the square. Play for 15 minutes (three rounds for each pair) and keep track of goals scored by each player.

### To Increase Difficulty

- Lengthen round to 90 seconds.
- Add neutral defender who joins with original defender to create 1v2 situation.

### To Decrease Difficulty

- Shorten round to 30 seconds.

### Success Check

- Be first to ball.

- Protect ball and maintain possession.
- Use body feints to unbalance defender.
- Be direct—attack nearer goal.

### Score Your Success

0 to 2 goals scored in three rounds = 1 point

3 or more goals scored in three rounds = 3 points

Your score ___

# INDIVIDUAL DEFENSE TACTICS

Individual defense tactics apply to the defending player located nearest to the opponent with the ball. This player, hereafter referred to as the *first defender,* is responsible for providing the initial line of defense by applying immediate pressure at the point of attack. Ultimately, the first defender hopes to win the ball, but that is not her sole objective. An essential responsibility of the first defender is to delay or slow the opponent's attack to provide teammates time to withdraw and reorganize behind the ball. The temptation to immediately jump in on the tackle must be tempered by the fact that a miscalculation will leave the first defender beaten and behind the play.

Top defenders always appear in complete control of their actions, and they don't sell themselves by recklessly diving in at every opportunity to challenge for the ball. Instead, they analyze the situation and, at the opportune moment, commit to the tackle with power and determination. Because your decisions on the soccer field ultimately dictate your actions, they will obviously play a critical role in your ability to defend in 1v1 situations. Good decisions are the stepping-stones that lead to solid individual defensive play. To win a majority of 1v1 battles when playing in the role of first defender, keep in mind the following general guidelines.

## Get in Goalside Position

The first step in the process of regaining possession of the ball is to assume the correct starting position in relation to the opponent, the ball, and your goal. Always get in position *goalside* (i.e., between the ball and the goal you are defending; see figure 7.3). From a goalside position, you can keep both the ball and the opponent you are responsible for marking in view at all times. It's generally to your advantage to position slightly to the inside of the opponent, shading him toward the center of the field. From there you can shut off the attacker's most direct route to goal.

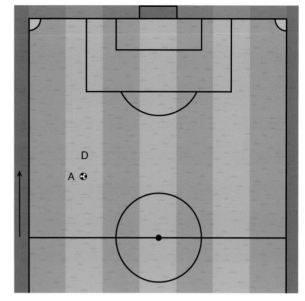

**Figure 7.3**  Goalside position.

## Choose a Good Starting Distance

How tight (close) should you mark an opponent when defending one-on-one? There are several variables to consider when faced with this decision. You must be close enough to prevent the attacker from turning with the ball to face you, but not so tight that she can spin off and dribble past you.

As a general rule, take a defending position a step or two off the attacker to give yourself a clear view of the ball. If the attacker tries to turn, you can quickly step in to tackle the ball. If you can prevent the turn and force the opponent to play the ball back or square, then you have done your job—delayed the attack and provided teammates with time to withdraw and organize behind the ball.

If the opponent you are marking does not have the ball, you must adjust your position accordingly because you are no longer fulfilling the role of first defender. In this situation your starting position should enable you to be first to any pass slotted into the space in front of the opponent, but it must also allow you to challenge for the ball or intercept the pass should the ball be played directly to that player. As a general rule of thumb, the farther your opponent moves from the location of the ball, the greater your marking distance can be (figure 7.4). If the ball is subsequently passed to the player you are responsible for marking, you can close the distance while the ball is in flight to challenge for the ball as it arrives.

Also take into account the area of the field and the ability of the opponent. As a general rule, the closer the opponent is to your goal, the tighter the marking distance should be. An opponent within scoring range must be denied the space and time needed to release a shot or pass the ball forward.

Finally, an opponent who has great speed and quickness should be afforded a bit more space to prevent him from merely pushing the ball past and outracing you. You can afford to mark more tightly if the opponent is highly skilled but relatively slow. In that situation you must deny the time and space required to use those skills to beat you.

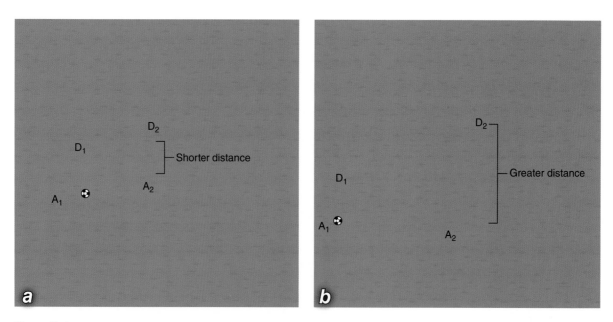

**Figure 7.4** Marking distance: *(a)* supporting the attacker close to the ball; *(b)* supporting the attacker farther from the ball.

## Deny Space and Time

Quickly reduce the distance between you and the opponent when you see that she is about to receive the ball. Ideally, you should arrive at about the same moment as the ball or just before. If possible, angle your approach to limit the attacker's options. For example, you can funnel the opponent into space along a touchline or force him into the space occupied by a covering defender. In all cases you must maintain good balance and body control.

Slow your approach as you near the attacker, shorten your strides, and shift into a slightly crouched posture with knees flexed (figure 7.5). Maintain a low center of gravity with your weight centered over the balls of your feet. Assume a staggered stance, with feet a comfortable distance apart and one foot slightly forward of the other. Having your feet in the staggered position eliminates the possibility of having the ball pushed between your legs, a dribbling maneuver commonly referred to as the *nutmeg*. You also will be able to respond more quickly to the opponent's sudden changes of speed and direction from this position.

**Figure 7.5** Assume a defensive posture: bent knees, staggered stance, vision on the ball.

## Prevent the Turn

Once an attacker turns with the ball to face your goal, his options dramatically increase and improve. The greatest danger is that he will now be able to serve a penetrating pass into the space behind you or attempt to beat you on the dribble. That being the case, it's in your best interest to prevent an opponent who has his back to your goal from turning with the ball. The marking position should be relatively tight but not so tight that the attacker can spin with the ball and roll off you. Get in position so that you have a clear view of the ball and are ready to step forward to tackle the ball if the opponent attempts to turn.

## Jockey and Delay

Despite your best efforts, there will be times when a talented attacker finds a way to turn on you. In that situation your immediate priority is to deny penetration. Try to jockey, or channel, the attacker into areas in which space is limited, such as toward the touchline or into a covering defender, or force her to pass the ball square or backward. If you can successfully deny or at least delay penetration, even for a few moments, then your teammates will have time to organize behind (on the goal side of) the ball.

## Commit to the Tackle

Always be alert for an opportune moment to win the ball. Step forward quickly and fully commit to the tackle if you sense that the attacker has allowed the ball to get too far from his feet. Use the tackling techniques described in step 1 to regain possession of the ball and go on the attack.

### MISSTEP

You arrive late and allow the opponent to turn with the ball to face you.

### CORRECTION

You must position at the appropriate distance to deny your opponent the space required for turning with the ball.

### MISSTEP

You jump in recklessly to the tackle and are beaten on the dribble.

### CORRECTION

Your first priority in a 1v1 situation is to prevent penetration, not necessarily win the ball. Get in position at an appropriate marking distance with feet in a staggered stance and weight evenly distributed. Challenge for the ball only when a teammate is covering the space immediately behind you or when you are extremely confident that you can successfully execute the tackle.

## Individual Defense Drill 1   Defend the End Line

Play on a 10- by 30-yard field area. Get in position on one end line as the defender; your opponent (attacker) stands on the opposite end line. The coach (server) begins play by kicking a ball to the attacker, who controls the ball and attempts to dribble it past you over your end line. Move forward quickly off the end line to close the distance to the ball. Score 1 point if you successfully tackle the ball or kick the ball out of the field area. After each round, return to your respective starting positions and repeat. Play 20 rounds as the defender; then switch roles and repeat.

### To Increase Difficulty for Defender

- Increase width of field.

### To Decrease Difficulty for Defender

- Decrease width of field to 5 yards.

### Success Check

- Quickly close distance to attacker.

- Maintain balance and body control.
- Use staggered defensive stance.
- Deny penetration.
- Tackle ball.

### Score Your Success

0 to 9 points = 1 point

10 to 14 points = 3 points

15 to 20 points = 5 points

Your score ___

## Individual Defense Drill 2
## Deny the Turn and Prevent Penetration

Six players participate in this drill. Four players stand an equal distance apart around the perimeter of the center circle, two in each half of the field. One player in each half (server) has a ball to begin; the other (target) does not. A single defender and an attacker are stationed within the circle.

The drill begins as one of the servers plays a ball to the attacker, who attempts to turn with the ball and play it to the target player positioned on the opposite half of the circle. The defender quickly closes the distance to the ball to prevent the turn and deny penetration. Play continues until the defender wins the ball or the attacker plays the ball to the target player. At this point the second server plays a ball to the attacker, and the round is repeated in the opposite direction. The defender earns 1 point for each round in which she prevents the attacker from turning and playing the ball to the target player on the opposite side of the circle. Play 10 rounds and keep track of points scored by defenders. Repeat until each player has taken a turn as the defender.

### To Increase Difficulty for Defender

- Increase size of area.
- Position two attackers within center circle.

### To Decrease Difficulty for Defender

- Reduce size of area.

## Success Check

- Assume goalside position.
- Quickly close distance to ball to deny turn.
- Maintain balance and body control.
- Deny penetration via dribble or pass.
- Tackle ball.

# Individual Defense Drill 3
## 1v1 to Multiple Mini-Goals

Play within a 40- by 40-yard area. Use markers to represent six to eight mini-goals, each 3 yards wide, spaced randomly throughout the field area. Divide the group into two equal teams. Each player pairs with an opponent on the opposite team for 1v1 competition. Each pair has a ball. Designate one team as the attackers for the first game. On the coach's command, the game begins. Once play begins, the attackers have 45 seconds to score as many goals as possible by dribbling though either side of a goal. An attacker may not dribble through the same goal twice in succession. If a defender steals the ball, he attempts to shield or possess it to prevent the opponent from scoring. After 45 seconds the attacking players total their goals scored to get a team total. After a brief rest, repeat the game with teams reversing roles. Play a series of 45-second games. The team scoring more goals wins the match.

## To Increase Difficulty for Defending Players

- Increase size and number of goals.

## To Decrease Difficulty for Defending Players

- Reduce width of field.
- Reduce size of goal.

## Success Check

- Maintain goalside position.

- Keep knees bent with low center of gravity.
- Place feet in staggered position.
- Apply immediate pressure on attacker with ball.
- Deny penetration via pass or dribble.

# Individual Defense Drill 4    1v1 Marking Game

Form two teams of three players each. Use markers to outline a playing area of 25 by 40 yards with a goal 4 yards wide at the center of each end line. Each team defends a goal. Do not use goalkeepers. Begin with a kickoff from the center of the field. Require strict 1v1 marking of opponents. Regular soccer rules apply except that the offside law is waived. Because goalkeepers are not used and shots may be taken from anywhere on the field, marking must be very tight to prevent long-range goals. Change of possession occurs when a defending player steals the ball, when the ball goes out of play, or when a goal is scored. The team scoring more goals wins the game.

### To Increase Difficulty for Defending Players

- Increase width of field.
- Place three small goals on each end line to provide attackers with additional scoring options.

### To Decrease Difficulty for Defending Players

- Reduce width of field.
- Reduce size of goal.

## Success Check

- Maintain goalside position.

- Keep knees bent and center of gravity low.
- Place feet in staggered position.
- Apply immediate pressure on attacker with ball.
- Deny penetration via pass or dribble.

## Score Your Success

Member of losing team = 1 point

Member of winning team = 2 points

Your score ___

# SUCCESS SUMMARY

Practicing one-on-one tactics is challenging and fun. The exercises are highly competitive and physically demanding, and they test your ability to execute skills and make decisions in gamelike conditions. Once you've sufficiently mastered the basics of individual attack and defense, get together with a group of teammates and organize a one-on-one tournament in which each player plays a two-minute 1v1 game (competition) against every other player. Players keep a tally of their 1v1 wins and losses to determine a tournament winner. Your coach can observe the tournament and analyze your performance.

Each of the drills in step 7 has been assigned a point value to help you evaluate your performance and measure your progress. Record your scores in the following chart. Total your points to obtain an estimate of your overall level of success.

## *Individual Attack Drills*

1.  1v1                                       _____ out of 5
2.  Turn and Play On                          _____ out of 5
3.  1v1 to a Common Goal                      _____ out of 3
4.  1 (+1) v 1(+1) to Mini-Goals              _____ out of 3
5.  Four-Goal Game                            _____ out of 3

## *Individual Defense Drills*

1.  Defend the End Line                       _____ out of 5
2.  Deny the Turn and Prevent Penetration     _____ out of 3
3.  1v1 to Multiple Mini-Goals                _____ out of 2
4.  1v1 Marking Game                          _____ out of 2

**Total**                                     _____ **out of 31**

A combined score of 23 or more points suggests that you have mastered the fundamentals of individual attack and defense tactics. You are ready to move on to group tactics. A score in the range of 16 to 22 is considered adequate. You should review and rehearse the individual attack and defense tactics once again before moving on to step 8. If you scored 15 or fewer points, you have more work to do. Review the material once again and perform all the drills at least one more time. When you are confident and competent in your ability to execute individual tactics, you can move on to the next step.

# Attacking as a Group

Although the individual tactics discussed thus far are essential for winning the one-on-one battles, the team as a whole will not experience success unless players can combine their efforts toward a common goal. Much like the pieces of a puzzle, individual players must fit together in the correct combinations to complete the picture. When players are willing and able to work together, when they complement one another, then team performance can far exceed the collective efforts of individual performances. Ultimately, that is the goal of all team sports—that the so-called whole (team) be greater than its individual parts (players). Conversely, when teammates cannot or will not work in combination, team performance suffers regardless of how talented the players are.

Group attack tactics typically involve two or more players working together to maintain possession of the ball, penetrate the opposing defense, and create scoring opportunities. Step 7 discussed in depth the role of the first attacker: to penetrate the opposing defense via the pass or dribble. In most cases the first attacker needs the help of teammates to accomplish that aim. That is where group tactics come into play.

Group attack involves the coordinated involvement of the first, second, and third attackers. The overriding objective is always to position more attacking players than defending players in the vicinity of the ball to create what is commonly referred to as a *numbers-up situation,* and then to exploit that numerical advantage. That exploitation happens through the implementation of tactical concepts that include support in attack, give-and-go (wall) passes, double passes, takeovers, and overlaps.

The second attacker's primary role is to provide immediate passing options, or *support,* for the player on the ball. He also plays an important role in executing the give-and-go pass, the double pass, and the takeover maneuvers. The third attacker's job is to provide passing options away from the ball, usually by making penetrating diagonal runs through the defense or overlapping runs behind the defense.

Successfully executing group attack tactics requires an understanding of each attacker's role in the specific situation coupled with the ability to perform the requisite skills involved. An adequate level of technical ability (skill) is a prerequisite for tactical execution. At the end of the day, it doesn't really matter that you know where to be, when to run, or how to perform a specific tactic if you are unable to pass, receive, dribble, and shoot the ball effectively. For that reason you must master the skills discussed in steps 1 through 5 before focusing on the tactical aspects of the game.

# SUPPORT IN ATTACK

Coaches often state that players without the ball must work harder than the player with the ball. That line of thought reinforces the fact that players off the ball are responsible for providing passing options for the player on the ball. This tactic, referred to as support in attack, serves to position more attackers than defenders in the vicinity of the ball and thus increase the likelihood that the team will be able to maintain possession. Conversely, failure to provide adequate support leaves the first attacker isolated with few options, a situation that shifts the advantage to the defense. When determining when, where, and how to get in position to provide optimal support, consider the number of support players needed for a specific situation, the most advantageous angle of support, and the proper distance of support.

Too few teammates in the vicinity of the ball (a lack of support) limits the first attacker's options, whereas too many can be a disadvantage because they draw additional defenders to the area. As the area around the ball becomes crowded with players, it becomes increasingly difficult to find the space and time required to develop passing combinations. Ideally, three attacking players should provide nearby support to the first attacker, one player positioned to each side and slightly ahead of the ball to provide width, and the third player positioned behind the ball to provide depth (figure 8.1).

Imagine three lines drawn from the ball, one to each of the support players. The angle formed between any two support players and the ball should be 90 degrees or greater (figure 8.2). A single defending player cannot possibly cover two or more support players when they are positioned at wide angles, but the defending player may be able to do so if the support players are positioned at a narrow angle (less than 90 degrees) of support.

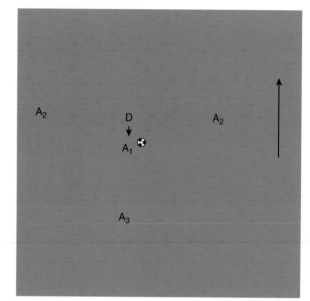

**Figure 8.1**  Support in attack. Attackers near the ball provide passing options for the player on the ball. A1 = player on the ball; A2 = support attackers; A3 = support behind the ball; D = defender.

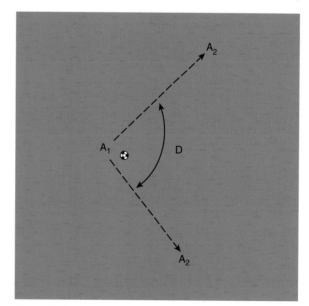

**Figure 8.2**  Wide angle of support.

How close to the ball should you be as a support players? It depends. Base your decision on the position of the defenders and the area of the field. As a general rule, position yourself within 3 to 4 yards of the ball when the first attacker is being challenged by an opponent, a situation in which the player may have to release the ball quickly. You can extend the distance of support, possibly to 8 to 10 yards, if a defender is not in position to challenge for the ball or if the space around the ball is not crowded with players. In all cases, support players should maintain a clear passing lane to the ball.

Reduce the distance of support as the ball moves closer to the opponent's goal. The defending team usually consolidates its players in the most dangerous scoring zone front and center of its goal to reduce the available space and time for attackers in that area. By employing tighter support positioning in that area, the attacking team improves its chances of successfully executing the give-and-go pass or takeover maneuver to penetrate a packed defense and create an opportunity for a strike at goal. The distance of support can be extended as the ball moves farther from the defending team's goal.

### MISSTEP

A single defender is able to close down the passing lanes to two or more attackers.

### CORRECTION

Support players should position at a wide angle (90 degrees or greater) from the ball to maintain open passing lanes to the ball. Support players should not position behind the defender or at a narrow angle, which may enable the defender to cut off a pass directed at a support player.

### MISSTEP

Support players fail to readjust position in response to the movement of the ball.

### CORRECTION

Soccer is a fluid game, and as such your position of support is in a state of constant flux. As the ball is passed from one attacker to another, the players providing support must adjust their positions accordingly. For this reason players "off the ball" must actually work harder than the player with the ball.

## Support in Attack Drill 1    3v1 Possession Game

A single defender plays against three attackers within a 12- by 12-yard grid. The attackers try to keep the ball away from the defender within the boundaries of the grid. Attackers are unrestricted in their movement within the grid and are allowed unlimited touches to pass and receive the ball. The emphasis is on proper support movement and positioning of the second attackers. Score 1 point for eight or more consecutive passes without a loss of possession. Play continuously for five minutes.

## To Increase Difficulty for Attackers

- Decrease size of grid.
- Limit attackers to two touches to receive and pass ball.
- Add defender to create 3v2 situation.

## To Decrease Difficulty for Attackers

- Increase size of grid.
- Add attacker to create 4v1 situation.

## Success Check for Attackers

- Get in position at wide angles of support.
- Prepare ball with first touch.
- Use correct pace and accurate passes.
- Readjust position with movement of ball.

## Score Your Success

0 to 3 points in five minutes = 1 point

4 to 6 points in five minutes = 2 points

7 or more points in five minutes = 4 points

Your score ___

# Support in Attack Drill 2   2v2 (+4) Support Game

Eight players participate in this drill. Use markers to outline a 25- by 25-yard playing area. A support player stands at the midpoint of each of the four sides. The remaining players are in two teams of two players each. One team has possession of the ball to begin. The objective is to maintain possession of the ball within the grid. The four support players join the team with the ball to create a 6v2 situation, or a four-player advantage for the attack. Support players, however, are restricted in their movements. They are permitted to move laterally along the sidelines but may not enter the field area. Support players may receive the ball from and pass the ball to central players only—they may not pass among themselves—and are limited to two touches to receive and pass the ball. Change of possession occurs when a defending player steals the ball or when the ball goes out of play. Score 1 team point for six consecutive passes without a loss of possession. Play for five minutes, after which central players switch positions with support players and repeat the game.

## To Increase Difficulty for Attackers

- Limit support players to one-touch (first-time) passes.
- Award 1 team point for 10 consecutive passes without loss of possession.

## To Decrease Difficulty for Attackers

- Permit support players to pass among themselves.

*(continued)*

Support in Attack Drill 2 *(continued)*

### Success Check for Attackers

- Move ball quickly to unbalance defenders.
- As support player, move laterally to provide passing options.

### Score Your Success

0 to 3 points in five-minute game = 1 point

4 to 7 points in five-minute game = 3 points

8 or more points in five-minute game = 5 points

Your score ___

# Support in Attack Drill 3
## 4v2 (+2) Double-Grid Game

Set up two adjacent 15- by 15-yard grids with a 5-yard space between them. Four attackers and two defenders are in grid A, and two additional players are in grid B. The four attackers in grid A attempt to keep the ball from the two defenders (4v2) by passing among themselves. Attackers are limited to three touches or fewer to receive and pass the ball. Once the attackers have completed a minimum of four consecutive passes, they can play the ball to the two players stationed in grid B. Two attackers from grid A immediately sprint to grid B to join the two players already there to create a four-player team in grid B. The two defenders in grid A also sprint to grid B to create a 4v2 situation in that grid.

If a defender wins the ball, she passes it to one of the players in the opposite grid. The two defenders follow the pass to form a new four-player attacking team in the other grid. Two of the original attackers sprint into the opposite grid to serve as defenders. Play for 10 minutes. The attacking team scores 1 point each time it completes four or more consecutive passes and plays the ball into the opposite grid.

### To Increase Difficulty for Attackers

- Reduce size of grid to 10 by 10 yards.
- Add third defender to create 4v3 situation in each grid.
- Limit attackers to two touches or fewer.

### To Decrease Difficulty for Attackers

- Increase size of grid.
- Add extra attacker to create 5v2 situation in each grid.

### Success Check for Attackers

- Get good first touch of ball to alleviate defensive pressure.
- Provide immediate support at wide angles to ball.
- Make hard support runs to opposite grid when ball changes location.

### Score Your Success

4 or fewer points as attacker = 1 point

5 to 9 points as attacker = 3 points

10 or more points as attacker = 5 points

Your score ___

# Support in Attack Drill 4
## 3v3 (+2) Possession Game

Use markers to create a 25- by 25-yard playing area. Organize two teams of three players each. Designate two additional players as a neutral players who always join the team with possession of the ball. Use colored vests to differentiate teams and the neutral players. One team begins with possession of the ball.

The team with the ball attempts to keep it from the opponents. The neutral players join with the team in possession to create a 5v3 situation, or a two-player advantage for the attack. Change of possession occurs when a defending player steals the ball or when the ball goes out of play and was last touched by a member of the attacking team. Play is continuous with teams switching from attack to defense and vice versa on each change of possession. There are no restrictions on the number of touches permitted to receive and pass the ball.

Score 1 point for eight consecutive passes without a loss of possession. The team scoring more points wins. As a support player, use quick ball movement along with proper positioning.

### To Increase Difficulty for Attackers

- Reduce size of grid to 20 by 20 yards.
- Add neutral defender to create 5v4 situation.
- Limit attackers to two touches or fewer.

### To Decrease Difficulty for Attackers

- Increase size of field to 30 by 30 yards.
- Add extra attacker to create 6v3 situation.

### *Success Check for Attackers*

- Get good first touch of ball to alleviate defensive pressure.
- Provide immediate support at wide angles to ball.
- Make hard support runs to opposite grid when ball changes location.
- Move ball quickly to change point of attack.

### *Score Your Success*

Member of losing team = 2 points

Member of winning team = 5 points

Your score ___

# GIVE-AND-GO (WALL) PASS

The most fundamental numbers-up situation is two attackers versus one defender. The give-and-go pass, or wall pass (figure 8.3), is an effective way to penetrate past the defender in a 2v1 situation.

The concept of give-and-go is simple. The player with the ball (first attacker) dribbles toward goal, causing the nearest defender to either withdraw or commit to the first attacker. As the defender closes to tackle, the attacker releases the ball to a nearby teammate (second attacker, or wall) and sprints forward into the space behind the defender to collect a return pass.

For the give-and-go pass to work, the two attacking teammates must each fulfill specific responsibilities and work in concert. Correct timing of the pass and run are essential for success. The player on the ball (first attacker) must initiate the action. Perform the following steps in this order:

1. *Take on the defender.* Dribble directly at (take on) the nearest defender when you recognize that a potential give-and-go situation exists. This action is designed to freeze the defender.

2. *Commit the defender.* Dribbling directly at the defender will draw him to you.

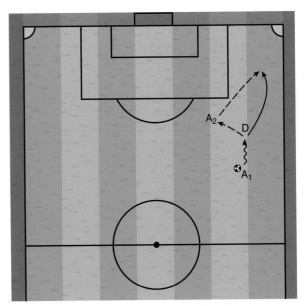

**Figure 8.3** Give-and-go pass. The first attacker passes to the second attacker and then runs forward into open space to receive a return pass.

3. *Release the ball at the opportune moment.* As the defender closes to tackle, pass the ball to the wall player's lead foot using the outside surface of your instep.

4. *Sprint forward.* After releasing the ball, sprint forward into the space behind the defender.

5. *Collect the return pass.* Receive a return pass from the wall player.

The wall player (support attacker) must perform the following steps in this order as the first attacker commits the defender.

1. *Move quickly to a position ahead and to the side of the first attacker.* Get in position 3 to 4 yards to the side of the defending player at an angle approximately 45 degrees from the ball.

2. *Get in position sideways in relation to the ball.* Use an open stance with your body angled sideways toward the first attacker. Use your lead foot to redirect the pass.

3. *Redirect the ball.* Position your lead foot to redirect the pass from the first attacker into the space behind the defender.

4. *Support the ball.* Sprint forward to support your teammate. Another give-and-go situation could develop immediately.

### MISSTEP

As the first attacker, you release your pass before committing the defender to you.

### CORRECTION

Dribble directly at the defender. Release the pass at the instant the defender steps forward to tackle the ball.

### MISSTEP

You commit the defender and pass to the wall player, but then that player is unable to redirect the ball into the space behind the defender.

### CORRECTION

This error can occur for two reasons. First, the wall player may be too far away from you. The proper support distance of the wall player is 3 to 4 yards to the side of the defender. Positioning at a greater distance will allow the defender sufficient time to readjust her position to block the passing lane. Execution of the give-and-go may also break down if you (the first attacker) release the ball too soon, before the defender has committed to the tackle.

# DOUBLE PASS

The double pass (figure 8.4) is simply a wall pass followed by a second entry pass to the original wall player. After redirecting the ball into the space behind the defender, the wall player makes a diagonal penetrating run ahead of the ball to receive a return pass from the first attacker. Each player has specific obligations.

As the first attacker (the player on the ball), your primary responsibility is to dribble at and commit the defender to you. As the defender closes, release the pass to the lead foot of the wall using the outside-of-the-foot technique and then sprint forward into space behind the defender to collect a return (wall) pass. After receiving the ball, complete the double pass by passing the ball forward to the original wall player, who has sprinted into position ahead of the ball.

As the support (wall) player, your initial responsibility is to get in position as the wall 3 to 4 yards to the side of the defending player while at the same time maintaining a clear passing lane to the ball. Position your body sideways to the first attacker. As the ball arrives, redirect the pass into the space behind the defender and then sprint forward ahead of the ball to receive a second pass from the first attacker to complete the double pass.

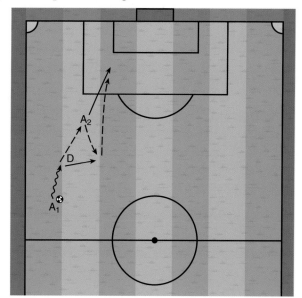

**Figure 8.4** Double pass. The first attacker passes to the second attacker (wall) and runs into open space past the defender. The second attacker returns the ball to the first attacker, runs ahead of the ball, and receives a return pass.

**MISSTEP**

The double-pass combination fails to materialize.

**CORRECTION**

You must first execute a successful wall pass to set up the double pass. Once the wall player has redirected the initial pass behind the defender, she must sprint ahead of the ball to receive a return pass.

## Wall Pass and Double Pass Drill 1   Off the Wall

Partner with a teammate. Execute the wall pass against an imaginary defender as you jog the length of the field. Score 1 point for each properly executed wall pass. Perform the drill at half speed to begin; then gradually progress to full speed. Execute 40 wall passes, playing 20 as the first attacker and 20 as the second (wall) attacker, for a possible maximum of 40 points.

### To Increase Difficulty for Attackers

• Add defender.

### To Decrease Difficulty for Attackers

• Practice wall passes off kick (rebound) wall.

### Success Check for First Attacker

• Dribble at imaginary defender.
• Release pass with outside surface of foot.
• Sprint forward into space.

### Success Check for Support Player (Wall)

• Get in position sideways-on to first attacker.
• Redirect pass into space behind imaginary defender.
• Move forward to support ball.

### Score Your Success

0 to 24 points = 1 point

25 to 34 points = 3 points

35 to 40 points = 5 points

Your score ___

## Wall Pass and Double Pass Drill 2   2v1 in Grid

Partner with a teammate to play against a third player (defender) within a 12- by 12-yard grid. Use dribbling, shielding, and passing skills to maintain possession within the area. Your team is allowed an unlimited number of touches to pass and receive the ball. Score 2 points each time you and your partner execute a give-and-go pass to beat the defender. Score 1 point each time you and your teammate combine for five or more consecutive passes. Play for five minutes; then switch defenders and repeat.

### To Increase Difficulty for Attackers

- Reduce size of grid.
- Score 1 point for seven consecutive passes.
- Limit attackers to three touches to pass and receive ball.

### To Decrease Difficulty for Attackers

- Increase size of grid.
- Score 1 point for three consecutive passes.

### *Success Check for Attackers*

- Commit defender.
- Move without ball.
- Maintain clear passing lane to ball.
- Execute one–two passing combination.

### *Score Your Success*

0 to 9 points in five-minute game = 1 point

10 to 14 points in five-minute game = 3 points

15 or more points in five-minute game = 5 points

Your score ___

# Wall Pass and Double Pass Drill 3
## 2v1 to the End Line

Use markers to outline a 15- by 25-yard field area. You and a teammate get in position on one end line of the field. A third player (the defender) stands on the opposite end line with a ball. The defender initiates play by serving the ball to you and immediately sprinting forward to defend.

You and your partner attempt to take on and beat the defender to the end line either by dribbling past the defender or by executing a wall pass or double pass. Score 1 team point if you and your partner beat the defender and penetrate the end line with the ball. If the defender wins the ball, the play is dead and players return to their original positions. Repeat 20 times for a possible maximum of 20 points.

### To Increase Difficulty for Attackers

- Restrict attacking team to 10-yard-wide zone when attempting to beat defender.

### To Decrease Difficulty for Attackers

- Add third attacker.

### *Success Check for Attackers*

- Attack at game speed.
- Commit defender.
- As support player, position ahead of ball and to side of defender.
- Execute wall pass or dribble past defender.
- Penetrate at speed to end line.

*(continued)*

Wall Pass and Double Pass Drill 3 *(continued)*

### *Score Your Success*

0 to 9 points = 1 point

10 to 14 points = 3 points

15 to 20 points = 5 points

Your score ___

# Wall Pass and Double Pass Drill 4
## 2v1 (+1) Transition Game

Organize into two teams of two players each. Use markers to outline a playing area 20 by 25 yards with a 4-yard-wide goal at the midpoint of each end line. Each team defends a goal and can score in the opponent's goal. Begin the game with a kick-off from the center of the field. The team with possession scores points by kicking the ball through the opponent's goal or by executing a successful wall pass. The defending team positions one player as a goalkeeper and one as a defender. Change of possession occurs when the defender steals the ball, the goalkeeper makes a save, the ball last touched by a member of the attacking team goes out of bounds, or a goal is scored.

When the defender gains possession of the ball, he must pass back to the goalkeeper, who can then sprint forward out of the goal to join in an attack on the opponent's goal. The team losing possession must now defend. One player sprints back to play as the goalkeeper while the other is the defender. The action is continuous as teams attack with two players and defend with one player and a goalkeeper. Teammates alternate playing goalkeeper. Score 1 team point for each wall pass that beats a defender and 1 additional point for each goal scored. Play for 15 minutes and keep track of points. The team that scores more points wins the game.

### To Increase Difficulty for Attackers

- Decrease size of goal.
- Decrease width of field.
- Limit players to three touches.

### To Decrease Difficulty for Attackers

- Increase size of goal.

### *Success Check for Attackers*

- Immediately transition from defense to attack.
- Take on and commit defender.
- Execute wall pass.
- Penetrate to goal.

### *Score Your Success*

Member of losing team = 0 points

Member of winning team = 2 points

Your score ___

# Wall Pass and Double Pass Drill 5
## Multiple Scoring Options

Form two teams of five players each. Use markers to outline a 40- by 50-yard playing area with a 4-yard-wide goal on the center of each end line. Each team defends a goal and can score in the opponent's goal. Do not use goalkeepers. Begin with a kickoff from the center of the field. Regular soccer rules apply except for the method of scoring. Teams are awarded points as follows:

- 1 point for a successful give-and-go pass
- 1 point for a successful double pass
- 2 points for a goal scored

Play for 20 minutes. The team scoring more points wins the game.

### To Increase Difficulty for Attacking Team

- Reduce size of field to limit space and time.
- Restrict players to three touches or fewer to pass and receive ball.
- Reduce width of goal.

### To Decrease Difficulty for Attacking Team

- Enlarge goals.

### Success Check for Attackers

- Recognize and exploit opportunities for give-and-go pass.
- Provide support for player on ball.
- Recognize opportunities for double pass.
- Maintain open passing lanes.
- Penetrate to goal.

### Score Your Success

Member of losing team = 1 point

Member of winning team = 3 points

Your score ___

# TAKEOVERS

The takeover maneuver, typically used to lose a tightly marking defender, can be likened to the pick in basketball. When executed properly, it is an excellent way to separate from an opponent who is attempting to limit your space and time on the ball.

To perform the takeover (figure 8.5) when you have the ball and are being marked tightly by the first defender, dribble laterally across the field toward a nearby teammate (receiver) who is moving toward you. As you pass the receiver, leave the ball. The receiver accepts the ball and continues forward in the opposite direction into the space you vacated. In the process of exchanging the ball, the opponent who was trailing you is momentarily screened from the ball. This crisscross, or scissors, sort of movement between you and your teammate creates an opportunity for the receiving player to get free of her marker and penetrate toward goal. As the original dribbler, you also have the option of decoying the takeover and keeping the ball, which may also confuse your marker.

As the dribbler, you need to shield the ball from the trailing defender at the moment the ball is exchanged. Because the defender is usually positioned goalside (inside), between you and the goal, you control the ball with your outside foot (i.e., the one farther from the defender. The receiving player angles her approach to collect the ball with her inside foot (the foot closer to you). This maneuver is sometimes referred to as the *same-foot exchange.* The right-foot-to-right-foot and left-foot-to-left-foot rule always applies when executing a takeover.

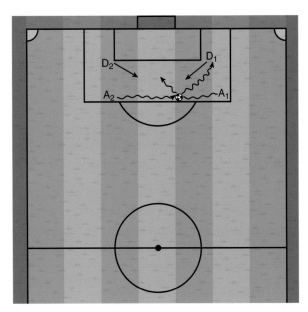

**Figure 8.5**   A takeover is used to lose a defender in a tight space.

### MISSTEP

The defender kicks the ball away as you attempt to exchange possession.

### CORRECTION

Control the ball with the foot farther from the trailing defender. In this manner you can maintain distance between the ball and your opponent, and you may also cause the defender to lose sight of the ball momentarily during the exchange of possession.

### MISSTEP

You collide with your teammate as you attempt to exchange the ball.

### CORRECTION

This error occurs when you and your teammate fail to use a same-foot takeover. If you are controlling with your right foot, then your teammate should collect the ball with his right foot, and vice versa.

# OVERLAP

The overlap maneuver is a two- or three-player combination designed to get a defender or midfielder forward (usually from, but not limited to, a wide position) into a more penetrating attacking position. Overlaps are generally used to get in on the flank to create a numbers-up situation, and typically involve wide midfielders or wide backs.

To execute an overlap (figure 8.6), dribble at the nearest defender to commit him, similar to when attempting to create a wall pass situation. As the play develops, a teammate sprints around and past (overlaps) you into a more forward position. This action creates space for you to play the ball diagonally forward for the overlapping player to run on to.

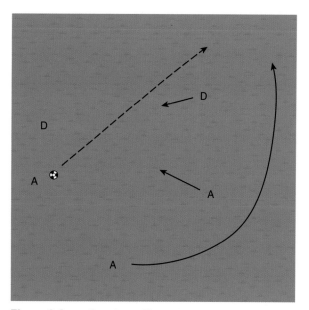

**Figure 8.6**   Overlap. The player bends his run around a teammate to overlap the ball and get in a more advanced attacking position.

### MISSTEP

You are stripped of the ball, and as a result the overlapping player is caught on the wrong side of the ball in a poor defensive position.

### CORRECTION

Do not execute an overlapping run unless you are in position to serve the ball forward. Once you are facing forward and are in no danger of losing the ball, your teammate can sprint ahead of the ball to receive the pass.

## Takeovers and Overlaps Drill 1
## Multiple Takeovers

Play within the penalty area in two groups (A and B) of equal numbers. Each player in group A has possession of a ball; group B players do not. On command, all players begin moving throughout the area. Those with a ball dribble, and those without a ball jog. Dribblers look to exchange their balls via a takeover move with a player who does not have a ball, and then immediately look to get a ball back by executing a takeover with a different player. All takeovers should adhere to the same-foot guideline—right foot to right foot or left foot to left foot. Each player performs a minimum of 50 takeovers.

*(continued)*

Takeovers and Overlaps Drill 1 *(continued)*

## To Increase Difficulty

- Execute takeover maneuver at game speed.
- Add three neutral defenders who try to prevent takeovers.

## To Decrease Difficulty

- Perform drill at half speed.

## Success Check

- Dribble at nearby teammate.
- Exchange ball using same-foot technique.

- Shield ball with your body when exchanging with teammate.
- Accelerate after collecting ball.

## Score Your Success

34 or fewer takeover maneuvers without error = 1 point

35 to 46 takeover maneuvers without error = 3 points

47 to 50 takeover maneuvers without error = 5 points

Your score ___

# Takeovers and Overlaps Drill 2
# Takeover to Goal

Two equal teams (A and B) of four to six players each play on one end of a field with a full-size goal centered on the end line. Teams get in single-file lines facing each other on opposite sides of the penalty arc at the outer edge of the penalty area. Each player on team A has a ball; team B players do not. A goalkeeper is in goal.

The first player from team A dribbles directly at the first player from team B and executes a takeover at the top of the penalty area. The team B player pushes the ball into the penalty area and shoots to score. The team A player who exchanged the ball bends her run toward goal to finish any rebounds off the goalkeeper. Players switch lines after each attempt at goal. Continue the drill until each player has executed 20 takeovers. Score 1 point for each successful takeover performed at game speed.

## To Increase Difficulty

- Add trailing defender who attempts to disrupt takeover.

## To Decrease Difficulty

- Perform drill at half speed.

## Success Check

- Control ball with foot farther from imaginary defender.

- Adhere to same-foot rule when executing takeover.
- Curl your run into penalty area after exchanging ball.
- Accelerate and shoot on goal.

## Score Your Success

0 to 13 points = 1 point

14 to 17 points = 3 points

18 to 20 points = 5 points

Your score ___

# Takeovers and Overlaps Drill 3
## Three-Player Weave

Three groups line up single file about 6 yards apart at the midline of the field facing a goal. Each player in the middle line has a ball. To begin, the first player with the ball passes to the first player in line in one of the other groups, and then overlaps the pass. The player receiving the ball dribbles diagonally inward, toward the center, and releases the ball to the first player from the third group, who has run diagonally ahead of the ball. The basic rule is that players must overlap (sprint around and ahead of) the teammate to whom they pass the ball. The movement is similar to the three-man weave drill in basketball. This restriction creates a continuous series of overlapping runs until the players get to the end line. Once each group of three has overlapped to the end line, repeat the exercise going back to the original starting point at the midline. Repeat 20 times from midline to end line and back. Score 1 point for each successful repetition of the three-player weave from midline to end line and back. Individual players keep track of the number of overlapping runs they execute.

### To Increase Difficulty

- Increase distance covered.
- Increase number of repetitions.

### To Decrease Difficulty

- Decrease distance covered.
- Decrease number of repetitions.

## Success Check

- Play ball accurately to teammate's feet.
- Overlap ball.

- Accelerate into open space.
- Look for return pass.

## Score Your Success

10 or fewer successful repetitions from midline to end line = 1 point

11 to 14 successful repetitions from midline to end line = 2 points

15 or more successful repetitions from midline to end line = 3 points

Your score ___

# Takeovers and Overlaps Drill 4
## Overlap to Goal

Play on a 25- by 35-yard field with a small goal at the midpoint of each end line. Form two teams of two players each. Each team defends a goal and can score in the opponent's goal. Designate one additional player as a neutral player who plays with the team in possession to create a 3v2 situation, or a one-player advantage for the attack. Do not use goalkeepers.

Regular soccer rules apply except for the following restriction: Players must overlap the teammate to whom they pass the ball whenever possible. This restriction creates a continuous series of overlapping runs throughout the game. Play for 15 minutes and keep track of goals scored. Individual players keep track of the number of successful overlapping runs they execute.

*(continued)*

Takeovers and Overlaps Drill 4 *(continued)*

### To Increase Difficulty

- Play even numbers (3v3).

### To Decrease Difficulty

- Play 3v1.

## Success Check

- Play ball accurately to teammate's feet.
- Overlap ball.
- Look for return pass.

## Score Your Success

19 or fewer successful overlapping runs = 1 point

20 to 24 successful overlapping runs = 2 points

25 or more successful overlapping runs = 3 points

Winning team player = 1 bonus point

Your score ___

# Takeovers and Overlaps Drill 5
## Three-Player Flank Overlap

Divide the team into three groups. Group A players, each with a ball, stand in single file on the midline next to the touchline. Group B players stand within the center circle. Group C players get in position 35 yards front and center of the goal, facing the center circle.

The drill begins as the first player in group A passes the ball to a player in group C and then sprints down the sideline. The receiving (target) player first-times the ball back to a group B player, who controls the ball and releases a diagonal penetrating pass to the overlapping player from group A. The overlapping player controls the ball, dribbles to the end line, and crosses it into the goal mouth. The group B and group C players involved in the three-player passing sequence sprint forward into the goal area to finish the cross. Players switch groups after each overlap attempt. The neutral goalkeeper attempts to save all shots. Continue until each player has executed 15 overlapping runs.

### To Increase Difficulty

- Place two defenders within penalty area to defend cross.

### To Decrease Difficulty

- Perform drill at half speed.

## Success Check for Attackers

- Play firm pass into target (group C player).
- Sprint forward to position ahead of ball.
- Receive ball and cross it into goal area.

## Score Your Success

9 or fewer successful overlapping runs at game speed = 1 point

10 to 14 successful overlapping runs at game speed = 2 points

15 successful overlapping runs at game speed = 3 points

Your score ___

# SUCCESS SUMMARY

The successful execution of group attack tactics depends in large part on your ability to read the situation correctly, choose the most appropriate action, and implement that action through precise skill execution. In other words, you must determine what to do and when to do it and then be physically able to do it.

Improved tactical awareness should be a continuing pursuit for all players, particularly those at higher levels of competition. You can improve your understanding of group attack tactics through exercises that simulate situations you will face in the match. Even veteran professionals can sharpen their decision-making skills through repetitive practice in game-simulated situations.

Each drill in step 8 has been assigned a point value to help you evaluate your individual and group performance. Record your scores in the following chart and then total the points to get an estimate of your overall level of competence.

## *Support in Attack Drills*

1. 3v1 Possession Game      _____ out of 4
2. 2v2 (+4) Support Game      _____ out of 5
3. 4v2 (+2) Double-Grid Game      _____ out of 5
4. 3v3 (+2) Possession Game      _____ out of 5

## *Wall Pass and Double Pass Drills*

1. Off the Wall      _____ out of 5
2. 2v1 in Grid      _____ out of 5
3. 2v1 to the End Line      _____ out of 5
4. 2v1 (+1) Transition Game      _____ out of 2
5. Multiple Scoring Options      _____ out of 3

## *Takeovers and Overlaps Drills*

1. Multiple Takeovers      _____ out of 5
2. Takeover to Goal      _____ out of 5
3. Three-Player Weave      _____ out of 3
4. Overlap to Goal      _____ out of 3
5. Three-Player Flank Overlap      _____ out of 3

**Total**      **_____ out of 58**

A combined score of 47 or more points suggests that you have sufficient mastery of the tactical concepts in step 8 and are ready to move on to step 9. A score in the range of 35 to 46 is considered adequate. Rehearse each tactic a few more times to become more comfortable with the maneuvers. If you scored fewer than 35 points, you need to review the material again, progress through the drills, and improve your point total before moving on to step 9.

# Defending as a Group

Attacking tactics are designed to create open space by stretching the opposing team both horizontally and vertically, to provide multiple options for the player on the ball, to penetrate the opposing defense through combination team play sprinkled with bursts of individual brilliance, and to culminate with a goal scored. Conversely, defending tactics are designed to compact the field vertically and horizontally, to reduce the space and time available for attacking players, to position a significant number of players behind the ball, to minimize the options for the player on the ball, and to deny penetration. Once a defender wins the ball, the team as a whole must make a quick transition from defense to attack. Conversely, the opposing team must immediately take on a defensive posture. From that perspective attacking and defending tactics can be likened to the opposite sides of the same coin. Although their objectives are mirror opposites, the two are forever linked in the sense that players must make quick and effective transitions from one to the other at each change of possession.

*Pressure, cover,* and *balance* are essential defensive tactics that apply to all systems and styles of play. Every player, including the goalkeeper, should understand the important role that each of these tactics plays in the team's overall defensive scheme. Just as attacking players must work together to create scoring opportunities, defending players must effectively combine to ensure defensive pressure, cover, and balance if the team is to deny opponents the space and time required for scoring goals.

## PRESSURE, COVER, AND BALANCE

The defender nearest the ball, referred to as the *first defender,* is responsible for applying immediate pressure at the point of attack (see step 7). The objective here is to deny the opposition immediately penetration via the pass or dribble so as to buy defending players sufficient time to recover to positions on the goal side of the ball.

As the first defender applies pressure on the ball, the *second (cover) defender(s)* get(s) in position to protect the space (cover) behind and to the side of the first defender. From this position, if the first defender is beaten on the dribble, the covering defender can step forward to close down the dribbler and deny penetration.

The second defender is also in position to cut off passes slotted through the space behind the first defender, and as such must be aware of support (second) attackers positioned near the ball. The covering defender (or defenders) functions somewhat like the free safety in American football, a player who is available to cover space and help teammates when needed. Keep in mind that the role of a defender may quickly change depending on the movement of the ball. For example, a covering defender may suddenly become the first defender if the ball is passed to the opponent he is marking.

*Defending players located a greater distance from the ball are typically referred to as third defenders and* are responsible for providing *balance* in defense. Defensive balance is designed to protect the vulnerable space ahead of the ball, particularly the open space behind the defense on the side of the field opposite the ball.

## First Defender

If you are the defender nearest the ball, you are responsible for applying immediate pressure on the opponent with the ball. To do so, you must quickly close the distance to the ball, ideally while the ball is in flight to the receiving player. When nearing the attacker, slow your approach to maintain optimal balance and body control. Your priorities are to limit the attacker's options by limiting the available space and time, force the opponent to pass the ball square or backward, or channel the attacker to dribble or pass the ball into space occupied by the second (covering) defender (figure 9.1). Your primary objective is not necessarily to win the ball, although you should attempt to do so if the opportunity presents itself.

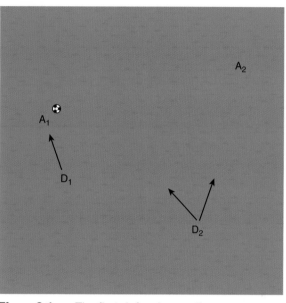

**Figure 9.1** The first defender applies pressure on the ball, while the second defender covers the space behind the first defender.

### MISSTEP

You are beaten on the dribble before a second defender is in cover position.

### CORRECTION

Your primary responsibility as first defender is to delay the attack to give your teammates time to organize behind the ball. Do not dive in on the tackle until a covering defender is in position to protect the space behind you. Attempt to jockey and delay the attacker until help arrives.

## Second (Cover) Defender

As the covering defender, you have two primary responsibilities. First, you must protect the space behind and to the side of the first defender. To accomplish that aim, you get in position to prevent an opponent's pass through that space, and you must be ready and able to step forward should the first defender be beaten on the dribble. Second, you must be aware of opponents (support attackers) in the vicinity of the ball. To fulfill both obligations, you need to be in position at the proper angle and distance from the first defender.

To achieve the proper angle of cover, get in position behind and to the side of, not directly behind, the first defender. From this starting position, you can cut off passes through that space and also close down a nearby support attacker if the ball is passed to that player. You should maintain a clear view of the ball and should be able to adjust your position quickly in response to the first defender's movements. Ideally, there should be a covering defender diagonally behind and to each side of the first defender. When properly positioned, the three defending teammates form a triangular shape (figure 9.2).

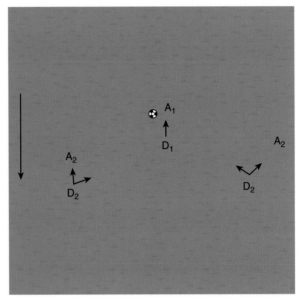

**Figure 9.2**    The proper angle of cover for the second defender. The second defender protects the space behind the first defender and can also apply pressure to the support attacker.

The distance of cover varies depending on the area of the field and the position of nearby opponents. Defensive coverage must be very compact (tight) in the dangerous scoring zone front and center of your goal, an area where opponents must be denied the time and space required to release a shot on goal. The distance of cover can be extended as the ball moves farther away from your goal. For example, when the ball is within 30 yards of goal, the appropriate cover distance may be as little as 2 yards, whereas 5 to 6 yards may be more appropriate when the ball is near midfield. It all depends on the situation. Keep in mind that as the covering defender you are also responsible for marking an opponent (second attacker) in the vicinity of the ball. As a general rule, the closer that opponent is to the ball, the tighter your coverage should be. The distance of cover can be extended as the opponent moves farther from the ball (figure 9.3).

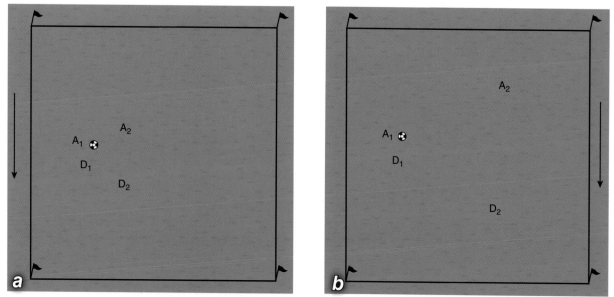

**Figure 9.3**  The distance of cover changes depending on whether the opponents are (a) closer to the ball or (b) farther from the ball.

## MISSTEP

As a cover defender, you get in position directly behind the first defender.

## CORRECTION

When you are directly behind the first defender, you cannot protect the space to the side of the first defender, and you are also in a poor position to step forward if the first defender is beaten on the dribble. Covering defenders should position *behind and to each side of* the first defender. The three players form a triangular shape with the first defender at the apex of the triangle.

## MISSTEP

As a cover defender, you get in position too far from the first defender.

## CORRECTION

Get in position at a distance from which you can provide tight cover for the first defender and also apply pressure on the ball should it be played to a second attacker in the vicinity of the ball.

# Defensive Pressure and Cover Drill 1
## 2v2 to Goals

Organize into two teams of two players each. Use markers to outline a 20- by 25-yard field area with a 4-yard-wide goal centered on each end line. Begin with a kickoff from the center of the field. Each team defends a goal and can score goals by kicking the ball through the opponent's goal below knee height. Do not use goalkeepers. Teams switch from attack to defense, and vice versa, on each change of possession. Teammates must play in combination defensively to ensure adequate pressure and cover. The first defender applies pressure on the ball while the second defender gets in position to prevent a penetrating pass through the space beside and behind the first defender. The second defender must also be in a position to immediately challenge for the ball should it be passed to a nearby support attacker. Play for 15 minutes continuously and keep a tally of goals scored.

### To Increase Difficulty for Defending Team

- Require teams to defend two small goals, one at each corner of each end line.
- Increase size of field to create more attacking space and time.
- Add neutral player who always joins team with possession to create 3v2 situation, or one-person attack advantage.

### To Decrease Difficulty for Defending Team

- Make goals smaller.
- Reduce width of field.

### *Success Check for Defenders*

- First defender applies immediate pressure at point of attack.
- Second defender positions at proper distance and angle of cover.
- Second defender steps forward to win ball when appropriate.
- Teammates readjust positions in response to movement of ball.

### *Score Your Success*

Concede 11 or more goals in 15 minutes = 1 point

Concede 6 to 10 goals in 15 minutes = 3 points

Concede 0 to 5 goals in 15 minutes = 5 points

Your score ___

# Defensive Pressure and Cover Drill 2
## Prevent the Killer Pass

Designate a team of two defenders and a team of four attackers. Use markers to outline a 15- by 15-yard playing grid. The attacking team attempts to keep the ball from the defending team within the grid. The attacking team scores 1 point each time attacking players complete six consecutive passes, and 1 additional point for each pass completed that splits (goes between) the defenders. This is referred to as a killer pass. The defending team scores 1 point each time defenders win possession of the ball or force the attackers to play the ball outside the field area. If the defenders win the ball, they immediately return it to the attacking team, and the game continues. Play for 10 minutes and keep track of points.

### To Increase Difficulty for Defenders

- Enlarge playing area.
- Add attacker to create 2v5 situation.

### To Decrease Difficulty for Defenders

- Reduce field area to 10 by 10 yards.
- Limit attackers to three touches or fewer to pass and receive ball.

### *Success Check for Defenders*

- As first defender, apply immediate pressure on opponent with ball.

- Limit attackers' passing options.
- Make play predictable.
- Cover positions to prevent pass that splits defenders.
- Switch roles depending on location of ball.

### *Score Your Success*

Defenders score fewer points than attackers = 0 points for each defender

Defenders and attackers score equal number of points = 2 points for each defender

Defenders score more points than attackers = 4 points for each defender

Your score ___

# Defensive Pressure and Cover Drill 3
## 3v2 (+1) Game

Form two teams of three players each. Play on a 20- by 30-yard field with a 4-yard-wide goal centered on each end line. One team has possession of the ball to begin. The team with the ball attacks with three players; the opponents defend with two field players and a goalkeeper. The attacking team scores 1 point by kicking the ball directly to the opposing goalkeeper. The defending team attempts to win the ball and prevent the opponent from scoring. If a defending player steals the ball, she must pass it back to her goalkeeper before the team can initiate an attack on the opponent's goal. The goalkeeper can then move forward to join her teammates in the

*(continued)*

**Defensive Pressure and Cover Drill 3** *(continued)*

attack. One player on the team that lost possession retreats into the goal to be the goalkeeper. The remaining teammates assume the roles of first and second defender. Teams switch between attack and defense with each change of possession. Change of possession occurs when a defender steals the ball, when a point is scored, or when the ball leaves the playing field last touched by the attacking team. Teammates alternate playing goalkeeper. Play nonstop for 15 minutes and keep track of points.

### To Increase Difficulty for Defenders

- Increase width of field.
- Increase size of goal.
- Add neutral player who always joins team in possession to create 4v2 (+1) situation.

### To Decrease Difficulty for Defenders

- Reduce width of field.
- Reduce width of goal.
- Limit attackers to three or fewer touches to receive and pass ball.

### *Success Check for Defenders*

- Apply immediate pressure at point of attack.
- Deny penetration via dribble.
- Position to prevent passes that split (go between) defenders.

### *Score Your Success*

Member of losing team = 1 point

Member of winning team = 3 points

Your score ___

# Defensive Pressure and Cover Drill 4
## Deny Penetration

Play within a 20- by 20-yard field area. Two defenders stand in the center of the area; one attacker gets in position at the midpoint of each sideline for a total of four attackers. The server (coach) stands outside the field area with an ample supply of balls.

To begin, the server passes a ball to one of the attackers. The player receiving the ball (first attacker) attempts to dribble directly across the square to the opposite sideline. The two defenders work in combination to deny penetration. The first defender steps to confront the dribbler while the second defender positions to provide cover (support) for his teammate. If the dribbler cannot immediately penetrate past the defenders, he passes the ball diagonally to an attacker on a different sideline. After receiving the ball, that player becomes the first attacker and immediately tries to dribble across the grid to the opposite sideline. Defenders immediately adjust position to deny penetration by the new attacker.

If a defender wins the ball or the ball is kicked out of the area, the server immediately plays another ball to a different attacker, and the exercise continues. An attacker who successfully dribbles across to the opposite sideline scores 1 point. The attacker returns to his original sideline by running along the outside of the grid. In the meantime, the server plays a ball to a different attacker, and the game continues. Play for five minutes; then designate two different defenders and repeat the drill. Play several rounds so that each player takes a turn as a defender.

## To Increase Difficulty for Defenders

- Increase size of grid.
- Place two attackers at midpoint of each sideline to create 2v2 situation.
- Allow attackers to penetrate by passing ball to player on opposite sideline, rather than dribble.

## To Decrease Difficulty

- Reduce size of grid to 10 by 10 yards.

## Success Check for Defenders

- First defender applies immediate pressure at point of attack.
- Maintain balance and body control.
- Second defender covers space behind first defender.

## Score Your Success

Concede 9 or more points in five minutes = 1 point for each defender

Concede 4 to 8 points in five minutes = 3 points for each defender

Concede 0 to 3 points in five minutes = 5 points for each defender

Your score ___

# Defensive Pressure and Cover Drill 5
## Numbers Up: Defending in the Box

Play within the penalty area with a regulation goal on the end line. Form two teams of two players each, and position a neutral goalkeeper in the goal. Both players from one team station within the penalty area, as defenders. One member of the opposing team also positions within the area, as the lone attacker. Her partner stations outside the area, as a server, with a supply of balls.

Play begins with the server kicking a ball to her teammate stationed within the penalty area. That player attempts to score by beating the two defenders on the dribble and kicking the ball past the goalkeeper. Immediately after a score or a save by the goalkeeper, or after the ball goes out of play, the server sends another ball into the area and play continues. Play for 90 seconds, after which the server switches places with her teammate and the round is repeated. Play a series of 90-second rounds, with teams switching roles every two rounds. Defenders should double down on the attacker to prevent penetration on the dribble and shots on goal. The size of the playing area should accommodate the age and ability of the players. An attacking player scores 1 point for a shot on goal saved by the goalkeeper and 2 points for a goal scored. Teammates total their points to get a team score. The team conceding fewer points wins.

## To Increase Difficulty for Defenders

- Increase size of grid.
- Add second attacker to create 2v2 situation.

## To Decrease Difficulty for Defenders

- Reduce size of grid.

*(continued)*

Defensive Pressure and Cover Drill 5 *(continued)*

### Success Check for Defenders

- First defender applies immediate pressure at point of attack.
- Maintain balance and body control.
- Second defender covers space behind first defender.

### Score Your Success

Concede 9 or more points in five 90-second rounds = 1 point for each defender

Concede 4 to 8 points in five 90-second rouinds = 3 points for each defender

Concede 0 to 3 points in five 90-second rounds = 5 points for each defender

Your score ___

# Defensive Pressure and Cover Drill 6
## 3v2 in Each Half

Use markers to outline a field area 35 by 50 yards, bisected lengthwise by a midline. Place a regulation-size goal at each end of the field with a goalkeeper in each goal. Organize two teams of five field players each. For each team, designate three players as attackers and two as defenders. The three attackers take positions in the opponent's half of the field, and the two defenders team up in their own half. This creates a 3v2 situation in each half. Each team defends its goal and can score in the opponent's goal.

Players are restricted to movement within their assigned half of the field. A defender who steals the ball passes it to a teammate in the opposite half to initiate the counterattack. Otherwise, regular soccer rules are in effect. The team conceding fewer goals wins.

### To Increase Difficulty for Defenders

- Increase size of field.
- Add attacker to each team to make situation 4v2 in defending zone.

### To Decrease Difficulty for Defenders

- Add defender to each team to make situation 3v3 in each half.
- Limit attackers to three or fewer touches to pass and receive ball.

### Success Check for Defenders

- Apply immediate pressure at point of attack.
- Deny penetration via dribble.
- Force attackers to go side to side with passes.
- Protect space behind first defender.
- Force attackers to take poor angle shots.

### Score Your Success

Member of team that concedes fewer goals than opponents = 2 points

Your score ___

# Third Defender

While the first defender applies pressure at the point of attack and the second defender positions to provide cover, the third defender's responsibility is to ensure defensive balance (figure 9.4). As a third defender, you position yourself diagonally behind the second defender along the line of balance, an imaginary diagonal line that begins at the ball and extends toward the goalpost farther from the ball. From a position along the line of balance, you can accomplish three important objectives: protect the space behind the second defender, keep the play in front of you, and keep the opponent you are responsible for marking in view.

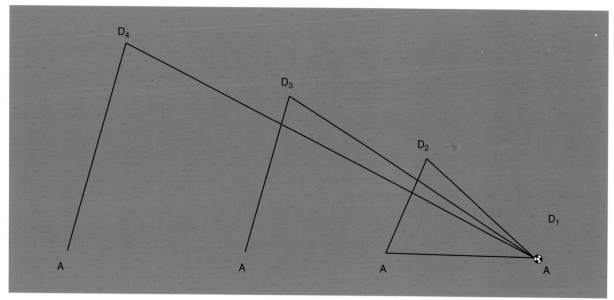

**Figure 9.4**    These defenders are in proper balance to deny a penetrating pass and at a correct distance to close in on the opponents they are marking.

## MISSTEP

You get in position square to the covering defender and are beaten with a long diagonal pass.

## CORRECTION

You should be positioned diagonally behind, not directly beside, the second defender along an imaginary line extending toward the far goalpost. From that position, you can cut off a ball played into the space behind the second defender. The line of balance changes with the movement of the ball. The farther from the ball you are, the deeper the line of balance will be.

**MISSTEP**

As a third defender, you take a position too tight to the second defender and, as a result, are vulnerable to a long diagonal pass directed into the space behind you.

**CORRECTION**

Don't be too concerned about providing tight cover for the second defender. If the ball is played into the space behind the second defender, but in front of you, then you should close the distance while the ball is in flight to apply pressure as the ball is received.

# Defensive Cover and Balance Drill 1
## 3v3 (+2) Possession Game

Use markers to outline a 25- by 25-yard playing area. Organize two teams of three players each. Two additional players are neutral and join the team in possession to create a 5v3 situation and a two-player advantage for the attack. Both teams and the neutral players are in the playing area. Use colored scrimmage vests to differentiate teams from each other and identify the neutral players. One team is in possession of the ball to begin.

The team with the ball (plus the neutral players) attempts to keep the ball and complete as many consecutive passes as possible without loss of possession. The three defenders work in combination to apply pressure, cover, and balance in an attempt to make play predictable and win the ball. Change of possession occurs when a defending player steals the ball or when the ball last touched by a member of the attacking team goes out of play. Teams are awarded 1 point for six consecutive passes without loss of possession and 2 points for 10 or more consecutive passes without loss of possession. Play for 15 minutes. The team conceding fewer points wins the game.

### To Increase Difficulty for Defending Team

- Increase size of playing area.
- Add third neutral player to create three-player advantage for attackers.

### To Decrease Difficulty for Defending Team

- Decrease size of playing area.
- Restrict attackers to three touches or fewer to pass and receive ball.

### *Success Check for Defenders*

- First defender applies immediate pressure on ball.
- Second defender provides coverage.
- Third defender provides balance.
- Teammates must move in unison to maintain proper defensive positions.

### *Score Your Success*

Member of team conceding fewer points = 2 points

Your score ___

# Defensive Cover and Balance Drill 2
## 5v3 (+2) Game

Play on a field 40 by 30 yards. Position two 5-yard-wide goals on each end line, approximately 10 yards apart. Organize two teams of five players each. Each team must defend the two goals on its end line and can score in either of the opponent's goals. One team has possession of the ball to begin. The team with the ball attacks with five players. The opponents defend with three field players and one goalkeeper in each goal. A defending player who steals the ball must pass the ball back to one of his goalkeepers before the team can initiate a counterattack. Both goalkeepers join the attack to create a 5v3 situation in the opposite direction. Teams switch from defense to attack, and vice versa, with each change of possession. Regular soccer rules apply except for the method of scoring. A team scores 1 point for eight consecutive passes without loss of possession and 2 points for each goal scored. Play for 15 minutes and keep track of points.

### To Increase Difficulty for Defending Team

- Increase length and width of field.
- Enlarge goals.

### To Decrease Difficulty for Defending Team

- Reduce size of goal.
- Reduce size of field.
- Limit attackers to two touches to pass and receive ball.

### Success Check for Defenders

- Apply pressure at point of attack.
- Deny penetration via dribble.
- Cover space behind and to sides of first defender.
- Force attackers to take shots from poor (narrow) angles to goal.

### Score Your Success

Member of team conceding fewer points = 2 points

Your score ___

# Defensive Cover and Balance Drill 3    6v6v6

Play within an extended (double) penalty area (44 by 36 yards). Organize three teams of 6 players each. Designate one team as the defending team; the remaining two teams combine to form a 12-player attacking team. Each team of 6 wears a different colored vest. The 12-player attacking team attempts to keep the ball from the 6-player defending team. Attackers are limited to two touches or fewer to receive and pass the ball. Change of possession occurs when a defender steals the ball, when an attacker plays the ball out of the area, or when an attacker uses more than two touches to receive and pass the ball. The team whose player error caused the loss of possession becomes the defending team; the original defending team becomes the attacking team. Defending teams are assessed 1 penalty point each time the attacking team completes eight or more passes in succession without a loss of possession. Play for 20 minutes. The team conceding fewer penalty points wins the game.

*(continued)*

Defensive Cover and Balance Drill 3 *(continued)*

### To Increase Difficulty for Defending Team

- Allow attacking team unlimited touches to receive and pass ball.
- Increase size of field area.
- Assess 1 penalty point for six consecutive passes.

### To Decrease Difficulty for Defending Team

- Reduce size of field.
- Require attackers to play one-touch soccer.

### *Success Check for Defenders*

- Defenders work in combination to compact space and limit attacking options.

- Defender nearest ball applies immediate pressure.
- Nearby teammates provide coverage behind and to side of first defender.
- Defender farthest from ball provides balance in defense.

### *Score Your Success*

Member of team conceding the most penalty points = 1 point

Member of team conceding the next-fewest penalty points = 3 points

Member of team conceding the fewest penalty points = 5 points

Your score ___

# Defensive Cover and Balance Drill 4
## 10v5 (+5) Over the Midline

Divide the group into two teams (A and B) of 10 players each. Play on an 60- by 50-yard field area, divided lengthwise by a midline. Teams A and B take positions in opposite halves of the field and are differentiated by the color of their scrimmage vests. The coach functions as the server and stands outside of the field near the midline with a supply of balls.

The game begins as the server kicks a ball into the half of the field occupied by team A. Team B immediately sends five players across the midline into team A's half to win the ball. Team A players attempt to maintain possession of the ball by passing among themselves. Players are limited to two touches or fewer to receive and pass the ball. If a team B player wins the ball, she kicks it across the midline to a teammate in the opposite half. The five team B players who won the ball immediately sprint into their half to join their teammates. Team A, which lost possession, sends five players into team B's half of the field to win the ball back.

Teams continue switching from one half to the other with every change of possession, playing 10 attackers versus 5 defenders in each half. The 5 defending players should work in combination to employ the group defense tactics of pressure, cover, and balance. The first defender to the ball applies pressure, covering defenders provide support behind and to the sides of the first defender, and remaining defenders get in position to provide coverage and balance. A team scores 1 point for 10 or more consecutive passes. The team conceding fewer points wins the game. Play for 15 minutes continuously.

### To Increase Difficulty for Defending Team

- Permit attackers four or fewer touches to receive and pass ball.
- Increase size of field.

### To Decrease Difficulty for Defending Team

- Restrict attackers to one-touch soccer (for high-level players only).
- Allow seven players to cross midline to attempt to win ball back.

## Success Check for Defenders

- Close distance to ball quickly.
- Deny penetration at point of attack.
- Compact space behind ball.
- Limit options for player on ball.
- Keep play in front of defense (prevent passes that split defense).

## Score Your Success

Member of team conceding greater number of points = 2 points

Member of team conceding fewer points = 4 points

Your score ___

# Defensive Cover and Balance Drill 5
## Defending Numbers Down

Organize one team of seven players and one team of five players. Use markers to outline a field area of 40 by 60 yards. Position a regulation goal at the center of one end line. Position two small goals, each 3 yards wide, at each corner of the opposite end line. Station a goalkeeper in the regulation goal; do not use goalkeepers in the small goals. The team with five players (numbers-down team) defends the large goal and can score in either of the small goals. The five-player team positions with four defenders and a defensive midfielder who fronts the back four. The seven-player team defends the two small goals and can score in the large goal, and its players are limited to three touches or fewer to receive, pass, and shoot the ball. The seven-player team is awarded 2 points for each goal scored in the large goal. The five-player team scores 1 point for each goal it scores in the small goals. Play for 15 minutes and keep track of points.

### To Increase Difficulty for Numbers-Down (Five-Player) Team

- Allow seven-player team unlimited touches to receive, pass, and shoot ball.

### To Decrease Difficulty for Numbers-Down (Five-Player) Team

- Make field narrower.
- Restrict seven-player team to two touches or fewer.

*(continued)*

209

Defensive Cover and Balance Drill 5  *(continued)*

### Success Check for Defenders

- Apply immediate pressure at point of attack.
- Prevent penetration via pass or dribble.
- Compact space behind ball.
- Balance on side of field opposite ball.

- Prevent shots front and center of goal.

### Score Your Success

Member of team scoring fewer points = 1 point

Member of team scoring more points = 3 points

Your score ___

# Defensive Cover and Balance Drill 6
## 6v6 to Full Goals

Organize into two teams of six field players and one goalkeeper each. Use markers to outline a 60- by 50-yard field. Position a regulation-size goal at each end of the field and a goalkeeper in each goal. One team has possession of the ball to begin. Each team defends a goal and can score in the opponent's goal. Regular soccer rules apply. The overriding emphasis is on group defense tactics. The defender nearest the ball applies pressure at the point of attack, nearby teammates (second defenders) provide cover, and defenders farthest from the ball (third defenders) provide balance. Defending players adjust their positions and responsibilities depending on the movement of the ball. Play for 25 minutes. The team conceding fewer goals wins the game.

### To Increase Difficulty for Defending Team

- Designate two neutral players who play with attacking team to create two-player advantage for attackers.

### To Decrease Difficulty for Defending Team

- Limit players to three touches or fewer to receive, pass, and shoot ball.

### Success Check for Defenders

- First, second, and third defenders coordinate play.

- Deny penetration at point of attack.
- Protect space behind and to sides of first defender.
- Third defender takes position along line of balance.
- Compact space and limit attacker's options.
- Make play predictable.

### Score Your Success

Member of team conceding more goals = 3 points

Member of team conceding fewer goals = 5 points

Your score ___

# SUCCESS SUMMARY

The successful execution of group defense tactics requires the properly coordinated efforts of two or more teammates. You must be prepared to fulfill the role of a first, second, or third defender, depending on the game situation, and understand the importance of each role as it relates to the other two. Teamwork is absolutely essential to your success, so communication among defending players is essential. For example, when playing as the covering (second) defender, you can verbally inform the pressuring (first) defender to channel the attacker in a specific direction or cue him when to challenge for the ball.

Each drill in step 9 has been assigned a point value to help you evaluate your performance and chart your progress. Some of the drills, by necessity, are evaluated on the play of the group rather than on the performance of each player. As a consequence, your point total may not reflect an accurate evaluation of your individual play. For example, a player in a 5v5 game may correctly apply the principles of the first, second, and third defenders but still receive a low score if the team as a whole does not perform well. However, an important responsibility when playing group defense is getting the group to perform as one, so each player should act as a coach on the field in that respect. Record your scores in the following chart and then total your points to obtain an estimate of your overall level of competence.

## *Defensive Pressure and Cover Drills*

| | | |
|---|---|---|
| 1. | 2v2 to Goals | ___ out of 5 |
| 2. | Prevent the Killer Pass | ___ out of 4 |
| 3. | 3v2 (+1) Game | ___ out of 3 |
| 4. | Deny Penetration | ___ out of 5 |
| 5. | Numbers Up: Defending in the Box | ___ out of 5 |
| 6. | 3v2 in Each Half | ___ out of 2 |

## *Defensive Cover and Balance Drills*

| | | |
|---|---|---|
| 1. | 3v3 (+2) Possession Game | ___ out of 2 |
| 2. | 5v3 (+2) Game | ___ out of 2 |
| 3. | 6v6v6 | ___ out of 5 |
| 4. | 10v5 (+5) Over the Midline | ___ out of 4 |
| 5. | Defending Numbers Down | ___ out of 3 |
| 6. | 6v6 to Full Goals | ___ out of 5 |
| **Total** | | **___ out of 45** |

A score of 37 or more points suggests that you have sufficiently mastered the defensive concepts covered in step 9 and are ready to move on to team tactics. A combined score in the range of 30 to 36 points is considered adequate. Review and rehearse each tactic a few more times before moving on to step 10. If you scored 29 or fewer points, you need to review the material again, progress through the drills, and improve your point total before moving forward.

# Attacking as a Team

Outstanding individual effort can sometimes break down a defense and create a scoring opportunity seemingly out of nothing (simply watch Lionel Messi work his magic as he weaves through opposing defenses with the ball seemingly glued to his feet). That is the exception rather than the rule, however. The majority of coaches and players alike will agree that in most instances a goal scored is ultimately the result of the coordinated efforts of teammates—a group of individuals thinking and playing as one.

Team tactics are designed to mesh the talents of 11 individuals into a collective effort, to ensure that everyone is focused and moving toward the same goal, so to speak. The fundamental objectives of team attack are to outnumber opponents in the area around the ball, to create and exploit gaps of open space within the opposing defense, and to ultimately finish the attack with a goal scored. The teamwork required to achieve those objectives occurs only when players have a clear idea of what the team is trying to accomplish when it has possession of the ball. That is where team attack tactics come into play.

Top-flight attacking teams are not simply a product of good fortune. For the team to create opportunities and score goals on a regular basis, its players must incorporate into their collective play specific principles of team attack that are universal to all game situations and systems of play. A summary of these principles follows.

## PLAYER MOBILITY

Time-motion studies demonstrate that, on average, a soccer player has the ball in possession only a few minutes of a 90-minute match. For the remaining 80-plus minutes or so, you will be playing without the ball; for this reason, your movement and actions without the ball need to be efficient and meaningful. The team cannot afford any spectators on the field—that is, players who are willing to work when they have the ball at their feet but tend to stand and watch the action when they don't. Even more so than in the past, player mobility and movement without the ball have become essential to individual and team success. Players should be moving constantly to make themselves available for passes and to create space for their teammates. Effective *off-the-ball* (i.e., without the ball) *movement* creates passing options for the player on the ball, draws opponents into poor defensive positions, and clears space for teammates to fill. It allows the team to possess the ball for long stretches of the game and eventually creates quality scoring opportunities. Spain's men's national team, which recently won the EURO 2012 championship, is an excellent model of how to incorporate all of these aspects to create a high-powered team attack.

## Diagonal Runs Off the Ball

*Diagonal runs* are player runs that penetrate diagonally through the opponent's defense. Diagonal runs can initiate from a wide area and travel diagonally through the center of the defense, or they can begin from a central area and travel toward the flank (figure 10.1).

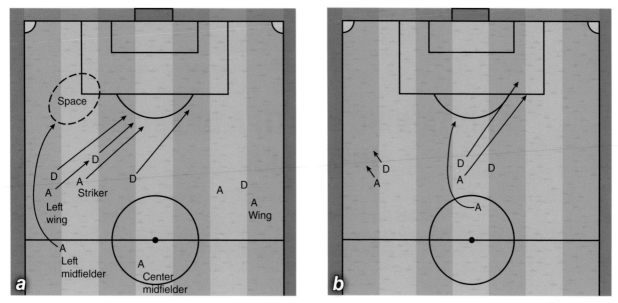

**Figure 10.1**   Diagonal runs: *(a)* from the flank through the center; *(b)* from the center toward the flank.

Diagonal runs have several advantages over square (flat) runs, which travel horizontally across the field. Because players executing diagonal runs penetrate toward goal and slice through the defense, they force opponents to mark them. This action can draw defenders into poor defensive positions and at the same time create open space for teammates to fill. Diagonal runs also position the player to receive the ball with her body between the trailing defender and the ball, because the defender is usually goalside and inside of an attacker. Finally, a diagonal run that originates from the flank and travels inward places the runner in an excellent position to receive a ball slipped through the center of the defense.

## Checking Runs Off the Ball

*Checking runs* are used to withdraw into open space to receive a pass, or simply to create distance between yourself and the defender marking you (figure 10.2). Initiate the movement with a short, sudden burst of speed forward, as if you were going to run past the defender to receive the ball. Defending players are schooled to maintain a goalside position between their opponent and the goal, so the defender will typically retreat (withdraw) in response to your movement. As the defender retreats, you suddenly check back toward the ball. This sudden change of direction will likely increase the distance between the marker and you, and create space in which you can receive, control, and turn with the ball.

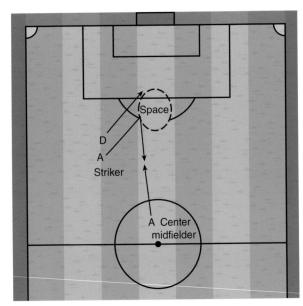

**Figure 10.2** An example of a checking run.

# MAINTAINING WIDTH AND DEPTH IN ATTACK

In step 8 we discussed how the player on the ball should have teammates positioned behind, to each side of, and ahead of him. The function of the player behind the ball is to provide depth (support) in attack and to do what the player with the ball is not always able to do—pass the ball forward. For example, if the player on the ball has her back to the opponent's goal, she can pass the ball back to the supporting teammate, who can then pass the ball forward to a different player. Teammates positioned slightly ahead and to each side of the first attacker provide short, relatively safe passing options; teammates positioned ahead of the ball provide options for the penetrating pass. This concept of group support can be extrapolated to the team as a whole.

The typical soccer field is approximately 120 yards long by 75 yards wide, significantly larger than an American football field, and one of the largest playing areas of any sport. When in possession of the ball, the team should attempt to stretch the field vertically and horizontally to maximize the use of the available space. Effective passing combinations coupled with proper player movement and positioning require the opposing team to cover a larger field area, thus creating gaps of space within the defense that the attacking team can exploit. Passes must vary in type, distance, and direction to keep opponents from closing down around the ball. The positioning of players to ensure width and depth in attack is commonly referred to as the *proper attacking shape* (see figure 10.3).

Depth in attack is achieved by positioning one or more players ahead of the ball at all times. These front-running players stretch the field vertically (north-south) and spearhead the attack. At the same time, the team has one or more players on each flank near the touchlines to stretch the field horizontally (east-west). Flank players (wingers) on the side of the field nearer the ball, and to some extent weak-side players on the side of the field opposite the ball, provide width in attack. Weak-side players are in particularly good positions to make diagonal penetrating runs through the center of the opponent's defense (figure 10.4).

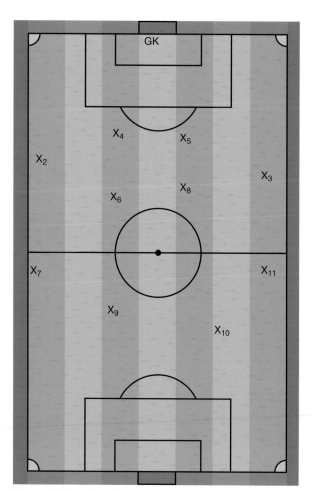

**Figure 10.3** Positioning for width and depth in attack.

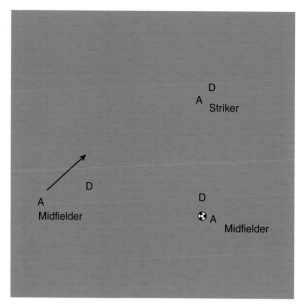

**Figure 10.4** Penetrating runs from the weak side.

# CREATIVE IMPROVISATION

Defending tactics are designed to make the opponents play as predictably as possible. It follows that when your team is on the attack, it is to your advantage, at times, to improvise and do the unexpected. Dribbling at opportune times and in specific areas of the field is an excellent means of incorporating improvisation in attack and can effectively break down an opposing defense. On the flip side, indiscriminate dribbling at inappropriate times can just as quickly destroy the continuity required to produce an effective attack. To clarify when and where to use dribbling skills to best advantage, we divide the playing field lengthwise into three zones—the rear (defending) third, the middle (midfield) third, and the front (attacking) third (figure 10.5).

A smart player always weighs the risk versus safety of dribbling in various areas of the field. The rear, or defending third, of the field, nearest your goal, is referred to as a no-risk zone because it is an area in which your team can ill afford to lose possession. Rather than attempt to advance the ball by dribbling past opponents in this area, it is safer to advance the ball by passing it to a teammate in a more forward position. Even if the pass is cut off or the player loses possession, you are still in position to defend the counterattack.

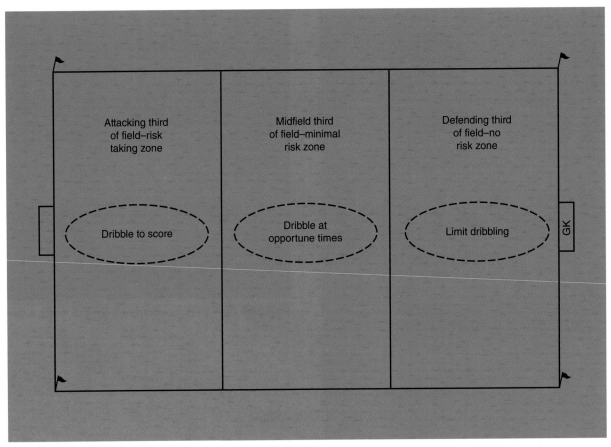

**Figure 10.5** Risk and safety in the three zones of the field.

In the middle third of the field, players are willing to accept a moderate risk of loss of possession. Most teams try to strike a balance between safety (passing) and risk (dribbling) in the middle third, so you will generally see dribbling skills used with somewhat greater frequency in that area of the field. Beat an opponent on the dribble and you immediately put that player on the wrong side of the ball and create a numbers-up situation for your team as you move forward into the front (attacking) third of the field. Even if you are stripped of the ball, you still have time to recover to a goalside position and defend, because the ball is 50 yards or more from your goal. Excessive dribbling in the middle third is never prudent because it tends to slow the attack and makes play predictable.

The attacking third of the field is the area in which players (and coaches) are most willing to accept the risk of possession loss to create a goal-scoring opportunity. Dribbling skills are used to best advantage in the attacking third of the field near the opponent's goal, an area where the benefits of beating an opponent on the dribble outweigh the potential negative consequences of loss of possession. If you can penetrate past an opponent by dribbling in the front third, you've probably created an excellent scoring opportunity for yourself or a teammate. Loss of possession in this area does not pose an immediate threat to your own goal. Learn to recognize situations that warrant the appropriate use of dribbling skills, and take advantage of them.

# COLLECTIVE TEAM SUPPORT

Soccer is sometimes referred to as a game of triangles. This refers to the general positioning of players in relation to their teammates as they move throughout the field area. If the 10 field players position themselves at the proper depth and angle of support with respect to nearby teammates, then the organization of players does resemble a series of interconnected triangles (figure 10.6a). These triangles are not static, however, because players constantly adjust their positions based on the changing location of the ball and movement of teammates (figure 10.6b). Spain's men's national team, the EURO 2008 and EURO 2012 title holder and 2010 World Cup champion, provides an excellent example of this attacking principle. The Spaniards employ a short and accurate passing game to dominate their time in possession in virtually all of their matches. They make their opponents "chase the ball" for much of the match, and eventually exploit the gaps of open space created in the opposing defense.

Total team support in attack is achieved only when teammates move up and down the field as a single, compact unit. As a general rule, there should be no more than 50 yards or so between the last defender in the back line and the foremost attacker at the front of the team.

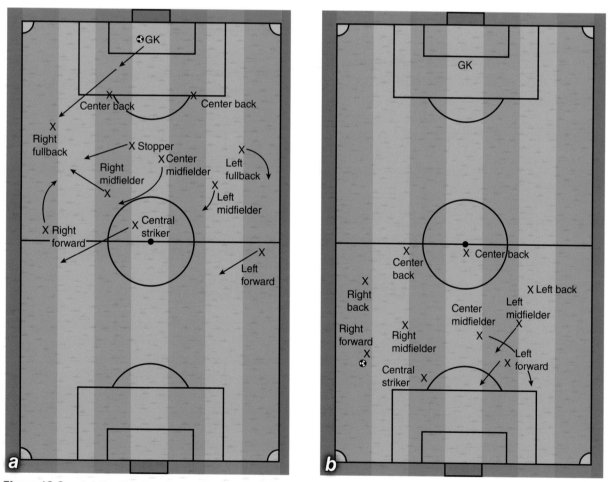

**Figure 10.6**  (a) Positioning for total team support: players are at the proper depth and angle. (b) Players adjust positions based on the movement of the ball.

# SHIFTING THE POINT OF ATTACK

Defending players cannot run as fast as the ball can travel, and clever attacking teams use this to their advantage. Playing the ball quickly from one area of the field to another, a tactic commonly referred to as *shifting the point of attack,* can unbalance the defense and create opportunities to penetrate and go to goal.

It's important to pass the ball quickly using a minimum number of touches, particularly in the defending and middle thirds of the field, and then to switch the play to attack the defense at its most vulnerable area. Two or three short possession-type passes will draw opponents toward the ball. At that point, a long cross-field or diagonal pass (figure 10.7) can leave defenders in poor position, unable to recover quickly enough to prevent penetration at the new point of attack.

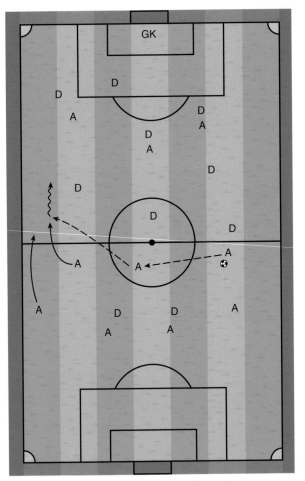

**Figure 10.7** Shifting the point of attack.

# CREATING AND FINISHING SCORING OPPORTUNITIES

Once the attacking team has created gaps of open space within the opposing defense, it must strike quickly before the opportunity is lost. It is generally to the team's advantage to create scoring opportunities in central areas that provide a wide shooting angle to goal (figure 10.8). Shots taken from areas front and center of the goal are most likely to find the back of the net, whereas shots taken from the flank where the shooting angle is narrower rarely beat a competent goalkeeper.

Creating scoring opportunities is only half the battle; the ability to take advantage of those opportunities ultimately determines team success or failure. In short, scoring goals remains the single most difficult task in soccer. Although sound tactics and coordinated group play can put players in positions to score, at the end of the day it is up to the individual to finish those opportunities. That is why players such as Mario Gomez of Germany, Lionel Messi of Argentina, and Wayne Rooney of England are among the most sought-after players in the soccer world. They can determine the outcome of a game with one magnificent strike.

On more than one occasion, I've heard coaches say that goal scorers are born, not made. They point to intangible qualities such as ability to anticipate, timing, field vision, composure under pressure, and the ability to be in the right place at the right time; traits that all great goal scorers seem to have. To an extent, I agree with that position, although I firmly believe that all players, regardless of their inherent strengths and weaknesses, can become more proficient goal scorers through dedicated practice. Develop the ability to shoot with power and accuracy. Learn to release your shot quickly and with either foot. Be able to recognize potential scoring opportunities,

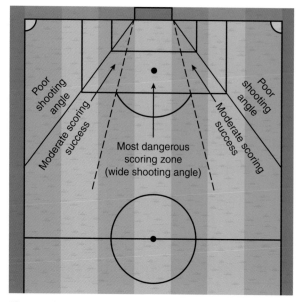

**Figure 10.8** Create scoring opportunities with a wide shooting angle to goal.

and learn to position yourself to take advantage of those situations. Work on your weaknesses and play to your strengths. If you are willing to commit to that goal, you can become your team's most lethal weapon, the player who can consistently put the finishing touch on a successful attack.

# Team Attack Drill 1
## Possess to Penetrate and Score

Use markers to create a 25-yard-wide by 40-yard-long playing area, with a full-size goal centered on each end line. Organize two teams of four players each, plus goalkeepers. Use colored vests to differentiate teams. One team has the ball and begins with a kickoff from the center of the field. Each team defends a goal and can score by kicking the ball through the opponent's goal or by completing eight consecutive passes without a possession loss. The defending team can win the ball by intercepting passes or tackling the ball from opponents. Except for the method of scoring, regular soccer rules apply. Score 1 point for a goal scored and 2 points for eight consecutive passes. The team scoring more points wins the match.

Be patient when organizing your attack. Try to keep possession of the ball until there is an opportunity to move forward and score. Because the defending team must apply pressure to win the ball, its players may be drawn into poor defensive positions, which will create gaps of open space within the defense that your team can exploit. These same concepts can be transferred to the full-sided (11v11) game.

### To Increase Difficulty for Attacking Team

- Add neutral player who always plays with defending team.

### To Decrease Difficulty for Attacking Team

- Add two neutral players who always join attacking team.

*(continued)*

Team Attack Drill 1 *(continued)*

### *Success Check*

- Move constantly to be available for passes.
- Play firm one- or two-touch passes back to supporting teammate.
- Go to goal when opportunity arises.
- Finish with strike on goal.

# Team Attack Drill 2
## Dribble to Score in the Attacking Third

Organize two teams of six field players and a goalkeeper. Use markers to outline a rectangular field area of 75 by 50 yards with a regulation goal on each end line. Divide the field lengthwise into three equal 25- by 50-yard zones. A goalkeeper gets in position in each goal.

Begin with a kickoff from the center of the field. Each team defends a goal and can score in the opponent's goal. Regular soccer rules apply except for the following restrictions: Players are restricted to three touches of the ball or fewer when within the defending zone nearest their goal. There are no touch restrictions in the middle zone, although players are permitted to dribble the ball forward into open space only; they are not permitted to take on and beat opponents on the dribble. In the front third of the field, players must dribble past an opponent before they can shoot on goal. Players are assessed 1 penalty point for each zone restriction violation and 1 penalty point for each loss of possession. A player who beats a defender on the dribble and scores is awarded 2 bonus points. Individual players keep track of their penalty points. Play for 25 minutes.

### To Increase Difficulty for Attacking Team

- Add two neutral players who join defending team to create numbers-up advantage for defense.

### To Decrease Difficulty for Attacking Team

- Add two neutral players who join attacking team to create numbers-up advantage for attack.

### *Success Check*

- Advance ball quickly with limited touches through defending third.

- Advance ball quickly through middle zone by passing or dribbling forward into open space.
- Create 1v1 situations in attacking third.
- Dribble to penetrate in attacking third.

# Team Attack Drill 3
## Dribble Over the End Line to Score

Organize two equal teams of six to eight players each. Do not use goalkeepers. Play within a 60- by 50-yard area. Each team defends an end line and can score by dribbling the ball over the opponent's end line. Regular soccer rules are in effect except for the method of scoring and the following restriction: Players may not pass the ball forward. Square or back passes are used to set up opportunities to advance the ball by dribbling. Teams score 1 point each time a player dribbles the ball over the opponent's end line. Play for 20 minutes. The team scoring more points wins.

### To Increase Difficulty for Attacking Team

- Decrease width of field to reduce available space.

### To Decrease Difficulty for Attacking Team

- Add three neutral players who play only with attacking team.

### Success Check

- Position for width and depth in attack.

- Pass ball quickly with limited touches.
- Unbalance defense to create openings.
- Dribble forward at speed when the opportunity presents itself

### Score Your Success

Member of losing team = 1 point

Member of winning team = 3 points

Your score ___

# Team Attack Drill 4    Switch the Field

Organize two equal teams of six to eight players each. Use markers to outline a 70- by 50-yard field area. Position flags to represent three 4-yard-wide goals on each end line. Place one goal at each corner and one in the center. Each team defends the three goals on its end line and can score in its opponent's goals. Do not use goalkeepers.

Begin the game with a kickoff from the center of the area. The team in possession should move the ball quickly and attack the goal least defended by changing the point of attack at the appropriate moment. Teams score by kicking the ball through a goal below waist height. Regular soccer rules apply except that the offside law is waived. Play for 20 minutes and keep track of goals.

### To Increase Difficulty for Attacking Team

- Limit players to three touches to pass, receive, and shoot ball.
- Add two neutral players who play with defending team to create two-player advantage.

### To Decrease Difficulty for Attacking Team

- Enlarge goals.
- Add two neutral players who play with attacking team to create two-player advantage.

*(continued)*

Team Attack Drill 4 *(continued)*

## Success Check

- Position for width and depth in attack to stretch defense.
- Draw defenders to ball with short passes and then quickly change point of attack.
- Stress quick transition from defense to attack.

## Score Your Success

Member of losing team = 1 point

Member of winning team = 3 points

Your score ___

# Team Attack Drill 5   Game With Neutral Wingers

Organize two teams of five field players and a goalkeeper. Designate two additional players who play as neutral wingers with the team in possession. Use markers to outline a field area 75 by 65 yards with a regulation-size goal at the center of each end line. Mark a zone 10 yards wide extending the length of the field on each flank. Station one neutral player (winger) in each flank zone and a goalkeeper in each goal. Begin the game with a kickoff from the center of the field.

Teams play 5v5 in the central zone. The neutral wingers join the team with the ball to create a two-player advantage for the attack. Wingers may move up and down the length of the field but only within their flank zones. Goals can be scored directly from the central zone or from balls crossed into the goal area by the wingers. When a winger receives a pass from a central player or the goalkeeper, he must dribble into the defending team's half of the field and cross the ball into the goal area. Otherwise, regular soccer rules apply. Play for 25 minutes. Score 2 points for a goal scored off a cross and 1 point for a goal scored from a shot originating within the central zone. Each team keeps track of its points.

### To Increase Difficulty for Attacking Team

- Restrict players to three touches or fewer to pass, receive, or shoot ball.
- Station neutral defending player in each flank zone to create a 1v1 situation on flank.

### To Decrease Difficulty for Attacking Team

- Station two additional neutrals in central zone who join attacking team to create two-player advantage in the central zone.

## Success Check

- Position players to ensure width and depth in attack.
- Create scoring opportunities in central areas.
- Execute timed runs into goal area to score off crosses.

## Score Your Success

Member of losing team = 1 point

Member of winning team = 3 points

Your score ___

# Team Attack Drill 6    Early Entry to Score

Organize two teams of eight players each. Play on a regulation field with a full-size goal centered on each end line. Position a goalkeeper in each regulation goal. Use flags to represent three 6-yard-wide entry goals on the front edge of each penalty area. Place one entry goal at each corner of the penalty area and one in the center. Do not use goalkeepers in the entry goals.

Teams play 8v8 between the two penalty areas. Attacking players are not permitted to enter the opposing team's penalty area until the ball has been entered (passed) through one of the entry goals. Once the ball is entered into the penalty area, three players from the attacking team sprint into the area to finish the attack. Defending players are not permitted to enter their own penalty area. Once the ball has entered, the attacking team must generate a shot on goal with two passes or fewer. Score 1 point for each entry pass into the opponent's penalty area, and 1 additional point for a goal scored. Play for 25 minutes and keep track of points.

## To Increase Difficulty for Attacking Team

- Require three touches or fewer to receive and pass ball.
- Reduce width of entry goals.

## To Decrease Difficulty for Attacking Team

- Add three neutral players who play with team in possession to create numbers-up situation.

## Success Check

- Play ball quickly and with limited touches to change point of attack.
- Use square or back passes to set up penetrating (forward) passes.
- Enter ball into scoring area (through entry goal) as early as possible.

## Score Your Success

Member of losing team = 1 point

Member of winning team = 3 points

Your score ___

# Team Attack Drill 7    Three-Zone Transition Game

Organize three teams (A, B, C) of four players each. In addition, designate one neutral player and two goalkeepers. Use markers to outline a playing area of 75 by 50 yards with a regulation goal on each end line. Divide the field lengthwise into three equal 50- by 25-yard zones. Teams A and C begin in the end zones; team B begins in the middle zone. A goalkeeper takes position in each goal. Team B in the middle zone begins with the ball. The neutral player joins the team in possession of the ball.

Team B, assisted by the neutral player, advances and attempts to score against team A. Team A gains possession by tackling the ball or intercepting a pass, after the goalkeeper makes a save, after a goal is scored, or when a ball last touched by a player from team B travels over the end line.

After winning the ball, team A players and the neutral player move forward from the end zone into the middle zone. Team B players remain in the end zone to play as defenders on the next round. Team A players quickly organize in the middle zone before advancing into the opposite end zone to attack team C. Regular soccer rules apply. Play for 25 minutes. The team scoring the most goals wins the game.

*(continued)*

Team Attack Drill 7 *(continued)*

### To Increase Difficulty for Attacking Team

- Limit attacking players to three touches or fewer to pass, receive, and shoot ball.
- Add one additional player to each team to decrease available space.

### To Decrease Difficulty for Attacking Team

- Add two additional neutral players who join attacking team.

### Success Check

- Make quick transitions from defense to attack.
- Position players for width and depth in attack.
- Move ball quickly and with limited touches through middle zone.
- Create quality scoring opportunities from central areas with wide shooting angles to goal.

### Score Your Success

Member of losing team = 1 point

Member of winning team = 3 points

Your score ___

# Team Attack Drill 8
# Game With End-Line and Sideline Neutrals

Use markers to outline a 50- by 60-yard field area with a full-size goal centered on each end line. Organize three teams (A, B, C) of six field players each. Teams A and B take positions within the field area; each defends a goal. A goalkeeper gets in position in each goal. Team C players stand along the perimeter lines of the field, one on each sideline and two along each end line (one on either side of the goal), to function as support players.

Teams A and B compete within the area. Players can use the sideline and end-line support players (team C) as passing options, creating a 12v6 situation, which is a six-player advantage for the attacking team. Sideline and end-line support players are not permitted to enter the field area, although they can move laterally along the perimeter lines. Sideline players have a two-touch restriction; end-line players have a one-touch restriction. Play for 10 minutes or two goals scored, whichever occurs first, after which one of the middle teams (A or B) switches positions with team C to become the sideline and end-line neutral players. Play a minitournament so that each team plays every other team once. Score 1 point for a goal scored. The team scoring the most goals wins the competition.

### To Increase Difficulty for Attacking Team

- Reduce size of field to limit time and space available.
- Restrict central players to two touches to receive and pass ball.

### To Decrease Difficulty for Attacking Team

- Permit unlimited touches for sideline and end-line support players.

## Success Check

- Use passing combinations for width and depth.
- Play quickly, using a minimum number of touches to move ball.
- Change point of attack to unbalance defense.

## Score Your Success

Member of third-place team = 1 point

Member of second-place team = 3 points

Member of winning team = 5 points

Your score ___

# Team Attack Drill 9
## Total Team Attack—Spanish Style

Organize two teams of seven players each, plus goalkeepers. Play on a 60- by 80-yard area divided by a midline with a full-size goal centered on each end line. Each team defends the goal on its end line and can score in the opponent's goal. Regular soccer rules are in effect except for the following restriction: All seven field players of the team in possession must move forward into the opponent's half of the field before the team can attempt a shot on goal. This rule ensures team compactness and combination play while moving forward in the attack. This style of play is exemplified by the Spanish men's national team, which recently won the 2012 European Championship, as well as other top national sides from around the world.

A score is disallowed if the attacking player is in her own half of the field when the shot is taken. Score 1 point for a shot on goal saved by the keeper and 2 points for a goal scored. Play for 20 minutes and keep track of points.

### To Increase Difficulty for Attacking Team

- Restrict players to three touches or fewer to receive, pass, and shoot ball.

### To Decrease Difficulty for Attacking Team

- Permit two members of attacking team to remain in their own half when shot is taken.

### Success Check

- Maintain team shape for width and depth.

- Use short, crisp passing combinations emphasizing total team support.
- Move ball quickly with limited touches.
- Dribble to beat opponent in attacking half.
- Move forward in a compact unit.
- Provide support at proper angle and distance.
- Create scoring opportunities with wide angles to goal.

### Score Your Success

Member of losing team = 1 point

Member of winning team = 3 points

Your score ___

## Team Attack Drill 10    4 (+4) v 4 (+4) to Full Goals

Play on a 30- by 60-yard- field area. Position a regulation goal on each end line. Organize two teams of eight players each, plus goalkeepers. Teams are differentiated by colored scrimmage vests. Four players from each team station within the field area. The remaining players from each team station along the perimeter lines of the offensive half of the field (the half of the field their team is attacking): one on each touchline and one on each side of the goal, on the end line. Outside players must stay outside the field boundaries, but may inter-pass with their teammates stationed within the field area. Outside players are limited to two touches or fewer to receive and pass the ball. Outside players may not enter the field area and are not permitted to pass the ball to one another. Outside players are encouraged to drive crosses into the goal area when possible. The defending team (i.e., the team without possession) defends with four players only; their outside players are inactive until their team gains possession and advances into the opponent's half of the field. Every few minutes the inside and outside players switch roles. Play continuously for 20 minutes. A team is awarded 1 point for a goal scored from the field and 2 points for a goal scored directly out of the air by a volley or header. The team scoring more points wins the game.

### To Increase Difficulty for Attacking Team

- Restrict players to three touches or fewer to receive, pass, and shoot ball.

### To Decrease Difficulty for Attacking Team

- Allow two outside players to enter field when they have ball.

### *Success Check*

- Maintain team shape for width and depth.
- Use short, crisp passing combinations emphasizing total team support.

- Move ball quickly with limited touches.
- Use outside players as support teammates.
- Dribble to beat opponent in attacking half.
- Move forward in a compact unit.
- Provide support at proper angle and distance.
- Create scoring opportunities with wide angles to goal.

### *Score Your Success*

Member of losing team = 1 point

Member of winning team = 3 points

Your score ___

## Team Attack Drill 11    7v5 on Half Field

Designate a five-player team, a seven-player team, and one goalkeeper. Play on half of a regulation field with a full-size goal centered on the end line. Use cones or flags to represent two 3-yard-wide goals positioned 20 yards apart on the midline of the regulation field. The goalkeeper plays in the full-size goal; do not use goalkeepers in the small goals. The seven-player team attempts to score in the full-size goal and defends the two small goals. The five-player team defends the large goal and can score by passing the ball through either of the small goals. The seven-player team has possession of the ball to begin the game. The coach serves as the official score-keeper. The seven-player team can earn points as follows:

- 1 point for eight passes in succession without loss of possession
- 1 point for a successful give-and-go (wall) pass that beats a defender
- 1 point for a shot on goal saved by the goalkeeper
- 2 points for a goal scored off a shot taken within the penalty area
- 3 points for a goal scored directly off a ball crossed from the flank
- 3 points for a goal scored from a shot taken 20 yards or more from the goal

The five-player team earns 2 points for making six passes without loss of possession or kicking the ball through either of the small goals on the midline. Play for 25 minutes and keep track of team points.

### To Increase Difficulty for Seven-Player Team

- Restrict players to three touches or fewer to receive, pass, and shoot ball.
- Add opposing player to create 7v6 situation.
- Reduce width of field to limit available space.

### To Decrease Difficulty for Seven-Player Team

- Add player to create 8v5 situation.

### Success Check

- Position for width and depth in attack.
- Change point of attack to unbalance opposing team.
- Create 1v1 situations in attacking third.
- Create scoring opportunities in most dangerous (central) areas.
- Exploit flank areas.

### Score Your Success

Member of losing team = 3 points

Member of winning team = 5 points

Your score ___

# SUCCESS SUMMARY

The principles of team attack apply to all systems and styles of play. They provide a framework on which players can base their decisions and subsequent actions. The teamwork required to create a formidable attacking side occurs only when individual players are willing and able to channel their efforts toward the common (team) good.

It is best to practice team attack tactics in competitive, matchlike situations. The games need not be full-sided (11 players per team), but they must include a sufficient number of players to incorporate all the principles of team attack.

The drills in step 10 involve large groups of players, so it is difficult to assign individual point scores. Each of the drills has been assigned a point value based on the group (team) performance. In most cases, all players on the winning team receive the same score, and all players on the losing team receive the same (lower) score. Although this method of scoring may not accurately reflect the performance of a very talented player on a very weak team, the scores portray how the group of players worked together to integrate the principles of team attack into their play. Record your scores in the following chart and total the points to get an evaluation of your group performance.

## Team Attack Drills

| | | |
|---|---|---|
| 1. | Possess to Penetrate and Score | _____ out of 3 |
| 2. | Dribble to Score in the Attacking Third | _____ out of 5 |
| 3. | Dribble Over the End Line to Score | _____ out of 3 |
| 4. | Switch the Field | _____ out of 3 |
| 5. | Game With Neutral Wingers | _____ out of 3 |
| 6. | Early Entry to Score | _____ out of 3 |
| 7. | Three-Zone Transition Game | _____ out of 3 |
| 8. | Game With End-Line and Sideline Neutrals | _____ out of 5 |
| 9. | Total Team Attack—Spanish Style | _____ out of 3 |
| 10. | 4 (+4) v 4 (+4) to Full Goals | _____ out of 3 |
| 11. | 7v5 on Half Field | _____ out of 5 |
| **Total** | | _____ **out of 39** |

A total score of 30 or more points indicates that you have successfully mastered the concepts and are ready to move on to step 11. A score in the range of 22 to 29 points is considered adequate. Review the principles of team attack once again before moving on to step 11. If you scored fewer than 22 points, you need a more substantial review of the material; repeat the drills and improve your overall performance before moving on to step 11.

# Defending as a Team

At this point you understand the roles and responsibilities of the first, second, and third defenders. The next step in the team-building process is to mesh these strategies into an overall plan for team defense. My years of experience as a player and coach have made me well aware of the fact that a group of talented individuals does not necessarily form a cohesive defensive unit. Effective team defense, even more so than team attack, requires teammates to work together in an organized, disciplined manner. Players must be physically fit. They must play with commitment and determination. They must be able to compete successfully in one-on-one situations. They must be able to outjump opponents to win air balls. They must understand the important roles of the pressuring (first), covering (second), and balancing (third) defenders. Above all, they must accept their roles in the team's defensive scheme and understand how those roles relate to the group as a whole. Although the most successful teams at all levels of competition demonstrate sound defensive play, arguably the greatest defensive sides at the international level are exemplified by the Italian National teams of the past 30 years, which provide a working model of how to play stifling team defense.

Successful team defense is predicated in large part on the decisions players make in response to changing situations during play, and how they apply defending tactics in those situations. Poor decisions eventually translate into goals scored against the team. Players can improve their decision-making skills by developing a clear understanding of what the team is trying to accomplish when the opponent has the ball. The following principles of team defense provide a general framework on which to base decisions and subsequent actions. These principles are universal to all systems of play and progress through a logical sequence from the moment the team loses the ball until the moment it regains possession and goes on the attack.

# PRESSURE AT THE POINT OF ATTACK

A team is most vulnerable to counterattack during the few seconds immediately after loss of possession. Even the most experienced players can lose focus and become disorganized as they make the transition from attack to defense.

To prevent the opponent from initiating a swift counterattack, the defending player nearest the ball (first defender) must apply immediate pressure at the point of attack. The challenge should not be a reckless attempt to tackle the ball, but rather calculated and controlled pressure designed to delay penetration via the pass or dribble. If the pressuring defender can force the first attacker to play the ball backward, or at least square across the field, defending teammates will have extra time in which to regroup and organize behind the ball.

# RECOVER GOALSIDE OF THE BALL

While pressure is applied in the area of the ball to prevent a swift counterattack, defenders away from the ball quickly withdraw to positions behind the ball, referred to as *goalside positions* (figure 11.1). From a goalside position, you will be able to keep the ball and the opponent you are responsible for marking in view. Also, you will be in position to provide cover for your teammates. As defending players relocate behind the ball, they can compress areas of open space between the ball and their goal, making it more difficult for the attacking team to penetrate and create scoring opportunities.

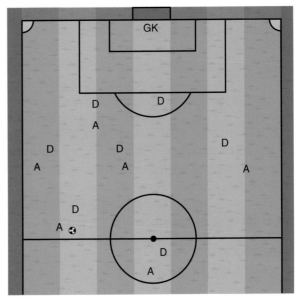

**Figure 11.1** Goalside position.

# LIMIT THE MOST DANGEROUS ATTACKING SPACE

The defending team's ultimate objective is to deny opponents space and time in the areas from which goals are most often scored. Toward that aim, consolidating players in the most dangerous (central) scoring zones has become an accepted tactic. As players retreat to a position goalside of the ball, they funnel inward toward the center of the field (figure 11.2). This pinching inward of players behind the ball is designed to eliminate gaps of open space within the center of the defense, thereby preventing opponents from slotting passes through the most vital scoring zones.

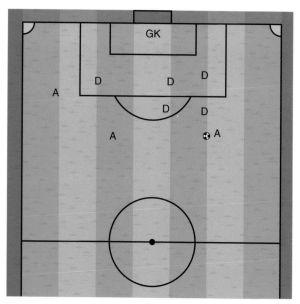

**Figure 11.2**   Concentration of defenders; defenders pinch inward to protect the most dangerous attacking space.

# ACHIEVE VERTICAL COMPACTNESS

The typical soccer field is approximately 120 yards long and 75 yards wide, significantly larger than an American football field. That is an extremely large area for 10 field players to cover when the opponent has the ball. The principle of team compactness is designed to compress the field vertically by reducing the distance between the defending team's back players and front players (figure 11.3). Team compactness eliminates gaps of open space within the defense to make it more difficult for the attacking team to penetrate through the defense. To achieve compactness, defending players must press toward the ball as one compact group. Defending players near the ball must apply immediate pressure on the first attacker to deny that player the opportunity to serve an early long ball behind a compact defense.

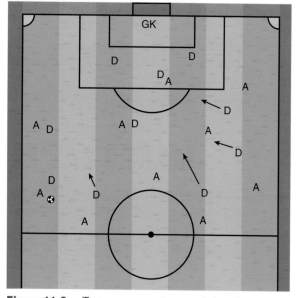

**Figure 11.3**   Team compactness; defending teammates are positioned to provide tight cover for one another.

# CONTROL THE SPACE BEHIND THE DEFENSE

As players get in position to reduce the open space within the defense, they must also take measures to protect the space between the deepest (last) defender and the goalkeeper. This is achieved through the principle of *defensive balance*. As discussed previously, balance in defense is provided by players away from the ball as they get in position along an imaginary diagonal line that begins at the ball and travels toward the far goalpost. From a position along the line of balance, defending players can keep the ball in view and also cut off passes directed into the space behind the defense. As a general rule, the farther a player is from the ball, the deeper her position along the line of balance should be (figure 11.4).

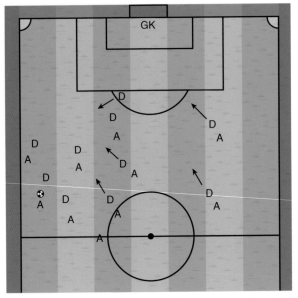

**Figure 11.4** Line of balance; players away from the ball positioned along the line of balance can cut off opponents' passes played behind or through the defense.

The goalkeeper can also help protect the vulnerable space behind the defense. He must be prepared to move forward to intercept passes that enter the space behind the last defender, much like the traditional sweeper back. When the goalkeeper leaves the penalty area, he must play the ball with his feet.

# MAKE PLAY PREDICTABLE

A primary goal of team attack tactics is to create as many options as possible for the player on the ball to make it difficult for the defending team to anticipate what that player will do. Conversely, defending tactics are designed to limit options through pressure at the point of attack coupled with tight marking of support attackers in the vicinity of the ball (figure 11.5). Immediate pressure on the ball forces the first attacker to play quickly and, because no short passing options are available, possibly attempt a longer pass with greater risk of losing possession.

Defending players can also eliminate passing options by getting in position to block the passing lanes between attackers, thereby forcing the player on the ball to play the ball through the air or back to a supporting teammate. In either case the advantage shifts to the defense. Lofted passes are generally less accurate than ground passes, and, from a defensive perspective, square and back passes provide additional time for defending players to organize and get in position goalside of the ball.

Finally, defending players can make play more predictable by funneling the first attacker into an area where the space is restricted. For example, when you force a flank attacker to dribble toward the sideline, you effectively reduce the space through which she can pass the ball forward (figure 11.6). In that sense you have limited her passing options and made play more predictable. You can achieve the same results by funneling the dribbler into the space occupied by a covering teammate.

The principles of team defense can be listed in a step-by-step progression, but the actual implementation of these principles must occur swiftly and simultaneously. At this point in the progression, the defending team should be in an excellent position to win the ball. There is pressure at the point of attack, defending players are in position to provide cover and balance for one another, the most dangerous scoring zones are protected, and the play of the attacking team has been made as predictable as possible. The final step in the sequence is for the first defender to challenge for and win the ball or force the opponent to play the ball into an area where a defending teammate can step forward to intercept the pass.

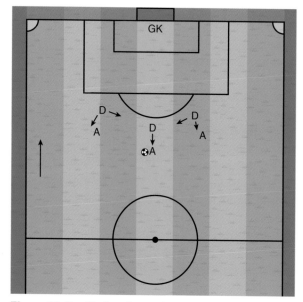

**Figure 11.5** Defending players can reduce attacking options by tight marking in the vicinity of the ball.

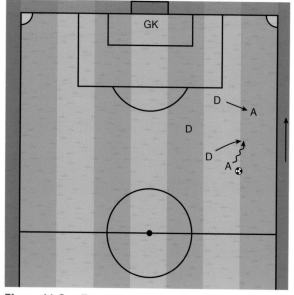

**Figure 11.6** Funneling the attacker into tight space along the touchline reduces her passing options.

# Team Defense Drill 1   Ball-Oriented Defending

Organize two teams of four players each. Play on a 20-yard-long by 35-yard-wide area. Divide the field widthwise into three zones. The end zones (1 and 3) are 10 yards wide and 20 yards deep; the middle zone (2) is 15 yards wide and 20 yards deep. Place cones or flags to represent a 2-yard-wide goal on opposite sides in each zone. (*Note:* Goals in each zone are 20 yards apart.) One ball is required per game. Use colored vests to differentiate teams.

Each team is responsible for defending the three goals on its end line (one goal in each zone) and can score in the opponent's three goals. One player from each team takes position in zones 1 and 3. Those players are responsible for defending the team's goal in their respective zones. Two players from each team take position in zone 2 and are responsible for defending the goal in that (the widest) zone. Defending players are restricted to movement within their zone and the adjacent zone. One player in the middle zone can slide sideways into an end zone to provide support (defensive cover) for the teammate in that zone, when appropriate. Likewise, defending players in the end zones can slide laterally into the middle zone to provide cover and balance for the central defenders. There are no restrictions on the team with the ball; attacking players can move between zones and do not have a touch restriction.

Pay attention to proper defensive shape and balance. Keep in mind that zonal positioning is based on the location of the ball and the position of defending teammates, not the position of opposing players. Players do not mark specific opponents. Regular soccer rules apply. Score 1 point for each goal scored.

## To Increase Difficulty for Defenders

- Increase width of zones.
- Increase width of goals.

## To Decrease Difficulty for Defenders

- Reduce width of zone.
- Restrict attackers to movement within a specific zone.

## Success Check

- Defender nearest ball applies pressure.
- Deny penetration via dribble.
- Defenders in adjacent zones slide toward ball to provide coverage and balance.
- Play ball-oriented defense—get in position according to location of ball.

## Score Your Success

Member of losing team = 2 points

Member of winning team = 5 points

Your score ___

## Team Defense Drill 2   Compact the Field Space

Play on a 90-yard-long by 75-yard-wide field. Place two lines of small discs to divide the field lengthwise into three 25-yard-wide vertical zones. Place two mini-goals (3 yards in width) on each end line, at the points where the end lines intersect with the disc lines. Organize two teams of nine players each. Both teams align in a 3-4-2 formation. No goalkeepers are required. Each team defends the two goals on its end line and can score in the opponent's goals. Regular soccer rules are in effect. The emphasis in this game is defensive compactness, so the defending team should attempt to compact the space on the side of the field where the attacking team is trying to score. To do so, all players on the defending team should slide toward that side of the field, so that all defenders are consolidated within two adjacent thirds (50 yards of width) of the field at the moment a shot is taken on goal. The overall emphasis is on compacting the field space to reduce the space available to attacking players.

A goal scored is worth 1 point. If a defending player is located in the far zone (farthest distance from the ball) at the moment goal is scored, then the attacking team is awarded 2 additional points. The defending team must use all of the fundamental principles of team defense to deny penetration and win the ball.

### To Increase Difficulty for Defending Team

- Enlarge area of field to create more available space for attacking team.
- Add two neutral players who play with attacking team.

### To Decrease Difficulty for Defending Team

- Reduce length and width of field to limit space and time available to attacking team.

### Success Check

- Apply immediate pressure at point of attack.
- Provide close support for teammates.
- Provide balance away from ball.
- Compact field vertically and horizontally.

### Score Your Success

Member of losing team = 2 points

Member of winning team = 5 points

Your score ___

## Team Defense Drill 3   Playing Out of the Back

Organize two teams of seven field players and a goalkeeper each. Play on a 50- by 80-yard field divided lengthwise by a midline. Place a regulation goal on each end line. Each team has four players (back line) in its defending half and three players in the opponent's half of the field; players are not permitted to cross the midline. Regular soccer rules are in effect except for the following restriction: Once the defending team wins the ball in its half of the field, it is permitted a maximum of three passes to send the ball to a teammate in the opponent's half. This restriction emphasizes the importance of moving the ball quickly and without risk of possession loss when in your own end. Violation of the three-pass restriction is penalized by loss of possession to the opponent. Play for 20 minutes. The team scoring more goals wins.

*(continued)*

Team Defense Drill 3 *(continued)*

### To Increase Difficulty for Defenders

- Add two neutral players who always join attacking team to create pressure in defending half.

### To Decrease Difficulty

- Allow five passes in defending half before entering ball into opponent's half of field.

### Success Check

- Defend as a compact unit.

- Deny opponents space and time to develop passing combinations.
- Make swift transition from defense to attack on change of possession.
- Limited touch to move ball and create passing options.

### Score Your Success

Member of losing team = 2 points

Member of winning team = 5 points

Your score ____

---

# Team Defense Drill 4   Defense Numbers Down

Organize two teams of seven field players and a goalkeeper. Designate two additional neutral players who join the team in possession to create a 9v7 situation, a two-player advantage for the attacking team. Play on a 60- by 90-yard field with a regulation goal centered on each end line. Each team defends a goal and can score in the opponent's goal. Regular soccer rules apply.

The defending team, being outnumbered, employs zonal (ball-oriented) marking and implements all principles of team defense. The player nearest the ball applies immediate pressure at the point of attack while the remaining players retreat to a position goalside of the ball. Defending players should compress the field vertically and horizontally to limit the time and space available to attackers. Play for 20 minutes. The team conceding fewer goals wins the game.

### To Increase Difficulty for Defending Team

- Increase size of field space.
- Designate three neutral players who play with attacking team to create 10v7 situation (three-player advantage for attack).

### To Decrease Difficulty for Defending Team

- Narrow field.
- Limit attacking players to three touches or fewer to receive, pass, and shoot ball.

### Success Check

- Apply immediate pressure on ball.
- Consolidate defenders in most dangerous scoring zones.
- Position for coverage and balance.
- Deny shots from central areas.

### Score Your Success

Member of losing team = 3 points

Member of winning team = 5 points

Your score ____

# Team Defense Drill 5    4v6 Transition to 6v4

Play on an 80-yard-long by 50-yard-wide field area bisected lengthwise by a midline. Position a regulation goal on each end line. Organize two teams of 10 players each, plus a goalkeeper. Each team positions six players in the opponent's half of the field and four players in its own half, creating a 6v4 situation in each half. Goalkeepers station in their respective goals. Differentiate teams with colored vests. One ball is required; an extra supply of balls in each goal is recommended.

The coach begins play by serving a ball to one of the six-player attacking groups; players in that group try to score on the four defenders and goalkeeper in their half of the field. If a defender wins the ball, he must pass it to a teammate in the opposite half of the field to initiate an attack on the opponent's goal. Play continuously for 20 minutes. Regular soccer rules are in effect. The team scoring more goals wins the game.

## To Increase Difficulty for Defenders

- Increase size of field.
- Add neutral attacker to create 7v4 situation in defending half.

## To Decrease Difficulty for Defenders

- Add defender to create 6v5 situation in defending half.

## Success Check

- Apply immediate pressure at point of attack.
- Close distance as ball is traveling.
- Limit passing options.
- Position for coverage and balance.

## Score Your Success

Member of losing team = 3 points

Member of winning team = 5 points

Your score ___

# Team Defense Drill 6    Deny Service

Organize two teams of eight field players and one goalkeeper. Play on a regulation field with a full-size goal centered on each end line. Use markers to designate an offside line 30 yards from each end line. Teams take positions on opposite halves of the field but between the two offside lines. Each team defends the goal on its end line and can score in the opponent's goal.

Begin with a kickoff from the center spot. Regular soccer rules apply, except for the following restrictions: An attacking player beyond the offside line (30 yards or more from goal) is not considered offside even if positioned behind the last defender, and defending players cannot enter the area between the offside line and their goal before the ball enters that area. These rule variations enable the team in possession to play the ball behind the last line of defending players to create breakaway situations. To prevent this, the defending team must deny the opponent the time and space required to serve long balls behind the defense. The emphasis is on immediate pressure at the point of attack coupled with defensive compactness to eliminate open spaces within the defense. Regular scoring is in effect. Play for 25 minutes. The team conceding fewer goals wins the game.

*(continued)*

Team Defense Drill 6 *(continued)*

## To Increase Difficulty for Defending Team

- Add two neutral players who always join attacking team to create 10v8 situation (two-player advantage for attack).

## To Decrease Difficulty for Defending Team

- Add two neutral players who always join defending team to create 10v8 situation (two-player advantage for defense).

## Success Check

- Maintain proper defensive shape.
- Apply immediate pressure at point of attack to deny long service.
- Tightly cover second defenders.
- Defenders away from ball provide balance.
- Defending players compress field lengthwise.

## Score Your Success

Member of losing team = 3 points

Member of winning team = 5 points

Your score ___

# Team Defense Drill 7    Protect the Lead

Play on a 60-yard-wide by 75-yard-long field, with a regulation goal on each end line. Organize a team of 10 field players and a team of 8 field players. Station a goalkeeper in each goal. One ball is required; a supply of extra balls in each goal is recommended. Teams station in opposite halves of the field and defend the goal on their end line.

The 8-player team begins the game with a 1-0 lead. The 10-player team gets possession of the ball to begin. Regular soccer rules are in effect. The game is 10 minutes long; the 8-player team attempts to protect the one-goal lead by using the defending principles of immediate pressure on the ball, cover and balance behind the ball, and defensive compactness. If the 10-player team scores before 10 minutes have expired, it wins, and the game ends. Repeat the game with teams switching roles (take two players from the 10-player team and add them to the 8-player team). Defending players must be organized to deny open space and time to the numbers-up attacking team. The defensive principles of pressure at the point of attack, cover, and defensive balance away from the ball should be emphasized.

## To Increase Difficulty for Defending Team

- Reduce defending team to 7 players

## To Decrease Difficulty for Defending Team

- Narrow field.
- Add defending player to create 10v9 situation.

## Success Check

- Apply pressure at point of attack.
- Back four defenders are linked in their movements.
- Position to provide coverage and balance.
- Deny most dangerous attacking space and shots from central areas.

## Score Your Success

Member of losing defending team = 0 points

Member of winning defending team = 2 points

Your score ___

# Team Defense Drill 8
# Defend and Recover Goalside

Play on a regulation field with a full-size goal on each end line. Place a line of markers the width of the field, approximately 35 yards from each end line, to divide the field into three zones. Organize two teams of eight players each. Station a goalkeeper in each goal. Use colored vests to differentiate teams. You'll need at least one ball, and an extra supply of balls is recommended.

Begin with a kickoff from center field. Each team defends a goal and may score in the opponent's goal. Regular soccer rules apply, except for the following variation: The coach or an assistant coach serves as referee and every few minutes whistles a stoppage in play and awards one team a direct free kick from within its defending zone (35 yards from its goal). When the kick is taken, all members of the opposing team must be stationed in the middle zone. The attacking team must serve a long pass off the free kick into the space behind the defending team. Players from the team defending the serve are not permitted to enter their defending zone, marked by the 35-yard line, until a player from the opposing team enters the zone and touches the ball. At that point defending players can immediately sprint back into their defending zone in an attempt to prevent a score. The attacking team scores 1 point for a shot on goal saved by the goalkeeper and 2 points for a goal scored. The team conceding fewer points wins.

## To Increase Difficulty for Defending Team

- Make restraining line 40 yards from goal.

## To Decrease Difficulty for Defending Team

- Narrow field.

## Success Check

- Take most direct recovery route to goalside position.
- Make hard, full-speed recovery runs.

## Score Your Success

Member of losing team = 0 points

Member of winning team (conceding fewer points) = 2 points

Your score ___

# ROLE OF THE GOALKEEPER

The goalkeeper plays an important role in organizing the team defense. The goalkeeper, more so than any other player on the team, is in an excellent position to view the entire field. From a vantage point behind the defense the keeper can view the action as it develops and communicate helpful information to the field players. Although excessive chatter is not welcomed or appropriate, verbal commands specific to the situation can be a valuable asset. To fulfill that role requires first and foremost that the goalkeeper possess a thorough understanding of the defending tactics employed on a group (area of the ball) and team basis. Goalkeeper communication and commands with the field players should reflect these guidelines. Commands should be delivered in a positive and precise manner, as there is little margin for error.

# SUCCESS SUMMARY

The principles of team defense apply to all systems and styles of play. They are designed to provide a framework on which individual players can coordinate their actions so that the performance of the group (team) exceeds the abilities of individual players. Establishing a strong team defense is accomplished by applying immediate pressure at the point of attack, by providing cover (support) for the first defender in the event she is beaten on the dribble, by compressing the field vertically and horizontally to limit open spaces between defending teammates, by limiting attacking options, and finally by winning the ball and initiating a counterattack.

The teamwork required for establishing a solid team defense occurs only when individual players are willing and able to fulfill their specific roles within the team's defensive scheme. This is best accomplished through repetitive practice in competitive, large-group situations.

The team defense drills in step 11 involve large groups of players playing in concert. Each drill has been assigned a point value based on the group performance. All players on the winning team receive the same point score and all players on the losing team receive the same (lower) point score. Although this method of evaluation may not accurately reflect the performance of a very talented individual on a very weak team, scores depict how the group of players worked together to integrate the principles of team defense into their play. Your coach can observe the training session and provide specific feedback on the strengths and weaknesses of your overall performance. Record your scores in the following chart and then total the points to get an estimate of your group performance.

## Team Defense Drills

1. Ball-Oriented Defending _____ out of 5
2. Compact the Field Space _____ out of 5
3. Playing Out of the Back _____ out of 5
4. Defense Numbers Down _____ out of 5
5. 4v6 Transition to 6v4 _____ out of 5
6. Deny Service _____ out of 5
7. Protect the Lead _____ out of 2
8. Defend and Recover Goalside _____ out of 2

**Total** _____ **out of 34**

A combined score of 25 or more points indicates that you have sufficiently mastered the defending concepts discussed in step 11. A score in the range of 18 to 24 points is considered adequate. Rehearse the principles of team defense once again as a group before moving on to step 12. A score of 17 or fewer points indicates that you and your teammates need to review the material again, repeat the drills, and improve both individual and group performance before moving on to step 12, the final step.

# Understanding Player Formations, Roles, and Responsibilities

The team's system of play (formation) refers to the organization, positioning, and responsibilities of the 10 field players. In my experience one of the first questions asked by enthusiastic young coaches seeking to expand their knowledge of the game is "What do you think is the best formation to play?" On the surface that sounds like a reasonable question, but in reality there is no clear-cut answer. The best answer I can offer is that it all depends—on the players and on the opponents.

At its most fundamental level, the game of soccer is not about formations. Soccer is about players—their strengths, their weaknesses, their personalities, their character. For that reason the system of play most appropriate for my team may differ from the system that works for your team. The best formation is one that maximizes players' strengths while minimizing or hiding their weaknesses, one that provides the team the best opportunity to succeed.

There are no magical formations that can turn ordinary players into great players or transform a weak team into a dominant team. No system of play will work effectively if the team is stocked with players deficient in technical or tactical abilities (or both), whereas virtually any formation can succeed with superior players if they are willing to accept their roles and responsibilities within the team structure. So although the system of play provides structure and defines a starting point for team tactics, it should never be the primary focus. Individual player development is and always will be the most important ingredient for success on the soccer field.

The individual, group, and team tactics you have learned to this point apply to all systems, although player roles and responsibilities may differ from one system to another. Within the team's system of play, each player has a clearly defined role. Some roles are narrower than others. In some cases players listed as playing the same position may be assigned different responsibilities. For example, two players may both be called *midfielders* but fulfill substantially different roles. One may function as a defensive, or holding, midfielder, whose primary responsibility is to anchor the defense and shut down the opposing team's playmaker; the other may be an attacking midfielder, whose primary role is to open up the attack and create scoring opportunities for teammates. To achieve the cohesive play necessary for successful team performance, all players must understand and accept their roles within the system.

Several formations were apparent at the 2010 World Cup tournament and the EURO 2012 tournament. Most teams used a back line of four defenders spread across the field in zonal coverage. One or sometimes two defensive (holding) midfielders were positioned in front of the four defenders. The defensive midfielder functions as sort of a front sweeper, whose role is to prevent penetration through the center of the defense, to act as a screen for the central defenders, and to initiate the attack through accurate distribution of the ball. One midfielder was typically stationed on each flank to provide width in attack, and one was usually assigned a central attacking role, playing underneath the forwards. Most teams played with one or two forwards, although a few played with three front-runners. Spain, 2010 World Cup and EURO 2012 champion, actually played without a true forward for stretches of time, in what has been termed a 4-6-0 formation. Virtually all teams played zonal (ball-oriented) defense or a combination of zone and one-on-one marking. I mention such differences in how teams were organized only to emphasize that no system of play is inherently better than any other. They all work if played correctly.

# SYSTEM ORGANIZATION

A system of play involves 10 field players and a goalkeeper. Field players are typically designated as defenders, midfielders, and forwards. Variations in how the field players are deployed result in different formations and players' responsibilities. In describing a system of play, the first number refers to the defenders, the second to the midfielders, and the third to the forwards. The goalkeeper is not included in the numbering of players.

The following provides a historical perspective on some of the more popular formations of the past 25 to 30 years. It concludes with a brief discussion of a few new variations that were prevalent at the 2010 World Cup and EURO 2012 championship.

## 3-5-2 System

Germany unveiled the 3-5-2 alignment (figure 12.1) with great success during the 1986 and 1990 World Cups and continued to use it throughout the 1990s. In its original form, the three defenders were organized with a sweeper playing behind two central markers. Teams using this system today generally deploy the defenders in zonal coverage as a flat back three.

One midfielder is usually stationed directly in front of the back three in a defensive role as the anchor player. His primary responsibility is to prevent opponents from penetrating through the center of the defense via the pass or dribble. This player also provides coverage for the remaining four midfielders who are deployed across the field in front of the anchor, two centrally and one on each flank. One of the central midfielders is usually assigned an organizer, or distributor, role while the other plays a slightly more attacking role. Two strikers spearhead the attack.

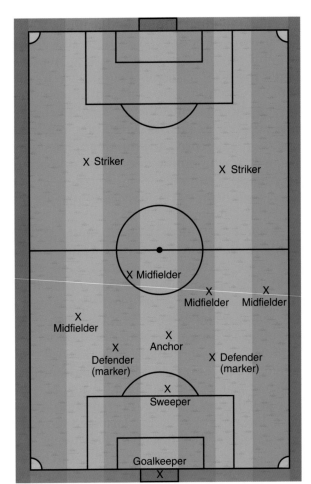

**Figure 12.1**  The 3-5-2 system.

Playing the 3-5-2 successfully requires quality flank players who can patrol the entire length of the touchline from one end of the field to the other. The two strikers must be very mobile and very active, constantly moving into positions where they can receive passes from midfielders and defenders. As a whole, the team must be able to possess the ball for stretches of time to dictate the tempo of the game, and to give flank midfielders ample time to move into more attacking roles.

## 4-4-2 System

From a tactical point of view, the 3-5-2 system places tremendous responsibility on the three defenders to cover the entire space behind the line of midfielders. To lighten the load, teams began to drop an extra midfielder into the last line of defenders to create a 4-4-2 alignment (figure 12.2). Theoretically, with a back line of four players, the defending team should be able to close down the space available to opponents more effectively.

When the 4-4-2 system first appeared, most teams played it with a sweeper, or free player, positioned behind the three other defenders. Today, most teams play a flat back four, with the four defenders playing flat across the field in zonal coverage. Four midfielders are positioned ahead of the back line. A wide midfielder patrols each flank, providing width in attack, while two midfielders set up in central positions.

The talents of the two inside midfielders should complement each other: one typically occupies a more attacking role; the other, a more defensive role. The abilities of the two forwards should also complement each other. Usually, one forward plays as more of a high target, looking to receive and hold passes from midfielders or defenders. The other forward usually plays in a complementary role off the target forward, darting into gaps of open space to receive passes and stretch the defense.

Traditional wingers—players who typically stay high and wide in the attack and who rarely withdraw to help on defense—are absent in the 4-4-2 system. The true wingers have been replaced by flank midfielders, players who withdraw into their own end to defend when the opponent has the ball and then move forward quickly into attack when their team gains possession. If the flank midfielders fail to make the quick transition from defense to attack, then the 4-4-2 can take on a defensive orientation.

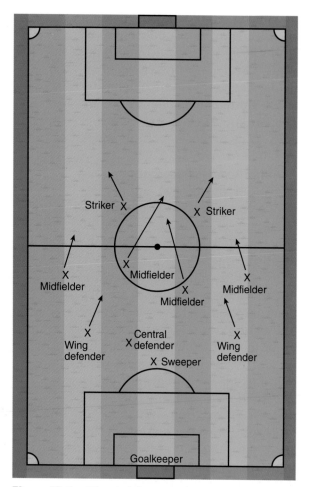

**Figure 12.2**   The 4-4-2 system.

Playing the 4-4-2 successfully requires quality midfielders who can control the ball and dictate the tempo of the game. It also requires forwards who can hold the ball under an opponent's pressure until midfielders can move forward in support. The four defenders are expected to support the midfielders when the team has possession of the ball. The primary role of the central defenders is to "stay home" and defend; as a general rule, they rarely make runs out of the back. Flank defenders, on the other hand, are expected to fulfill a more attacking role and should move forward at the appropriate time to overlap their midfield teammates to add additional players to the attack.

## 4-3-3 System

The 4-3-3 system (figure 12.3) evolved out of efforts to create a balance between attack and defense while placing greater emphasis on players' mobility, interchanging positions, and wide attacking play. The four defenders can be organized as a flat back four or with a sweeper playing behind the two flank defenders and stopper (marking) back. Three midfielders are responsible for controlling the middle third of the field, and can be organized in several ways.

Some teams play the three midfielders in a flat line across the field. In this alignment the center midfielder is the key player in this system. She must be a creative playmaker, have good passing and dribbling skills, and have the ability to move forward and score goals. On defense the center midfielder must be a strong ball tackler and a dominant player in the air. The flank midfielders provide coverage of wide areas, both in attack and defense.

Other teams choose to play one or two of the central midfielders in a more defensive role, and the remaining midfielder(s) in a more attacking role. In this alignment the defensive midfielders position centrally in front of the back line, while the attacking midfielder(s) usually floats underneath the central striker to function primarily as a distributor of the ball to the forwards. This type of formation lacks true wide midfielders; the three midfielders are positioned centrally to control that critical area of the field.

Three forwards spearhead the attack in the 4-3-3 system. A central striker is flanked on each side by a winger, or wide striker. Typically, the wingers are players who are very good on the dribble, play-

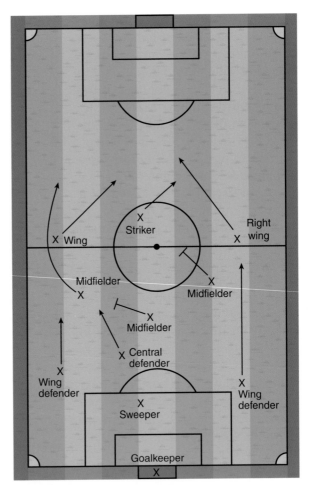

**Figure 12.3**   The 4-3-3 system.

ers such as Arjen Robben of the Netherlands and Welsh International Ryan Giggs. Such players are able to penetrate opposing defenses via the dribble to create scoring opportunities for themselves or their teammates. Although many teams play their wingers wide, almost to the touchlines, others prefer to pinch their wide players in tighter to the central striker. This player alignment leaves the wide spaces open into which the wing midfielders or flank defenders can push forward at opportune times. In either case the three forwards must exhibit a great deal of movement both with and without the ball. Through intelligent off-the-ball (third-player) running and interchanging positions, the front-running players can create space in which midfielders and defenders can move forward.

Playing the 4-3-3 system successfully requires players who are very fit, very skillful, and comfortable playing various roles. Midfield players must be willing and able to push forward into the attack at opportune moments to assume the role of either striker or winger. Likewise, flank defenders must have the technical ability and level of fitness required for overlapping midfielders to push forward into more attacking roles. The three forwards are expected to interchange positions through diagonal and looping runs and be comfortable playing both as central strikers and as wingers. In short, playing the 4-3-3 system effectively requires complete soccer players who are willing to expand their roles as the situation dictates.

# RECENT VARIATIONS

Major international competitions such as the World Cup, European Cup, and Confederations Cup often showcase the most up-to-date playing styles and systems of play. A significant observation gleaned from the 2010 World Cup and EURO 2012 championship was that all systems of play were based on tactical flexibility, which enabled teams to change their playing styles quickly. For example, it was not uncommon to observe teams switching from a 4-3-3 to a 4-4-2 to a 4-5-1 all within the same game (figure 12.4).

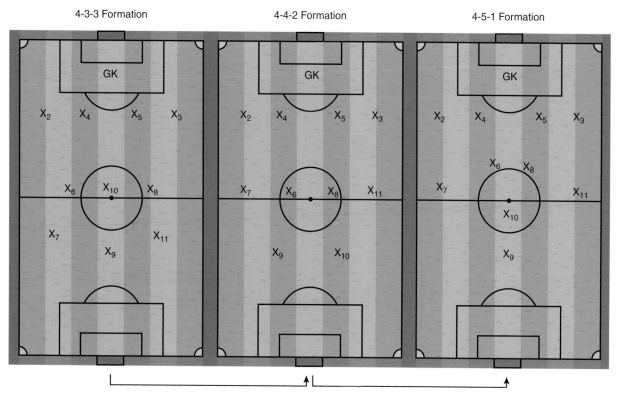

**Figure 12.4** Tactical flexibility; teams can quickly switch from one formation to another during the run of play.

The two most commonly played formations observed at the recently completed EURO 2012 championship were the 4-4-2 and 4-2-3-1. We have already discussed the 4-4-2; the 4-2-3-1 can be considered a variation of that alignment.

## 4-2-3-1 System

The 4-2-3-1 formation is actually not new to the international scene, having first appeared in Spain a decade or so ago. However, it has gained widespread popularity over the past few years and is now used by many national teams throughout the world. The back line of four players basically fulfills the same roles and responsibilities as those required in a 4-4-2 or 4-3-3 formation. The center backs stay home to anchor the defense, and the wide backs must be good 1v1 defenders and also have the ability to move forward in attack (figure 12.5).

The midfield is arranged with two holding, or defensive, midfielders who sit in front of the back four to form a block of six defenders. One of the two holding midfielders usually pushes forward into a higher position when the team has possession of the ball. The three midfielders stationed ahead of the block of six are typically aligned flat across the field. These players must be creative, mobile attacking players who can push forward quickly from withdrawn positions to support the high striker. The central striker in the 4-2-3-1 system must be a strong, skilled, and mobile player who can spearhead the attack. He must have the strength and ability to hold the ball until the midfielders arrive in support, and must also be a potent goal scorer. A classic example of this type of player is Mario Gomez of Germany.

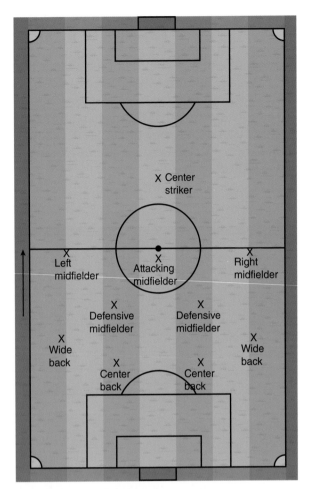

**Figure 12.5**   4-2-3-1 system.

## Future Systems

The game of soccer is constantly evolving, and we should expect to see new and innovative formations in each successive major tournament. Coaches are always looking to get that little extra advantage that will translate into success on the field. That being the case, I believe it is safe to say that any new formations that we may see in the next few years will still adhere to the age-old principles of attack and defense discussed in steps 10 and 11. Teams will attempt to be compact on defense, limiting the time and space available to their opponents. Defending players will immediately withdraw to positions behind the ball and will funnel inward to protect the most dangerous attacking space. When in possession of the ball, teams will attempt to use a mix of long and short passes to alleviate pressure and unbalance their opponents. The speed and tempo of play will continue to increase as players move the ball with a minimal number of touches, so individual mobility and level of skill will be at a premium. The only real differences between future systems and the present favorites will be the roles and responsibilities assigned to individual players. That is one aspect of the game that will never change—players must be willing and able to accept specific roles within a system of play to ensure that the performance of the whole (team) is greater than the sum of its parts (individuals).

# COMMUNICATING FOR SUCCESS

The soccer field is not a quiet place, nor should it be. It is usually filled with constant chatter as teammates communicate with one another during play. Verbal commands can provide important information to teammates that will help them make decisions that are in the team's best interests. Follow these general guidelines when verbally communicating with teammates:

- Keep your comments simple and concise.

- Call early to give teammates sufficient time to respond.

- Call loudly and clearly—you probably won't have time to repeat what you said.

Teams should adopt a standard set of verbal signals to avoid misunderstandings. The following terminology is common in soccer and should be understood by all players.

Use these verbal signals when your team has the ball:

- "Man on" when a teammate is about to be challenged from behind as she receives the ball. This will alert the player to protect the ball as she receives it and to control the ball into the space away from the defender.

- "Turn" to indicate that a teammate has sufficient space to turn with the ball as he receives it.

- "One time" to inform your teammate to pass the ball with her first touch.

- "Hold it up" to indicate that your teammate should shield the ball until supporting teammates arrive as passing options.

- "Dummy it" when you want a teammate to let the ball roll past him to you.

- "Switch" to indicate a long cross-field pass to change the point of attack.

Use these verbal signals when the opponents have the ball:

- "Mark up" to instruct a teammate to lock onto an opponent.

- "Step up" to instruct a teammate to reduce the space between herself and the opponent with the ball.

- "Close it up" to instruct teammates to compact the distance (space) between them.

- "Runner" to indicate that an opponent is running diagonally through or behind the defense.

Experienced players often use visual cues in addition to verbal instructions to communicate with teammates. Obvious signals include pointing to where you want the ball to be passed or where you want a teammate to move. You can also communicate with teammates in more subtle ways. A sudden glance in a certain direction or a slight nod of the head can alert teammates that you want the ball.

# TEAM ORGANIZATION DRILLS FOR REHEARSING SYSTEMS OF PLAY

The system of play is only a starting point. Once the game begins, the alignment of players is in constant flux. In reality, if players adhere to the principles of team attack and team defense, all systems end up looking very similar during the general run of play. The only real differences are the roles and responsibilities assigned to individual players. Consequently, there are no specific drills or exercises for practicing the individual systems. However, you and your teammates can use the shadow drill to become familiar with the movement patterns of the various alignments.

## Team Organization Drill 1
### Shadow Drill for Team Attack

Play on a regulation-size field with goals. Select a system, such as 4-4-2, and position players accordingly in half of the field. The goalkeeper stands in the goal. The coach stands about 30 yards from the goal with a supply of balls. The coach begins the exercise by driving a ball into the goalkeeper, who immediately distributes it to a defender or midfielder. From that point teammates collectively pass the ball down the field unopposed and shoot it into the opposing goal. Do not involve any opponents. Focus on proper attacking movement in relation to the movement of the ball as the team advances toward the goal. Begin the drill at three-quarter speed and gradually progress to game speed. Players are limited to three touches or fewer to receive, pass, and shoot the ball to keep the play fluid and moving. After each score, players sprint back to their original positions, and the coach serves another ball to the keeper. Repeat the exercise 30 times at game speed. Score 1 point for each shot on goal.

### To Increase Difficulty for Attacking Team

- Add six defenders to the drill who defend against the attacking team.

### To Decrease Difficulty

- Work ball down field at half speed unopposed.

### Success Check

- Position to ensure width and depth in attack.

- Provide short passing options for player on ball.
- Frequently change point of attack.
- Adjust positioning in relation to movement of ball and teammates.

### Score Your Success

0 to 19 shots on goal without error = 1 point

20 to 24 shots on goal without error = 3 points

25 to 30 shots on goal without error = 5 points

Your score ___

# Team Organization Drill 2
## Shadow Drill for Team Defense

Use the same setup as the shadow drill for team attack, but add an opposing team to the exercise. Your team gets in position to defend a goal. Your opponents take positions in the opposite half of the field.

The opposing goalkeeper has the ball to begin. The goalkeeper initiates play by distributing the ball to a teammate. The team then tries to move the ball down the field to shoot at your goal. Attacking players are limited to three touches or fewer to receive and pass the ball.

As defending players, work together to deny penetration, prevent shots with a wide angle to goal, and ultimately gain possession of the ball. Closely shadow your opponents to close space and deny penetration. You may intercept errant passes, but are not permitted to tackle the ball.

The attacking team scores 1 point for each shot on goal. After a shot on goal, or if your team wins the ball, immediately return it to the opposing goalkeeper and repeat. Repeat 30 times at game speed.

### To Increase Difficulty for Defending Team

- Defend with only eight field players (10v8).

### To Decrease Difficulty for Defenders

- Attacking team uses only seven players to create 10 defenders v7 attackers situation, or a three-player advantage for defense.

### Success Check

- Position to ensure pressure, coverage, and balance.

- Reduce space between players to ensure team compactness.
- Position to deny penetration and block passing lanes.
- Anticipate opponents' movements to intercept passes.

### Score Your Success

Concede 10 or more shots on goal = 1 point

Concede 6 to 9 shots on goal = 3 points

Concede 0 to 5 shots on goal = 5 points

Your score ___

# SUCCESS SUMMARY

Every system of play has inherent strengths and weaknesses. It is the responsibility of the coach to select a system most appropriate for the team, one that will highlight players' strengths and minimize their shortcomings. As a player, you are responsible for becoming familiar with the team's system of play, understanding your role within the system, and accepting that role for the overall good of the group. Your opportunities for individual as well as team success will be greatly enhanced if you do assume these responsibilities.

At this point of your development, you are ready to fulfill an important role within the team. The drills in step 12 involve the entire team playing as one, so it is difficult to determine performance scores for individual players. Each drill has been assigned a point value based on the group (team) performance. All members of the team receive the same point score. Your coach can provide more specific feedback with respect to your individual strengths and weaknesses. Record your scores in the following chart and then total your points to get an estimate of your team performance in executing the various systems of play.

## Team Organization Drills

1. Shadow Drill for Team Attack _____ out of 5
2. Shadow Drill for Team Defense _____ out of 5

**Total** _____ **out of 10**

Your total score will depend on how many systems your team rehearses in the shadow drills. As a general rule, the team should average at least 3 points per drill per system of play. Scoring fewer than 3 points indicates that the team does not fully comprehend the system and how it should be executed on attack or defense. Decide how your team wants to play, and then rehearse that system, or systems, until the movements become routine. As the saying goes, "Perfect practice makes perfect performance."

# About the Author

Joe Luxbacher, PhD, has more than 30 years of experience playing and coaching soccer at all levels. An expert in the fields of health, fitness, and competitive athletics, he holds a doctorate in health and physical and recreation education. A former professional and collegiate soccer player, he has played in the North American Soccer League, American Soccer League, and Major Indoor Soccer League. He currently serves as the head men's soccer coach at the University of Pittsburgh, a position he has held since 1984. His teams have won more than 200 games at the Division I level.

Widely respected by soccer coaches and players alike, Luxbacher has twice been named Big East Conference Soccer Coach of the Year. He has also earned an A coaching license from the United States Soccer Federation. Luxbacher was inducted into the Beadling Sports Club Hall of Fame in 1995, the Upper St. Clair High School Athletic Hall of Fame in 2002, and the Western Pennsylvania Sports Hall of Fame in 2005. He was also honored in 2003 when he was selected as a University of Pittsburgh Letterman of Distinction.

Luxbacher is the founder and director of coaching for Shoot to Score Soccer Academy, an organization that offers educational camps, clinics, and tournaments to players ages 7 to 18. Hundreds of young soccer players participate in Shoot to Score programs each year. (See www.shoot2score.net.) He has also written and produced the DVD series Winning Soccer in association with SportVideos.com.

Luxbacher, wife Gail, daughter Eliza, and son Travis live in Pittsburgh, Pennsylvania.